A Contested Terrain

RECONSTRUCTING AMERICA
Andrew L. Slap, series editor

A Contested Terrain

Freedpeople's Education in North Carolina During the Civil War and Reconstruction

AnneMarie Brosnan

FORDHAM UNIVERSITY PRESS
NEW YORK   2025

Copyright © 2025 Fordham University Press

All rights reserved. No part of this publication may be reproduced, stored in a retrieval system, or transmitted in any form or by any means—electronic, mechanical, photocopy, recording, or any other—except for brief quotations in printed reviews, without the prior permission of the publisher.

Fordham University Press has no responsibility for the persistence or accuracy of URLs for external or third-party Internet websites referred to in this publication and does not guarantee that any content on such websites is, or will remain, accurate or appropriate.

Fordham University Press also publishes its books in a variety of electronic formats. Some content that appears in print may not be available in electronic books.

Visit us online at www.fordhampress.com.

Library of Congress Cataloging-in-Publication Data available online at https://catalog.loc.gov.

Printed in the United States of America

27 26 25   5 4 3 2 1

First edition

Contents

List of Abbreviations   ix

Introduction | 1

1   The Civil War and Early Reconstruction Period in North Carolina | 11

2   To "Enjoy the Benefits of a School": Black North Carolinians and the Quest for Education | 20

3   A Diverse Group of Educators: Freedpeople's Teachers in North Carolina | 41

4   Answering the Call to Teach: Interrogating Teacher Motivations | 68

5   The Textbooks Used in North Carolina's Schools for the Freedpeople | 96

6   Life in Reconstruction North Carolina | 109

Epilogue   The Struggle for Educational Equality Continues | 125

Acknowledgments   131
Notes   133
Bibliography   173
Index   195

List of Abbreviations

ABFMS	American Baptist Foreign Mission Society
ABHMS	American Baptist Home Mission Society
ACS	African Civilization Society
AFUC	American Freedmen's Union Commission
AMA	American Missionary Association
ATS	American Tract Society
FFA	Friends' Freedmen's Association
FTP	Freedmen's Teacher Project
NEFAS	New England Freedmen's Aid Society
NFRA	National Freedman's Relief Association
PCMF	Presbyterian Committee on Missions for Freedmen
PEFC	Protestant Episcopal Freedman's Commission
PFRA	Pennsylvania Freedmen's Relief Association
WFAC	Western Freedmen's Aid Commission

A Contested
Terrain

Introduction

During the American Civil War and Reconstruction period, 1861–1877, formerly enslaved North Carolinians demanded access to education. From as early as 1862, enslaved people in North Carolina fled their masters' homes for the safety of Union lines in the easternmost part of the state. Despite arriving cold, hungry, and often entirely destitute, education was high on their list of priorities and North Carolinian freedpeople immediately began organizing and mobilizing to create a network of schools for themselves and their children. For these men and women, the meaning of freedom was inextricably intertwined with access to education and in the face of mounting poverty, overt hostility, and inadequate support from the federal government, Black North Carolinians relentlessly persevered in their quest for education.

Inspired by the freedpeople's profound thirst for knowledge, northern aid and missionary societies began sending teachers to the Union-occupied areas of North Carolina in 1863. Two years later, the United States Congress established the Bureau of Refugees, Freedmen, and Abandoned Lands, more commonly known as the Freedmen's Bureau, to "systematize and facilitate" these efforts. After the Civil War, white North Carolinians began entering the classroom, albeit tentatively at first, and many played an important role in the growth and development of freedpeople's education. Collectively, these collaborative efforts fostered the development of a state-wide public school system for both Black and white children, the professionalization of Black teachers, and an extensive network of Historically Black Colleges and Universities (HBCUs) throughout the state. The educational landscape was far from uniform, though, and as the following pages will demonstrate, each of the individuals and organizations involved had their own distinct vision regarding the nature and purpose of freedpeople's education.[1]

The growth and development of freedpeople's education is well-documented in the historical literature. During the early twentieth century, southern white historians associated with the Dunning school of thought criticized the development of schools for the freedpeople and those who elected to teach them. In their eyes, former slaves did not have the capacity to succeed in education and those who attempted to teach them were foolish and naïve, at best. Described by Edgar W. Knight as "messianic" invaders, freedpeople's teachers were frequently mischaracterized as northern white women which helped to cement the "Yankee schoolmarm" epithet in the historical literature for decades to come. As the twentieth century progressed, a new wave of historical revisionism emerged. Influenced by the Civil Rights Movement of the 1950s and 1960s, this generation of historians framed freedpeople's education in a more positive light. Although the teachers continued to be portrayed as predominantly northern white women, they were championed as pioneers of civil rights and racial activism, a view which was challenged some years later by post-revisionists who argued that the developments initiated during the Reconstruction period did not allow the formerly enslaved community to achieve meaningful freedom.[2]

Although historical interpretations of freedpeople's education changed significantly over the course of a century, the image of the freedpeople's teacher as a northern white schoolmarm remained remarkably unchanged until the beginning of the twenty-first century when historians such as Heather Andrea Williams, Christopher C. Span, and Hilary Green began to focus their work on the significant role that southern Black communities played in growing and sustaining a system of education in the war-torn South. Building upon decades of historical revision, including some of his own work, Ronald E. Butchart's seminal study of freedpeople's education, *Schooling the Freed People: Teaching, Learning, and the Struggle for Black Freedom*, successfully combined quantitative and qualitative research to demonstrate that southern Black men and women were the driving force behind the educational endeavors of the Reconstruction period.[3]

Building upon this work, *A Contested Terrain* uses North Carolina as a case study to interrogate the growth and development of freedpeople's education. Like some of the more recent studies, it similarly argues that Black North Carolinians were instrumental to the growth and development of southern Black schooling. In spite of limited financial resources, freedmen and women throughout North Carolina built schoolhouses, hired teachers, and purchased classroom supplies. Many former slaves taught in the first Black schools. By juxtaposing these efforts with the work of northern aid and missionary associations and white North Carolinians, it concludes that freedpeople's education was a contested terrain, fraught with conflicting visions of Black freedom and the role that education should play. For many white northerners, emancipation represented a destabilizing threat to society, and education was viewed as one of the ways in which this threat could be ameliorated. To that end, northern educators, missionaries, and government officials often viewed education as a means of reforming the freedpeople by inculcating them with nineteenth-century middle-class ideals and values. The desire to restore the antebellum hierarchal southern social order remained high on the list of priorities for many white North Carolinians who gradually began to accept the role that education could play in achieving this vision. Not surprisingly, southern Black men and women had a very different vision of freedom and the role that education would play. While the former slaves were no less concerned about defining their place in American society, citizenship and economic freedom were central to their definition of freedom. Thus, Black men and women saw education as a means of securing civil and political equality, upward mobility, and financial security.

A Contested Terrain uses North Carolina as a case study for three reasons. First, antebellum North Carolina was home to an incredibly diverse white population, the majority of whom were nonslaveholders. Due to the abundance of fertile land, eastern North Carolina developed a plantation-based society similar to that of the Deep South. Western North Carolina, on the other hand, was dominated by nonslaveholding yeomen farmers, many of whom were northern immigrants of German or Scotch-Irish descent. Due to the rural nature and rugged terrain of this region, settlements were widely dispersed, often hours apart, and many immigrant communities retained their native languages, cultures, customs, and religious beliefs. Moreover, this region of the state also boasted a significant population of Unionists who opposed secession and the formation of the Confederacy from the outset. Understanding this diverse landscape, then, provides a valuable insight into the complexities of freedpeople's education in North Carolina and the extent to which regional disparities may have influenced or hindered its development.[4]

Second, central North Carolina was home to a large Quaker population who were widely recognized for their anti-slavery sentiment and support for Black schooling. Formally known as the Religious Society of Friends, Quakers first settled in the Albemarle region of northeastern North Carolina during the late seventeenth century. According to William T. Auman and J. Timothy Allen, an increased number of Quaker immigrants, mostly from Pennsylvania, fled to North Carolina during the mid-eighteenth century in search of cheaper land and to escape religious persecution, political strife, and rising tension with Native Americans. The majority of these Quakers settled in the central Piedmont region, an area that is commonly known as the Quaker Belt (see Figure 1). Comprising fifteen counties—namely Randolph, Chatham, Moore, Guildford, Forsyth, Yadkin, Davie, Surry, Wilkes, Montgomery, Orange, Alamance, Stokes, Davidson, and Iredell—North Carolina's Quaker Belt was a center of anti-slavery activism during the antebellum era.[5]

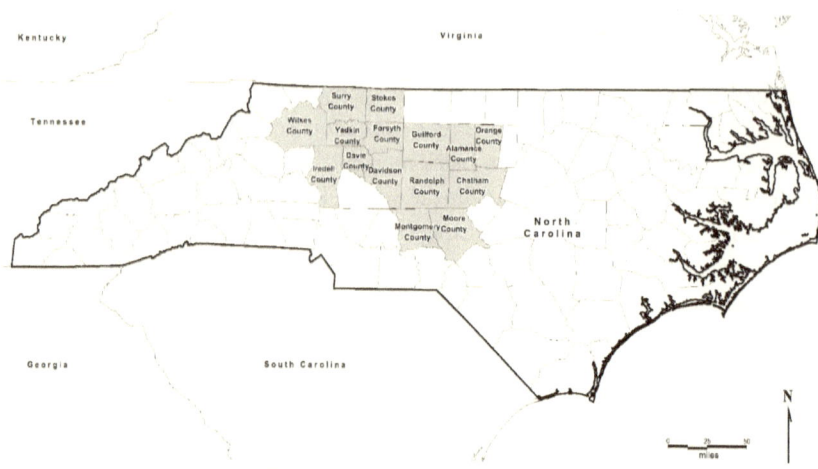

Figure 1 North Carolina's "Quaker Belt."

Although many Quakers owned slaves during the seventeenth and eighteenth centuries, the 1778 sitting of the North Carolina Yearly Meeting of Friends forbade church members from buying or selling enslaved people and those who refused were disowned by the church. Although North Carolinian Quakers began freeing their slaves on a rapid basis, proslavery lawmakers were quick to respond by passing legislation that impeded legal manumission and even forced some previously freed slaves back into bondage. Delphina E. Mendenhall, a Quaker teacher of the freedpeople from Guilford County, had great difficulty emancipating her slaves. Prior to his death in 1860, her husband George emancipated fifty slaves. By will, he emancipated thirty more. However, Mendenhall struggled to remove these slaves safely from the state. "In 1860 I succeeded in removing a part of these [slaves] to Ohio," she wrote. "In 1861 I started with all the remainder, & was turned back by an armed mob – There was great rejoicing among the proslavery part of the community." By 1864, Mendenhall had "12 men and boys still on hand," eight of whom were previously enslaved to her. "I had no power to emancipate them by will," she explained, "that power being taken away by our Legislator, the next session after the death of my Husband." When the war ended in 1865, Mendenhall attempted to obtain passports for each of these men so that they could safely relocate to Ohio.[6]

In addition to adopting an anti-slavery stance, North Carolinian Quakers also actively supported Black educational advancement. According to John Hope Franklin, Quakers were teaching slaves in North Carolina from as early as 1771.

In 1821, Levi Coffin and his cousin Vestal established a Sabbath school near their home in New Garden, Guilford County, to teach slaves to read. This was done with the permission of the slaves' masters who, according to Coffin, were more lenient than others. In spite of the students' progress, local slaveholders forced the Coffins to shut their school down after just a few months. Threatening to report the school for violating North Carolina's anti-literacy slave law, these men visited the slaves' masters and demanded their immediate removal. "They said it made their slaves discontented and uneasy," Coffin recalled, "and created a desire for the privileges that others had." Although Coffin was forced to shut his school down, he remained committed to anti-slavery activism and during his lifetime he helped thousands of enslaved people escape to the North. Such efforts ultimately earned him the nickname "President of the Underground Railroad." "I had the honor of wearing that title for thirty years," he wrote, "and it was not until the great celebration of the Fifteenth Amendment to the Constitution, by the colored people at Cincinnati, that I resigned the office, and laid aside the name conferred on me by Southern slave-hunters."[7]

Finally, antebellum North Carolina was home to a relatively large population of free people of color. Unlike other southern states which boasted large urban centers, there were "no sizeable towns" in antebellum North Carolina which meant that over 90 percent of these men and women lived in rural locations throughout the state. North Carolinian free people of color were not a homogenous group and recent research by Warren E. Milteer found that they came from a variety of mixed-heritage backgrounds, including African, Native American, and European. Although many North Carolinian free people of color suffered from poverty and discrimination, they also experienced a degree of freedom, and propertied free men of color had the right to vote until 1835. Due to their dispersal throughout the state, many free people of color developed close social ties with members of the white community which was uncommon in many other southern states. According to Milteer, "They not only lived side by side with whites, but also prayed with them, served with them in the militia, and voted with them at the polls." Indeed, between 1808 and 1832, John Chavis, a free Black Virginian, operated a successful school for both Black and white children in Raleigh until he was forced to close it down due to the introduction of new anti-literacy laws in the wake of Nat Turner's rebellion. After emancipation, North Carolinian free people of color used the social, cultural, and, at times, economic capital they had developed during the antebellum period to maintain a network of self-supporting schools, particularly when federal or benevolent aid was not forthcoming.[8]

A Contested Terrain draws on a wide range of traditional archival sources, including the records of the Freedmen's Bureau, nineteenth-century newspapers and periodicals, census records, slave narratives, college catalogs, the archives of northern aid and missionary societies, and the letters, memoirs, and diaries of the teachers themselves. Different sources were useful for telling the stories of different groups of teachers. The records of the aid and missionary societies, such as the American Missionary Association archives, give an important insight into the lives and work of those who secured employment with such organizations. Predictably, most of these teachers were white northerners which partly explains their overrepresentation in the historical literature until recently. A significant number of teachers, namely white and Black North Carolinians, worked in independent schools that were supported by local freedpeople, aid from the Freedmen's Bureau, or a combination of both. For these teachers, the records of the Freedmen's Bureau can offer a window into their lives and work, especially if they applied to the federal agency for aid. Many teachers left a record of their work in the form of letters, memoirs, and diaries and the digitization of sources means that these are now more accessible than ever. Periodicals published by northern aid and missionary societies regularly featured letters from their teachers in the South. These should be interpreted with caution, though, and may not always represent a reliable source of historical fact because they were explicitly intended to generate interest, funding, and support among northern readers. Similarly, letters of application for teaching positions, which are inherently biased in nature, may not accurately reflect the reasons why an applicant was seeking work among the freedpeople. Southern white teachers, it would appear, left less evidence of their work in the South and Butchart intimates that this may have been because they were ashamed of their work.[9]

The Freedmen's Teacher Project (FTP), a large-scale database providing biographical information on over 12,000 individuals who taught the freedpeople between 1861 and 1875, was used to supplement this research. According to the database, a total of 1,419 men and women taught the freedpeople in North Carolina. Although complete data is not available for every teacher, the database can identify their full name, gender, race, birth year, family relationships, religion, parents' occupation, the teacher's occupation before and after teaching in the freedpeople's schools, changes in marital status, educational level attained, institution they attended, years they taught (with location of each year), and home state. For southern white teachers, the database may also indicate if they or their parents had been slaveholders, were immigrants, or were of northern extraction. A supplemental database, known as the wealth database, provides information relating to the teachers' relative economic status in 1860 and 1870. However, this database only provides information on the Black and white teachers who were natives of North Carolina and partial information is provided for just 190 of the 751 teachers.[10]

Although the FTP was primarily used to construct the teachers' biographical profile, it was also useful for clarifying and redressing many of the misconceptions held about the freedpeople's teachers. The idea that northern white teachers were committed to Black educational advancement, for instance, was undoubtedly affirmed by the words of Massachusetts native Frances E. Bonnell who, in 1865, expressed her delight at teaching the freedpeople. "I think I could work among these people all my life," she wrote in a letter to her sponsoring organization. However, an analysis of the FTP reveals that Bonnell did not continue teaching in New Bern for more than one year, suggesting that she may have been less committed to freedpeople's education than her correspondence suggests. Additionally, the FTP could be used to provide some initial clues to the teachers' motivations. The length of time an individual spent in the classroom, for example, was often indicative of their commitment to freedpeople's education, particularly when this data was used alongside information from other archival sources. The teachers' religion, education, sponsoring organization, and previous occupation could also be used to interpret their attitudes toward and expectations of Black freedom, as will be demonstrated throughout the pages of this book.

Although the FTP was a valuable source, it is important to remember that each of the teachers included in the database are listed because there was some record, however partial, of their work in a Black school. This is particularly important when we consider the work of southern white teachers who may not have left a record of their work. As such, Butchart maintains that "far more southern white teachers worked in Black schools than can currently be fully identified for inclusion" in the database. Indeed, in the course of researching this topic, a number of teachers who were not included in the database have been identified and it is possible that more will come to light as further research is conducted. Moreover, although the home state has been identified for almost every teacher, the race for 191 teachers is as yet unknown.[11]

A Contested Terrain is divided into six chapters. Chapter 1 provides an overview of the Civil War and early Reconstruction period in North Carolina in order to contextualize the experiences of Black and white North Carolinians and elucidate some of the reasons why they elected to become teachers. It begins by examining the impact of the war on the state's socioeconomic landscape before interrogating conflicting views of Black freedom, the changing status of Black

North Carolinians, and how white southerners responded to emancipation. Key political developments, such as the formation of the Republican Party and the enfranchisement of Black men, are also examined. In this chapter, I argue that the right to vote was central to the freedpeople's definition of freedom and they used enfranchisement as an opportunity to legitimize their demands for education.

Chapter 2 examines the school-building process in North Carolina. It begins by examining the various ways in which Black North Carolinians organized and mobilized from the earliest days of freedom to create a network of schools for themselves and their children. In an effort to elucidate how competing ideologies within the postwar educational landscape intertwined to create a complex network of schools across the state, this chapter also analyzes the role of the Freedmen's Bureau and northern benevolent organizations. The practicalities of establishing schools, from funding requirements to teacher recruitment, and how these efforts ultimately gave rise to a public school system for both Black and white North Carolinians, is also examined.

Chapters 3 and 4 are specifically focused on the freedpeople's teachers. Chapter 3 develops the profile of the men and women who engaged in southern Black schooling. Using a combination of traditional archival material as well as data from the FTP, this chapter categorizes the freedpeople's teachers into four distinct groups: northern white, southern white, northern Black, and southern Black. It finds that most of the teachers in North Carolina were southern Black men and women, the vast majority of whom were natives of the state. The northern white teaching force, which represented about 26 percent of the entire teaching cohort, was dominated by young, unmarried women, so the "Yankee Schoolmarm" archetype is not entirely unfounded. Although white southerners represented a distinct minority of the freedpeople's teaching force, approximately 10 percent to be precise, an overwhelming number of these men and women were members of a Quaker church and their role in education often represented a genuine interest in and commitment to Black educational advancement.[12]

Chapter 4 moves on to interrogate the reasons why these men and women elected to become teachers. Although the teachers of the freedpeople can be categorized into four distinct groups, their motives were complex and fluid, often evolving over time, and defy such neat categorization. Shared experiences within the broader social, political, and cultural landscape, as opposed to regional identities or racial backgrounds, often shaped the teachers' decisions to seek work in a southern Black school. Moved by the didactic ideals of the northern common school system, for instance, northern Black and white teachers were often motivated by the desire to inculcate the former slaves with nineteenth-century middle-class ideals and values. Similarly, mounting poverty resulting from the postwar economic climate drove many North Carolinians, both Black and white, into the classroom. The desire to reform the freedpeople and maintain social control was a goal shared by many white teachers, both northern and southern, who were influenced by a combination of racial paternalism and idealistic notions of their own racial superiority. While dominant motivations occasionally emerged within a specific group of teachers, such as a commitment to racial elevation among Black teachers, the complex array of motivations transcends simplistic categorizations and reductive overgeneralizations by reflecting the dynamic interplay of social, political, and cultural factors that guided their work.

An analysis of the textbooks used in southern Black classrooms provides the basis for Chapter 5. It provides a textual analysis of a selection of northern common school textbooks and those that were specifically created for the freedpeople, otherwise known as freedmen's texts or textbooks. Although textbook analyses tell us little about what was actually taught or learned in the classroom, they provide important insights into the ideologies of the dominant race, gender, and social class. Ultimately, this chapter argues that both sets of textbooks portrayed Black people as racially inferior to whites, principally in an effort to maintain white supremacy. Such a portrayal indicates that nineteenth-century white Americans subscribed to the notion that mankind was naturally divided into distinct racial groups and, more significantly, that the white race was inherently superior. It also suggests that the powerful white Americans of this period were committed to perpetuating the racial subordination of Black people, both before and after the Civil War period.

Finally, Chapter 6 provides an overview of what life was like in Reconstruction North Carolina for the freedpeople's teachers. Regardless of whether they were northern or southern, teaching the freedpeople was a challenging occupation that required the utmost strength and resilience. In addition to classroom teaching, educators often engaged in a multitude of activities which ranged from the distribution of aid to the organization of labor. Life in Reconstruction North Carolina was not without merit, however, and many teachers used their work in the South as an opportunity for adventure while others forged strong relationships that lasted a lifetime. The rise of white paramilitary organizations, such as the Ku Klux Klan, as well as localized acts of violence toward freedpeople's schools, teachers, and students looms large in this chapter because it played such a pivotal role in shaping the trajectory of southern Black schooling.

In 1877, Reconstruction officially drew to a close when the last military troops were withdrawn from North Carolina. Yet the struggle for educational equality continued. When southern Democrats regained political dominance of the state, the gradual process of reversing the educational gains made during Reconstruction began. Although "Redeemers" were initially prevented from making any drastic changes due to the legal and constitutional provisions established during Reconstruction, attacks on Black schooling accelerated as the nineteenth century progressed, ultimately resulting in a racially segregated school system and an emphasis on industrial education for Black youth. The history of freedpeople's education, then, is bittersweet. On the one hand, it illuminates how the struggle for educational equality began from the earliest days of freedom, as localized acts of aggression, white paramilitary violence, and restrictive interpretations of Black freedom combined to prevent Black North Carolinians from accessing quality schooling. On the other hand, this history also serves as a testament to the determination and resilience of North Carolina's Black community to grow and develop a network of schools for themselves and their children. Through their activism, Black North Carolinians and their allies succeeded in establishing a public school system for both races, professionalizing the Black teaching force, and creating an extensive network of HBCUs throughout the state. While this process was not easy and the struggle for educational equality continued well into the twentieth century, it highlights the extent to which Black North Carolinians remained steadfast in their quest for education.

1 The Civil War and Early Reconstruction Period in North Carolina

When the Civil War ended in 1865, North Carolina lay in ruins. Not only had emancipation completely transformed the region's social, political, and economic landscape but the widespread destruction left in the wake of both the Union and Confederate armies meant that most of the population emerged from the war in poverty. Although few major battles occurred in North Carolina, the Union army waged many aggressive campaigns in the state. Brigadier General Ambrose E. Burnside's expedition during the spring and summer of 1862 was particularly successful in capturing many strategic locations along North Carolina's coastal plains, including Roanoke Island, New Bern, Fort Macon, and Beaufort. When news of the fall of Roanoke Island reached nearby Elizabeth City in February 1862, panic-stricken residents attempted to burn the town to the ground in an effort to subvert the growing expansion of the Union army into North Carolina's interior. Although the fire only succeeded in burning a very small section of the town, Elizabeth City rapidly deteriorated as the Civil War progressed. Once described as "a busy and beautiful little city," a *New York Times* correspondent noted that by the end of the war, Elizabeth City was deserted, overgrown, and laid to ruins "by vandal Georgian troops."[1]

In December 1863, Brigadier General Edward A. Wild launched a three-week raid on the northeastern region of North Carolina. According to Barton A. Myers, Wild's raid grew progressively "more aggressive, and far more destructive" in an attempt to crush guerrilla warfare in the region. During this three-week period, homes were burned, farms and infrastructure were destroyed, and livestock was confiscated. On one occasion, Wild sent Colonel Draper to Knott's Island along North Carolina's eastern seaboard to burn as many guerrilla houses as he could find. "As we left the village," wrote a northern journalist accompanying Wild's expedition, "smoke was seen rising from several points on Knotts island, showing that Col. Draper was carrying out the order of the General, 'to burn pretty freely.'"[2]

General William T. Sherman's march through Georgia and the Carolinas on route to Virginia during the winter of 1864–1865 was equally destructive. After employing a scorched earth policy in Georgia and South Carolina, white North Carolinians fearfully awaited Sherman's advance. "What the fate of our pleasant towns and villages and of our isolated farmhouses would be, we could easily read by the light of the blazing roof-trees that lit up the path of the advancing army," reflected Cornelia Phillips Spenser of Chapel Hill in 1866. White North Carolinians were right to be anxious. Approximately three months into the campaign, forty miles of countryside from Savannah, Georgia, to Goldsboro, North Carolina, "had been laid to waste."[3]

The use of foraging by both armies was often as destructive as Union raids and left North Carolina both physically and economically devastated. Prior to commencing his "March to the Sea," Sherman issued Special Field Order No. 120 which advised his army to "forage liberally." Soldiers were instructed to gather corn, meat, vegetables, horses, mules, and wagons as well as "whatever is needed by the command." They were also given permission to destroy mills, houses, and cotton gins. If guerrillas or hostile civilians attempted to obstruct the march, Sherman permitted the army commander to "order and enforce a devastation more or less relentless, according to the measure of such hostility." Although Sherman warned that the destruction of property was not permitted in areas "where the army is unmolested," few men adhered to this rule. As John Barrett found, "The majority of officers and men in Sherman's army neither engaged in indiscriminate looting nor condemned the actions of those who did." Jane Constance Hinton, the sister of a former slaveowner, Confederate soldier, and freedpeople's educator, could certainly attest to this and on April 15, 1865, six days after Confederate General Robert E. Lee surrendered at the Appomattox Court House in Virginia, Hinton's plantation home was ransacked and raided by "bummers," or foragers, of Sherman's army.[4]

In addition to the physical destruction, Sherman's total war campaign had a devastating effect upon the Confederate army. "Sherman's march through Georgia and South Carolina has disheartened the troops from those states & the mighty desertions from our skeleton Regiments are frightful," confessed one Confederate soldier two months prior to the collapse of the Confederacy. "I am telling you a simple truth, it is far from my wish, but it is nevertheless true. Some report to Grant & some go home."[5] Admittedly, desertion had been pervasive among North Carolina's regiments from as early as 1863, largely due to the strains of war on the home front, and Sherman's march through North Carolina merely exacerbated an already problematic situation.[6] As the Civil War progressed, Union troops extended into North Carolina's interior and in late March 1865, General George Stoneman also led raids in the western region of the state. Clearly, then, it was not until the final stages of the Civil War that "the full fury of war became a reality" for many North Carolinians. Finally, on April 26, 1865, seventeen days after Lee surrendered at Appomattox, the Confederate army under General Joseph E. Johnston surrendered to Sherman at Bennett Place in Durham, North Carolina, thus signaling the end of Sherman's "Carolinas Campaign."[7]

In the midst of the Civil War and before formal emancipation was announced in 1863, enslaved people in North Carolina fled their masters' homes for the safety of Union lines in the easternmost part of the state. By 1865, it is estimated that over 17,000 Black North Carolinians "had sought refuge in the Union-held areas of the state." Some traveled hundreds of miles to escape slavery and many died or were re-enslaved along the way. Often escaping from bondage with little more than the clothes on their backs, North Carolinian freedpeople had amassed little, if any, material possessions and most were entirely destitute. Upon reaching Union lines, they quickly realized that the Union army was barely equipped to support itself let alone the growing number of self-emancipated people. Overcrowded, unsanitary, and rampant with disease, Union camps lacked adequate medical facilities, food, shelter, and clothing. Freedmen and women were often forced to sleep in the streets or camp in the woods and many died from starvation, disease, and exposure. Over the course of three days in 1864, sixteen freedpeople died on Roanoke Island, "not from any prevailing disease," wrote Elizabeth Havard James, a white teacher from Medford, Massachusetts, "but from 'deep colds' as [the freedpeople] expressed it."[8] The previous winter, James reported visiting a household which contained almost thirty men, women, children, and infants living in one room which was filled with so much smoke from a stove without a chimney that it was impossible to see across it. "Many of the babies were sick," she reported, "and two died the next day from exposure." Conditions were as deplorable in Trent Camp near New Bern and northern white teacher J. W. Burghduff reported that he regularly received requests for food and clothing that he simply could not meet. "My heart aches for them," he lamented, "but we have not an article of clothing for them, and surely cannot feed them." On Roanoke Island, the supply of clothing was so poor that freedpeople's teacher Sarah P. Freeman openly worried about how she would clothe an orphaned boy who was brought to her wearing "nothing but the remnant of an old flannel shirt to cover him." After much effort, six-year-old Jim was finally "fitted out in a new suit of clothes" which included a pair of pants made of twelve pieces.[9]

Poverty was pervasive in postwar North Carolina. Although North Carolina never retained a plantation system quite like neighboring South Carolina or Virginia, much of its economic system was nonetheless heavily reliant upon slave labor; by 1860, slaves made up one-third of North Carolina's population, the vast majority of whom were situated in the eastern region of the state. In addition, the banking system had all but collapsed. Just before the outbreak of war, the Confederate dollar, commonly known as the "greyback," went into circulation. As the war waged on, the number of banknotes increased, inflation occurred, Confederate currency lost its value, and by 1865 the greyback was virtually worthless. Reflecting on the difficulties that she faced during the postwar period, Delphina Mendenhall, a Quaker teacher of the freedpeople, wrote, "I did not suffer any losses by either army – But by the destruction of the Banks, and State Stock, this means my Husband left for my support in old age, is gone, and person's indebted to my Husband's estate, were made insolvent by the war."[10]

Economic recovery was a slow process in Reconstruction North Carolina and all areas of the state were affected. Eight months after the Civil War ended, Samuel S. Ashley, an American Missionary Association (AMA) superintendent in North Carolina, admitted that there was "much suffering" in the southeastern town of Fayetteville. "Indeed there is suffering everywhere in the county," he concluded. In 1866, a Scottish-born Presbyterian minister echoed Ashley's observations, reporting that "a great deal" of property had been destroyed in North Carolina and that the property holders were now more or less impoverished. One year later, Joel Ashworth, a native of the state, confided in a Quaker missionary that "Times are rather hard in Randolph at this time money and provisions both scarce." By 1869 matters had not much improved and a Black teacher from Pennsylvania wrote, "there is scarcely any money in the country."[11]

Although Union victory succeeded in abolishing slavery, Black labor was still needed in the fields and on the plantations. This meant that many white residents attempted to reestablish a system of labor that closely resembled slavery. Commenting on the white population near his headquarters in Raleigh, Freedmen's Bureau Assistant Commissioner for North Carolina Colonel E. Whittlesey said, "I think they would re-establish slavery just as it was before, if there was no fear of any evil consequences from the government or from the people of other states. If not that, they would enact laws which would make the blacks virtually slaves. I have no doubt of that."[12] Whittlesey was proven correct. In January 1866, North Carolina's first postwar legislature enacted "the notorious Black Codes," a series of laws which, in the words of Eric Foner, "denied African Americans political rights and equality before the law, and imposed on them mandatory yearlong contracts, coercive apprenticeship regulations, and criminal penalties for breach of contract."[13] Although the Civil Rights Act of 1866 essentially invalidated these codes, the withdrawal of federal troops from the South in 1877 allowed southern legislatures to enact a series of new, racially discriminatory state laws which served to relegate Black people to a position of second-class citizenship and uphold white supremacy.[14]

According to Lieutenant George O. Sanderson, a Union veteran and Freedmen's Bureau official, many white North Carolinians refused "to recognize the condition of the former slaves as freedmen." Some, Sanderson reflected, threatened to "make it worse" for the freedpeople once military troops were withdrawn from the state, "that is, to make their freedom of no avail to them."[15] Even in the face of military occupation, some white southerners succeeded in holding their former slaves in a condition of servitude after the Civil War had ended. In Gates County, a local man named David Parker offered his former slaves board and clothing if they continued to work for him. Fearful of the repercussions if they refused, the freedpeople reluctantly agreed. When Superintendent of Negro Affairs Horace James learned of the situation he went to investigate. "There was no complaint of the food, nor much of the clothing," he reported, "but they were in constant terror of the whip." One man was kept in chains during the night and the rest were too afraid to run away. "Some were beaten or whipped almost every day," James concluded. Tellingly, Gates County was located "on the northern border of the State, far away from any influence of troops, and where the military power of the government had been little felt." Thus, as James observed, this incident reflected, to some degree, the difficulties that Black men and women in "similar localities" faced in the aftermath of emancipation.[16]

According to James, some of the freedpeople who continued to work for their former masters complained that they "were treated with more cruelty than when they were slaves."[17] Two months after Confederate defeat, in rural Wilson County, two freedwomen testified against their former master for beating them. Determined to ensure that "no d-d nigger should be free under him," William Barnes tied one of these women outstretched between two trees and cut her hair off. Three dogs were then set upon her before she was given two hundred lashes with a paddle, "a strap made purposely for whipping negroes."[18] Although violent acts of aggression such as this had been pervasive during times of slavery, the freedwomen's ability and willingness to testify against their former owners reflects not only the power struggle that ensued between former master and slave in the aftermath of emancipation, but the sheer determination of North Carolina's freed population to shape the contours of their newfound freedom.

Reluctance to perceive the former slaves as free men and women was coupled with an unwillingness to view Black people as intelligent and autonomous individuals. Rooted in the prevailing assumptions of Black inferiority, the freedpeople were regarded as lazy, ignorant, and submissive, on the one hand, or violent, aggressive, and predisposed to criminality on the other.[19] The freedpeople "are idle, thriftless and improvident," reported *The North Carolinian* in March 1868, "and we can see no hope for an improvement in their condition as a class."[20] In addition, many white North Carolinians steadfastly believed that "a free negro cannot be made to work," a belief which, in their eyes, justified the enforcement of restrictive labor contracts.[21] Deep-rooted notions of Black inferiority made it even more difficult for the former slaves to assert their new rights and, as later sections of this book will demonstrate, many freedpeople struggled to gain control of their own institutions, including their schools.

In spite of the prevailing racial attitudes, North Carolinian freedpeople grew increasingly hopeful that freedom would yield new possibilities, new opportunities, and a life that was altogether different from the one they led in slavery. This hope appeared to become a reality when, on March 2, 1867, the Radical Republican-dominated US Congress passed the First Reconstruction Act. Marking the beginning of Congressional, or Radical, Reconstruction, this act divided ten of the eleven former Confederate states into five military districts and demanded the creation of new state constitutions that would ratify the Fourteenth Amendment and enfranchise all male citizens over the age of twenty-one "of whatever race, color, or previous condition," except for those who participated in the rebellion or were guilty of committing a felony. At a time when only seven northern states allowed Black men to vote, these constitutions, which were to be "framed by a convention of delegates" elected by said citizens, was shaping up to be one of the most liberal in the history of the United States.[22]

On March 27, 1867, the Republican Party was formed in North Carolina under the leadership of former provisional governor, William Woods Holden, and it immediately made plans to register all eligible voters, resulting in the registration of 72,932 Black voters out of a total of 179,653. An election was held on November 20, 1867, to decide whether there should be a state constitutional convention and elect delegates to it. This was the first election in which Black men enjoyed the right to vote. 93,006 voted in favor of the convention, 32,961 opposed it and 53,686 registered voters did not vote either way; due to the disenfranchisement of ex-Confederates, the abstaining voters believed that they were underrepresented and rendered the convention undemocratic. One hundred and twenty delegates were elected, the majority of whom were Republican. Teachers of the freedpeople were particularly well-represented and such delegates included the northern white educator, lawyer, and politician Albion W. Tourgée, AMA Superintendent Samuel S. Ashley, northern Black educators James Edward O'Hara and James Walker Hood, and the formerly enslaved James Henry Harris.[23]

Arriving in North Carolina in 1864 as a missionary with the African Methodist Episcopal Zion (AMEZ) Church, James Walker Hood was instrumental to the growth and development of freedpeople's education. In addition to serving as a delegate to the state's constitutional convention, which was responsible for ratifying a new public school system for both Black and white North Carolinians, Hood also served as the chairman of the Freedmen's Convention of North Carolina two years earlier. In 1868, he became the state's first Black assistant superintendent of Public Instruction, a position which he held for three years until the Democratic "Redeemer" government abolished the post. Although Hood gradually withdrew from political affairs during the period of "Redemption," he continued to work for the religious and educational elevation of Black North Carolinians. In 1872, Hood became the seventeenth bishop of the AMEZ church and seven years later, in 1879, he helped establish the Zion Wesley Institute in Concord, North Carolina, which eventually relocated to Salisbury and became known as Livingstone College, an AMEZ-sponsored HBCU (Historically Black Colleges and Universities).[24]

In January 1868, delegates gathered in Raleigh to draft North Carolina's new constitution. Three months later, freedmen were given the opportunity to vote for its ratification. Many Black people heralded this momentous event as a new beginning for the Black race, not least because the new constitution provided for the implementation of state-funded public schools for both Black and white children. Reflecting upon his experience at the polls, northern Black teacher Robert G. Fitzgerald optimistically viewed the event as signaling the end of racial discrimination in the southern United States, despite overhearing "a white man say today is the Black man's day. Tomorrow will be the white man's." This election ultimately resulted in the adoption of North Carolina's "most liberal constitution" by a vote of 93,086 to 74,016. On July 20, 1868, after ratifying the Fourteenth Amendment, North Carolina was readmitted to the Union.[25]

The right to vote was central to the freedpeople's definition of freedom and on November 3, 1868, Black men in seven former Confederate states were given another opportunity to vote in the presidential election between Ulysses S. Grant, the Republican candidate, and Horatio Seymour, the Democratic nominee. In North Carolina, Robert Fitzgerald was exuberant about this new opportunity and on voting day he wrote:

> The great epoch in the history of our race has at last arrived, and today the colored citizens of these southern [states] are casting their votes for the presidential candidate U.S. Grant & Schuyler Colfax. The citizens of Hillsboro are

jubilant and their votes are going in like snowflakes, silently and surely. Everything is quiet and there seems to be the best feeling all around.[26]

The enfranchisement of Black men and their very obvious desire to exercise this right ultimately resulted in increased calls for freedpeople's education. Although the loudest calls came from northern whites and, in a couple of instances, the northern Black elite who were "worried that [the freedpeople] were not yet ready for such responsibility," the freed population also recognized that political responsibility necessitated schooling. "The negroes strongly aspire to the common rights of citizens," wrote Horace James. "[They] want to buy and sell and get gain, to select and favor their own church and school, and party, to defend themselves, to litigate with and implead one another, to hold written documents instead of verbal promises, and to manage their own affairs."[27]

Although education was central to the realization of each of these goals, the freedpeople's profound desire to become educated was multifaceted. On the one hand, many freedpeople understood that education was central to securing citizenship in postwar American society while others viewed it as a safeguard against re-enslavement. "If we are *educated,* they can't make slaves of us again," declared one Black student in New Bern. Others recognized the privileges that education could bring and sought to use schooling as a means of securing economic independence. Many freedpeople were more pragmatic in their approach toward education. Some endeavored to become literate in order to read the Bible while others learned the hard way that basic literacy skills were required in order to read, understand, and negotiate contracts. This function of schooling became significantly more pressing as more and more freedpeople were compelled to seek work in the fields or on the plantations. Rather than working for subsistence such as food, clothing, and lodging, as many employers offered, the freedpeople demanded wages or, at the very least, a portion of the crops which necessitated the creation of labor contracts. Taking advantage of the freedpeople's illiteracy, many employers successfully cheated the freedpeople out of their wages by creating complex labor contracts that were purposely confusing or misleading. In 1866, Freedmen's Bureau General Superintendent of Education John W. Alvord reported that he saw one labor contract "in which it was stipulated that 'one-third of seven-twelfths of all corn, potatoes, and fodder, &ce. Shall go to the laborers.'" In an address to the first Constitutional Convention of 1865, the Freedmen's Convention of North Carolina asked for friendly relations between whites and Blacks, particularly in terms of labor. "Our first and engrossing concern in our new relation is, how may we provide shelter and an honorable subsistence for ourselves and families. You will say, work; but without your just and considerate aid, how shall we secure adequate compensation for our labor?"[28] It was within this context, fraught with mounting poverty, racial discrimination, and unprecedented political transformation, that the freedpeople actively endeavored to establish a system of schooling for themselves and their children. This work was not done by the freedpeople alone. On the contrary, it required the collaborative efforts of multiple organizations and individuals, each with their distinct vision of Black freedom and the role that education would play.

2

To "Enjoy the Benefits of a School": Black North Carolinians and the Quest for Education

Growing a network of schools for the freedpeople was a collaborative effort that required the input of multiple individuals and organizations, including the Bureau of Refugees, Freedmen, and Abandoned Lands, more commonly known as the Freedmen's Bureau, northern aid and missionary societies, and, of course, the freedpeople themselves. Within this intricate educational landscape, the freedpeople emerged as the driving force and persistently demonstrated their commitment to education despite mounting obstacles which included postwar poverty, racial discrimination, rising hostility, and inadequate support from the federal government. The resulting network of freedpeople's schools ultimately gave rise to a public school system for both Black and white children as well as an extensive network of Historically Black Colleges and Universities (HBCUs). Yet, the educational landscape was far from uniform and each of the individuals and organizations involved had their own distinct vision regarding the nature and purpose of freedpeople's education.

From the earliest days of freedom, Freedmen's Bureau officials, school superintendents, and other members of the public often commented on the freedpeople's profound desire to learn. "The people are in great poverty," wrote Michael P. Jerkins, a Black teacher from Beaufort, North Carolina, "still there is a strong thirst for knowledge." H. S. Beals of the American Missionary Association (AMA) made a similar observation and while stationed in Beaufort he wrote, "All around us the Freedmen are struggling hard against poverty, some against actual starvation, yet they beg harder for a school than for food or clothing." While stationed in New Bern during the spring of 1862, North Carolina Superintendent of the Poor Vincent Colyer was utterly amazed to find that in spite of their poverty "the colored refugees evinced the utmost eagerness to learn to read." Thus, with the permission of Union General John G. Foster, Colyer established two schools for Black children and one for poor whites. According to one northern soldier, who also served as teacher, the two Black schools were always "full to overflowing."[1]

According to Freedmen's Bureau General Superintendent of Education John W. Alvord, the freedpeople's thirst for knowledge was not exaggerated and in his first semiannual report on schools he wrote:

> This is a wonderful state of things. We have just emerged from a terrific war; peace is not yet declared. There is scarcely the beginning of recognized society at the south; and yet here is a people long imbruted by slavery, and the most despised of any of earth, whose chains are no sooner broken than they spring to their feet and start up an exceeding great army, clothing themselves with intelligence. What other people on earth have ever shown, while in their ignorance, such a passion for education?[2]

In her assessment of freedpeople's education, Harriet Beecher Stowe, the bestselling author of *Uncle Tom's Cabin*, reiterated Alvord's observations and acknowledged that throughout history, no other group of formerly enslaved people have demonstrated such a profound thirst for knowledge. "Their enthusiasm and impulse was not for plunder, or for revenge, or for drink, or any form of animal indulgence," she wrote, "but for *education*." Tellingly, Stowe's remark betrays some of the concerns that white northerners had about Black freedom. While some feared that the freedpeople would invade the North, others worried that they would seek revenge on those who were complicit in perpetuating racial slavery. Most, however, were worried that the former slaves would form a permanent dependent class or become a destabilizing threat to society. Such fears were ultimately rooted in the conflicting racial stereotypes that permeated American culture throughout the nineteenth century. Perpetuated by literature, the sciences, theater, and the press, these racial stereotypes constructed Black people as unintelligent, lazy, and childlike, on the one hand, or uncivilized, dangerous, and predisposed to criminality on the other.[3]

When the Civil War ended in 1865, Black North Carolinians continued to organize and mobilize to create a sustainable system of education for themselves and their children. On the grassroots level, this involved building schoolhouses, hiring teachers, purchasing land, leasing property, and securing classroom supplies. Very often, this work necessitated the creation of local committees which assumed responsibility for raising the requisite funds. In 1867, freedmen and women in Burke County organized "to solicit funds for the education of our ignorant brethren." One year later, freedpeople in Lincolnton raised ten dollars "by voluntary contribution" for the local school. In Beaufort, local freedpeople raised over

$800 toward the construction of a new school building which they were "naturally rather proud of." "Let those who say that the Freedmen will never learn to help themselves visit Beaufort," wrote Samuel J. Whiton from Westford, Connecticut, "and listen to the story of this people's self-denial and toil in erecting this building." Sometimes, individual Black North Carolinians took it upon themselves to fund a school in their community. In 1867, a Black resident in Alamance County rented a schoolhouse at the expense of four dollars per month so that his neighbors could have access to education. That same year, North Carolina Superintendent of Education, F. A. Fiske, reported that "a poor colored man . . . who has no family of his own, built a log school house with his own hands, and hired a teacher on his own responsibility in order that his neighbor's children, in the depth of their poverty and ignorance, might enjoy the benefits of a school."[4]

The former slaves also organized politically to ensure greater access to education, which was no small undertaking considering the significant opposition that many faced in their attempts to do so. In October 1865, 117 Black men from forty-two different counties gathered at the African Methodist Episcopal Church in the state's capital of Raleigh to open the first postwar Freedmen's Convention in the South. Elected at meetings held throughout North Carolina, but particularly in the Black-majority counties along the eastern region of the state, these Black delegates consisted of those who were literate before the war as well as those who "don't-know-A-from-B." At this convention, delegates outlined their hopes and visions of Black freedom. Adopting a predominantly conservative stance, and praised by the press as a result, delegates called for friendly relations with whites, increased access to education, equal employment opportunities, and "to have all the oppressive laws which make unjust discriminations on account of race or color wiped from the statutes of the state." Reporting on the event from Raleigh, *The New York Times* wrote, "Some of the delegates, particularly Mr. J. H. Harris, of this county, exhibit intelligence of an extraordinary character, and all, with a few exceptions, have evinced a remarkably conservative and conciliatory spirit in their references to their late masters."[5]

James Henry Harris was a key political figure in North Carolina during the Civil War and Reconstruction era. A prominent member of the Union League, he also taught the freedpeople in Raleigh between 1865 and 1867. Appointed president of the State Equal Rights League, an organization founded at the first Freedmen's Convention, Harris organized a second freedmen's convention in Raleigh on October 2, 1866.[6] The focus of this convention was on education, race relations, and politics and it succeeded in establishing the Freedmen's Educational Association of North Carolina, the aim of which was to "aid in the establishment of schools, from which none shall be excluded on account of color or poverty and to encourage unsectarian education in this State especially among the freedmen." The convention's efforts appear to have paid off. Two months later, in December 1866, F. A. Fiske reported that of the ninety-five reported schools for the freedpeople, fifteen were "sustained by freedmen" while another twenty were "sustained in part by freedmen." Twenty-two school buildings were owned by the freedpeople.[7]

Nowhere was the freedpeople's educational activism more evident than in Fayetteville which boasted a thriving community of free people of color during the antebellum period. In 1867, seven local residents expended $136 on the purchase of a site for the construction of a school. Although the Freedmen's Bureau financed the building of the schoolhouse, the Black community actively participated in the growth and development of two local Black schools, the Philips School for primary grades and the Sumner School for intermediate level. Supported by prominent Black leaders such as James W. Hood and brothers Robert and Cicero Harris, who were freeborn Fayetteville natives, Black residents were committed to achieving "financial self-sufficiency" in order to protect and preserve their institutions in the face of growing uncertainty and financial instability. Such efforts ultimately culminated in the graded Howard School in 1869, present-day Fayetteville State University, which went on to become North Carolina's first State Colored Normal School in 1877.[8]

While the freedpeople's efforts were undeniably commendable and clearly demonstrate that they did not passively wait for the assistance of northern organizations, their role in the establishment of schools reflects wider issues relating to inadequate funding and a lack of support. As F. A. Fiske reported in January 1868, more than two-thirds of the schools in North Carolina were "sustained without aid from Northern Societies and need some assistance from the bureau in the form of rent or otherwise." On a tour of North Carolina in 1866, John W. Alvord frequently encountered formerly enslaved men and women who were actively attempting to educate themselves. On one occasion, he reported visiting a "native school" in Wayne County that was established by "Two young colored men, who but a little time before commenced to learn themselves." The school was attended by 150 pupils, "all quite orderly and hard at study," who paid a small tuition fee to attend. Alvord was told that he was the first white person to visit the school. Not long after, he visited a similar institution in Halifax County which was "the first of *any kind* which had been opened in that county since the war."[9]

From the federal perspective, the Freedmen's Bureau played an instrumental role in the growth and development of freedpeople's education. Established by an act of Congress on March 3, 1865 as a temporary agency under the leadership of Maine-born Major General Oliver Otis Howard, the Freedmen's Bureau, in the words of Ira C. Colby, "provided federally mandated social welfare programs to the former rebellious states and their localities primarily to assist and protect the freedmen in their new social status within white America." The Bureau's assistance was not limited to formerly enslaved men and women and it also attempted to aid displaced southern whites.[10] Although one of the Bureau's primary functions lay in the field of education, it also provided food, clothing, and medical aid, settled labor disputes, investigated claims of racial violence and, prior to President Johnson's order that abandoned or confiscated property must be returned to their southern white owners, facilitated land redistribution among the former slaves.[11] In his analysis of the Freedmen's Bureau in North Carolina, Gregory P. Downs found, "In the first six months [of operation], the Freedmen's Bureau certified contracts for more than 5,300 freedpeople, moved fifty criminal cases to trial, heard at least 5,000 complaints, oversaw several thousand sick people in hospitals, apprenticed 400 orphans, and rented out large tracts of abandoned lands to freedpeople." The regulation of labor was one of the Bureau's most pressing goals and by enforcing a labor-contract system, it attempted to push the former slaves back into the fields and onto the plantations as a subservient labor force.[12]

From the outset, the Freedmen's Bureau was significantly underfunded and understaffed. According to Paul A. Cimbala and Randal M. Miller, not more than 900 Bureau agents were working throughout the entire southern region at any one time. Because it was initially established as a temporary agency, Congress did not provide the Bureau with any funding, believing instead that the sale of abandoned plantations and rents from the surrounding lands would be enough to finance the agency's operations. Although other sources of funding came "from the quartermaster, commissary and medical departments of the army," as well as taxes on salaries and cotton, fines in the provost courts, donations, and the sale of clothing, food, and farm produce, the amount of money at the Bureau's disposal varied from state to state. After President Johnson authorized the return of confiscated land to its former owners, the Bureau's primary source of funding was drastically reduced. In 1866, North Carolina's budget was ranked the second smallest in the entire southern region. Its per capita spending, at a mere eighty cents, was also the lowest in the South. Arkansas' per capita spending, for comparison, was the highest in the South at $3.59. Such inconsistent figures across the former Confederacy, as Colby wrote, "suggests that the quantity and quality of the Bureau's programs also varied on a state by state basis."[13]

In North Carolina, the educational division of the Freedmen's Bureau was under the control and management of two successive superintendents of education, F. A. Fiske and H. C. Vogell. Although both agents were committed to growing and sustaining a system of southern Black schooling, financial limitations, a lack of manpower, and volatile race relations ultimately meant that when the Bureau finally ceased operations in 1870, less than half of North Carolina's Black, school-aged population had gained access to education. Funding constraints and a limited mandate were two of the greatest obstacles the Bureau faced in terms of educational provision. Although it could pay for a teacher's transportation to and from the South, as well as the rent of a school building which was often used to supplement the teachers' wages, the Bureau could not hire teachers or pay their salary. Instead, this responsibility fell to the northern aid and missionary associations which, as will be discussed shortly, experienced their own budgetary limitations. As a result, countless Black children throughout North Carolina were unable to gain access to education. In 1867, six schools were ready in Orange County "but no teachers were available." Similar situations existed in Harnett, Halifax, and Northampton counties. Although there were 17,419 freedpeople in eastern North Carolina by 1864, the average school attendance for the months of December, January, February, and March 1863–1864, was just 2,290.[14]

The rural nature of North Carolina compounded this issue. Settlements were widely dispersed, and northern aid and missionary societies preferred sending teachers, especially white teachers, to schools near the towns and cities, specifically New Bern, Raleigh, Goldsboro, Greensboro, and Charlotte. In 1869, James Walker Hood, North Carolina's first Black assistant superintendent of Public Instruction, reported that he was unable to visit many schools in the interior of the state because they were inaccessible by either rail or stagecoach. It was impractical and often impossible, he claimed, to find private transportation. Due to this inaccessibility, Hood found that there was not "a single day school" beyond the Blue Ridge Mountains in the western region of the state. "There are Sabbath Schools at several points," he reported, "and the people seem anxious to have day schools, but complain that they can neither obtain books or teachers."[15]

A limited supply of appropriate schoolhouses also hindered the Bureau's educational efforts. Although it could provide financial assistance for the establishment of Black colleges, provide books and furniture, and fund repairs, it was not authorized to finance the establishment of elementary schools. In 1867, F. A. Fiske reported that "not more than about fifty percent" of the freedpeople in Fayetteville could enjoy the benefits of education. "Should a new building be erected there," he continued, "I am confident that . . . a large school might be gathered and permanently sustained."[16] Likewise, in Nash County, 500 children were waiting to learn but there were no schools. In 1866, Sidney A. Busbee, a Black North Carolinian teacher, reported that the "rude" schoolhouse constructed by the freedpeople in Snow Hill, Greene County, was not sufficient to permit educational activities during the winter period, drastically reducing the potential time Black students could spend in school.[17] As a result, teachers conducted school in whatever space was available. In Trent Camp near New Bern, classes were first held in "old deserted churches, in abandoned hospitals, in old sheds, or under the shadow of a tree." Although schoolhouses were later located, Caroline Waugh, a white New Yorker, complained that the buildings were "not what they ought to be." "You can see through them in every direction and *many, many* places you can put your hands through, which in a cold, rainy day make it impossible for scholars or teacher to keep comfortable." In the absence of a suitable schoolhouse, former slave Charles Hunter taught his students in the Protestant Episcopal Church while northern Black teacher James E. O'Hara conducted school in his own home. Due to a lack of space, O'Hara was reluctantly forced to turn several students away.[18] A myriad of other practical considerations, such as poverty, a lack of suitable clothing, precarious weather conditions, overt hostility, and the necessity to labor, also affected school attendance. Nevertheless, according to Michael Goldhaber, the Bureau's educational efforts in North Carolina were relatively successful compared to the broader southern region where only 10 percent of Black, school-aged children succeeded in gaining access to education during the Bureau's lifetime.[19]

A lack of funding also plagued the efforts of the northern aid and missionary societies which first began sending teachers to North Carolina during the 1862–1863 school year. Working in collaboration with the Freedmen's Bureau which, in the words of Oliver O. Howard, intended to "systematize and facilitate" their work, these organizations consisted of a combination of secular and denominational societies, many of which were established at the onset of the Civil War to aid the freedpeople's transition from slavery to freedom. Other organizations, such as the American Baptist Home Mission Society (ABHMS) and the AMA had been in operation during the antebellum period as Christian missionary societies and simply extended their efforts to the southern missionary field. Only one aid society examined in this study was established in the South. Tellingly, it was established by the North Carolina Yearly Meeting of Friends in 1869 under the direction of Dr. Tomlinson.[20]

At least seventeen aid societies operated in Reconstruction North Carolina (see Table 1). The major organizations operated with the assistance of local branches or auxiliary agencies. In January 1865, the New England Freedmen's Aid Society (NEFAS) recorded fifty-six branch societies operating in various towns and cities throughout New England. Members of these societies sent donations of food, clothing, bedding, tools, textbooks, classroom materials, and household goods to their headquarters in the South. They also raised money through donations, fundraisers, and membership subscriptions to sponsor teachers. For the purposes of cohesion, uniformity, and increased productivity, the secular organizations were federated into one large national organization in 1866, eventually becoming known as the American Freedmen's Union Commission (AFUC).[21]

The major difference between the secular and religious organizations was their approach to religious conversion. Unsurprisingly, most of the religious societies viewed their work in the South as an extension of their prewar missionary activity and many used their schools as a means of attracting new members into the church's fold.[22] To this end, religious aid societies attempted to employ only those who were members of their churches. "As a rule," the Presbyterian Church only employed Presbyterian teachers because "they seem in general to feel that their mission to the Freedmen is *religious* as well as educational." The Presbyterian Committee on Missions for Freedmen (PCMF) appears to have adhered

Table 1 A list of the aid societies that operated in North Carolina between 1863 and 1875

Religious aid societies	Secular aid societies
American Baptist Foreign Mission Society	American Freedmen's Union Commission
American Baptist Home Mission Society	Delaware Association
American Missionary Association	National Freedman's Relief Association
The Baltimore Association (Quaker)	New England Freedmen's Aid Society
Friends' Freedmen's Association	Northwestern Freedmen's Aid Commission
Methodist Episcopal Freedmen's Aid Society	Pennsylvania Freedmen's Relief Association
Presbyterian Committee on Missions for Freedmen	Other (public schools, Michigan Freedmen's Aid Commission, Nat. Theological. Inst. etc.)
Protestant Episcopal Freedman's Commission	Western Freedmen's Aid Commission
Quaker Yearly Meetings	

Source: Butchart et al., "The Freedmen's Teacher Project" (2022)

to this rule and only three non-Presbyterian teachers in North Carolina were sponsored by the organization between 1863 and 1875. One of these teachers was the aforementioned Caroline Waugh, a Baptist. In 1869, Waugh was sponsored by the Presbyterian Church to teach in New Bern. The remaining eight years she spent in the South were under the sponsorship of the secular NFRA, an undetermined organization, and the interdenominational AMA.[23]

Although the Quaker-led Friends' Freedmen's Association (FFA) can be classified as a religious aid society, it did not attempt to convert the freedpeople to Quakerism. As James W. Hood remarked in 1869:

> In educating the Freedmen, the Friends are doing a work of praiseworthy benevolence. Without expectation of fee or reward; without attempting to teach the peculiar tenets of their faith; without any apparent desire to advance the interest of their own denomination, they are laboring to dispel the mist of ignorance which has so long hung over the colored people of the South. The Bible is introduced into all of their schools, but is read without comment.[24]

In addition, the FFA was willing to sponsor teachers from other denominations. Eliza A. Bahel, a Methodist from Pennsylvania, taught the freedpeople in Washington, D.C., and Salisbury, North Carolina, over a period of five years, all of which were under the sponsorship of the FFA. Similarly, Frances A. Gorham, a Methodist from New York, taught the freedpeople for a total of three years, two of which were under the sponsorship of the FFA. In contrast, most of the Quaker teachers taught under the auspices of the FFA while others were sponsored by individual Quaker churches located throughout the country.[25]

The Baltimore Association for the Moral and Educational Improvement of the Colored People was another Quaker organization that was active in North Carolina, and it employed a total of six men and women, both Black and white, from the North. Interestingly, the Baltimore Association was one of the few organizations that focused its efforts upon the establishment of white, rather than Black, schools. Although other organizations did not prohibit white children from attending their schools, few whites were willing to be educated alongside Blacks. Reflecting upon his failed attempt to establish a school for both whites and Blacks in Raleigh, northern white educator Fisk Parsons Brewer observed that whites were willing to go without schooling "rather than bear up against the ridicule that meets them for going to a freedman's school." Brewer's subsequent attempt to establish a college preparatory school for poor white men also failed "when [the students] found out that I was so much engaged with the 'niggers.'" In an effort to overcome such biases, the AMA opened a school for poor whites in the coastal town of Beaufort during the winter of 1866. However, the Black community criticized the decision to exclude Black students, arguing that a white-only school served to perpetuate preexisting racial prejudices. Caught between conflicting ideals, the AMA attempted to uphold its commitment to education for all and argued that the white school could serve as a means of promoting racial harmony. To avoid further controversy, though, the AMA eventually transferred the school to the county commission and the teacher, Amy Chapman, resigned her position with the AMA to continue teaching the white students.[26]

There were exceptions, of course, and in 1863 AMA teacher Susan Hosmer reported that some poor whites in New Bern were seeking the organization's assistance. "Being earnestly requested by a mother, a white child was permitted to become a member of our school," she wrote in September of that year. "Since then several others have come in without permission and as we come to work for all, they have not been turned away." Incidents such as this often inspired freedpeople's teachers to seek funding for the establishment of white schools. Former slaveholder and Confederate soldier Willis L. Miller often petitioned the Freedmen's Bureau for aid for this very purpose, usually with limited success. As Judkin Browning explained, "Northern agents determined that the native white hostility to Black education would prohibit any full welcoming of those same whites to the privileges of education." Shortly after arriving in North Carolina in 1863, white northerner Jennie S. Bell became aware of the destitution suffered by poor whites in the Harker's Island region of the state. Failing to get any support from the Freedmen's Bureau, Bell took it upon herself to establish a school and dwelling house at her own expense. In addition to teaching basic literacy and numeracy skills, Bell placed particular emphasis on teaching agricultural and industrial skills which, according to one journalist, completely transformed both the island and its residents.[27]

The AMA was the premier aid society in North Carolina, and it was responsible for sponsoring 15 percent of the teachers examined in this study at one point in their southern missionary careers. Established as an interdenominational abolitionist organization in 1846, the AMA developed close ties with the Congregational Church during the Civil War period. Although proselytization was not the AMA's initial priority, by 1870 the conversion of freedpeople to Congregationalism became an explicit goal. This was primarily because the AMA succumbed to pressure from within the Congregational Church to gain more religious converts, even though few former slaves were attracted to the Congregational style of worship. Fearful of losing the church's financial support, the AMA began establishing churches alongside schools. As an interdenominational organization, the AMA was open to employing any teacher from an evangelical Protestant background, providing such teachers possessed a strong "missionary spirit." Applicants from a Unitarian, Universalist, or Roman Catholic church were refused sponsorship.[28]

Although secular organizations were not linked to any particular religion, they were no less concerned about the former slaves' religious development. One of the aims of the National Freedmen's Relief Association (NFRA), for example, was "to instruct the Freedmen in . . . the principles of Christianity [and] their accountability to the laws of God and man." Similarly, the object of the AFUC was to aid "in the improvement of [the freedpeople's] condition upon the basis of industry, education, freedom, and Christian morality." Thus, regardless of their sponsoring organization, the teachers often facilitated "general religious exercises" in which all Christians could unite. Many also taught Sunday school while others engaged in religious meetings outside of normal school hours. As a result, secular organizations also exercised great care over the selection of their teachers.[29] Although James Hood claimed that secular organizations deemed the teachers' evangelical background "immaterial," they nonetheless attempted to employ only those who possessed "the spirit of true religion." At the same time, AFUC teachers were warned that they were "not missionaries, nor preachers, nor exhorters." "You have nothing to do with churches, creeds, or sacraments," advised Reverend O. B. Frothingham of the AFUC, "you are not to inculcate doctrinal opinions, or take part in sectarian propagandism of any kind." His words appear to have generated some criticism from the religious organizations and the AFUC was forced to defend its position in relation to the provision of religious instruction. This was partly because northern churches believed that freedpeople's education could only be successful in the hands of religious organizations. "It was natural and praiseworthy that many temporary agencies should spring into life," reported Samuel Haskell of the ABHMS in 1863, "But we believe that only the sober second thought is needed to convince wise Christian men that general denominational Societies are the bodies into whose hands the work should be permanently taken." Another Baptist missionary reiterated Haskell's point of view and argued that freedpeople's education should be "under the control of religious principle." This rivalry emerged in the teachers also and Mary Ann Burnap, who worked for the AMA, was known to be quite difficult toward those who worked for secular organizations. "I am pained every day by remarks by teachers from the other societies," she complained to AMA secretary George Whipple, "they can see that there is *something* that gives success to the christian, and it makes them feel *envious*."[30]

Although the religious and secular societies differed in their approach to religious conversion, both types of organizations perceived education as a means of reforming the freedpeople, protecting society, and restructuring the former Confederate states. As the Protestant Episcopal Church warned its northern congregants in 1866, the former slaves must be educated to protect the country "and especially our Southern country, from the constant danger of revolt." Uneducated freedpeople, they provoked, were at risk of shattering the "whole social fabric." That same year, Freedmen's Bureau agent Horace James argued that the only way in which the South could be "regenerated" and "rejuvenated" was by remaking it in the image of the North.[31] Later, in 1868, the AMA went a step further and argued that freedpeople's education was needed to save the world:

> Let it be remembered that the work is not alone for the people of color, but for the whole South, and, in the final outlook, for the country, and the world. This land is worth more to civilization, christianity and missions, than any other. For the sake of the world, then, it must be saved – saved from ignorance, vice, and infidelity, from intemperance, Romanism and the unsubdued spirit of rebellion.[32]

As the AMA intimated, the Roman Catholic Church was viewed as a significant threat to southern Black schooling. Although Catholic missionaries did not sustain a significant number of schools in the South, the AMA often framed its educational efforts as a war against the expansion of Romanism, primarily in an effort to gain the financial support of northern Protestants. "Rome is already [in the South] with a thousand sisters of charity, with scores of priests, building churches and schools for white and Black, and expending in her work more than a million of dollars, per annum," argued the AMA in 1868. "The Association then has no choice, but to meet her on her chosen field, with all her advantages of men and money." The following year, the AMA claimed that approximately 200,000 Black children were being educated in Catholic schools throughout the South and in 1872 it reported that Catholic missionaries had raised $600,000 for freedpeople's schooling some years previously. According to Ronald E. Butchart, these figures were "fabricated nonsense." Although Catholic schools had been established in Baltimore, Maryland, Savannah, Georgia, and St. Augustine, Florida, they were taught by a "handful of nuns" and "without significant results."

Ultimately, as Butchart concluded, "The Catholic bogey was used to stimulate contributions to the denominational societies."[33]

Regardless of the veracity of these claims, it appears as though the AMA's scare tactics achieved the desired effect and in 1868 Reverend Crammond Kennedy, secretary of the New York branch of the AFUC, was forced to address rumors that Catholic schools were driving AFUC schools from the southern missionary field. Although Kennedy admitted that some Black parents in St. Augustine, "being papists," sent their children to Catholic schools, he steadfastly maintained that AFUC schools were flourishing. Moreover, Kennedy claimed that parents often removed their children from the Catholic schools because "they did not learn to read and write so well." Catholic missionaries, he argued, were primarily focused upon teaching "the Catechism and ceremonies of the church," much to the frustration of local Black parents who were more concerned about literacy instruction.[34]

In order to limit the perceived threat that southern Black people imposed upon society, northern aid and missionary organizations attempted to replicate the northern common school system in the South by implementing a curriculum that focused on literacy and numeracy instruction as well as religious and moral values. Within this framework, northern aid and missionary societies embarked on a broader mission of what James Patterson termed "cultural reform" by attempting to reform the freedpeople's religious practices, personal relationships, organization of labor, gender ideologies, and domestic affairs. In this sense, northern involvement in freedpeople's education represented a form of cultural colonialism or, in other words, a deliberate attempt to impose the dominant society's culture, values, and way of life upon a recently liberated people.[35]

Viewing freedpeople's education through the lens of cultural colonialism, northern involvement in southern Black schooling was driven by two key objectives. The first was to inculcate the former slaves with northern ideals and values and the second was to mold them into a reliable labor force. As Janice E. Hale explained:

> In a system of colonialism, the colonizer has a dual purpose for educating the colonized. The first is socialization into accepting the value system, history, and culture of the dominant society. The second is education for economic productivity. The oppressed are treated like commodities imbued with skills that are bought and sold on the labor market for the profit of the capitalists.[36]

Shaped by a fundamental belief in Black inferiority, each of these objectives served the wider aims of reforming the freedpeople, protecting society, and restructuring the former Confederate states. Not surprisingly, Black southerners had a very different vision of freedom and the role that education would play. While the former slaves were no less concerned about defining their place in American society, citizenship and economic freedom were central to their definition of freedom. Thus, Black men and women saw education as a means of securing civil and political equality as well as upward mobility and financial security.[37]

As northern aid and missionary schools continued to expand throughout North Carolina, southern whites became concerned that the educational needs of white children were not being met. Although a system of public education had been in existence in North Carolina since the mid-1840s, the exigencies of the Civil War resulted in its collapse. After emancipation, North Carolina's postwar legislature was reluctant to reinstate a system of public schooling. Although North Carolina's General Assembly claimed that there was no money to support public schools, fears of racial integration were the primary cause. As the University of North Carolina professor, Charles Phillips, wrote in 1866, "Our common school fund has been swept away ... and our legislators fear to lay a tax for the support of the schools – lest agitation disturb us and claim that as negroes pay this tax they must also go to school." As a result, in March 1866, North Carolina abolished the entire public school system by abolishing the office of superintendent of common schools, knowing that one could not survive without the other. Lamenting this decision, the *Raleigh Sentinel* described the passing of the bill "as almost a total abandonment of the Common School System in the State – a result more ruinous than any thing which could have befallen us." Spurred by growing concerns that Black children were being educated in private missionary schools while white children were going without an education, in November 1866 North Carolina's General Assembly made plans to reinstate a public school system for white children only. Although the legislature did not envision implementing a public school system for Black children, the Black community was not taxed to support these schools.[38]

Efforts to establish a system of free public schooling for both Black and white children began in 1868 at North Carolina's constitutional convention. On January 14, 1868, delegates gathered in the state's capital of Raleigh to draft the new constitution and a committee on education, comprising eleven Republicans, two Democrats, and headed by AMA Superintendent Samuel S. Ashley, was quickly organized. Two months later, Ashley presented the committee's report to the convention, authorizing North Carolina's General Assembly to establish "a general and uniform system of Public Schools, wherein tuition shall be free of charge to all the children of the State between the ages of six and twenty-one years." The report also mandated that schools should be in operation for four months of the year, supported by "taxation or otherwise," and made available to "every child of sufficient mental and physical ability."[39] This report, with minor amendments, later became Article IX of North Carolina's constitution.

Unsurprisingly, many white North Carolinians opposed the new constitution's article on education, principally because no provision was made for segregated schools. Although the two Democratic delegates appointed to the committee suggested amendments to provide for separate schools, neither of these amendments were adopted. Plato Durham, "a leading Conservative from Cleveland County (and later Klan chieftain)," suggested including an additional section into the article that would provide for separate schools. In response, Samuel Ashley proposed the following amendment: "It being understood that this section is not offered in sincerity, or because there is any necessity for it, and that it is proposed for the sole purpose of breeding prejudice and bring-about a political re-enslavement of the colored race [sic]." Ashley's amendment was adopted but Durham's proposed section, as amended, was rejected. Later, when John Graham also suggested amending a section to provide for separate schools and colleges, Albion W. Tourgée's substitute amendment stated that separate schools could be provided so long as "there shall be as ample, sufficient and complete facilities afforded for the one class as for others." Foreshadowing Tourgée's defense of Homer A. Plessy in the renowned *Plessy v. Ferguson* US Supreme Court case, both the amendment and substitute were rejected. Ultimately, the delegates' refusal to provide for segregated schools led to the charge that North Carolinian Republicans were "committed to the dogma of the social equality of the races."[40] Reporting on the event in March 1868, the *Raleigh Sentinel* wrote:

> We are tired and disgusted with detailing the dirty doings of the Scalawag Convention. The decent people of the state will not be surprised to see, by the report of proceedings on yesterday, that the negrophilists, Yankee and native, on two distincttest [sic] issues, voted down propositions to insert, in the Article on Education, a prohibition of the mingling of white and negro children in Schools and white and negro youth in Colleges.... So that the negro worshipping hybrids in the Convention have then voted, virtually and emphatically, *to force the attendance of white children in schools with the negroes.*[41]

Although few delegates wanted integrated schools, Ashley and Tourgée both feared that the constitutional provision of separate schools would work to undermine the educational prospects of North Carolina's Black community in the years to come. Moreover, Republicans argued that it was not necessary to insert the terms "white" or "black" into the constitution because "black people did not want to go to white schools, nor did the white people wish it." James W. Hood, who also served as delegate, supported the creation of separate schools on the grounds that Black schools would only be taught by Black teachers. Finally, Republicans pointed out that the legislature would ultimately decide on the issue of integration. As the ex-Confederate Republican William B. Rodman argued, section two of the article on education "left the matter of separate schools open to the Legislature." "Thus," Rodman concluded, "the highest officers of the state, elected by white majorities would have control of this matter." Toward the final days of the convention, a resolution was adopted that declared, "the interests and happiness of the two races would be best promoted by the establishment of separate schools."[42] Although this resolution did not form part of the constitution, the fear of integrated schools subsided and in April 1868 the constitution was ratified by a vote of 93,086 to 74,014.[43] Samuel Ashley was appointed superintendent of Public Instruction while Hood served as the state's first Black assistant superintendent. One year later, in April 1869, North Carolina's Republican-controlled legislature passed the school law which provided for a segregated, tax-supported school term of four months for all children between the ages of six and twenty-one. Thus, Ashley and Hood were required to sustain and develop not one school system but two.[44]

North Carolina's public school system officially went into operation in 1869. At this time, the state was home to a total of 330,581 school-aged children, 223,815 of whom were white and 106,766 of whom were Black. Establishing a system of schooling for both races was no small undertaking. Schoolhouses had to be built, while others had to be repaired. Teachers had to be trained and hired, and resources had to be purchased. In 1869, out of a total of 1,906 schoolhouses, the condition of 178 was characterized as "good" while 685 were reported as "bad." In order to finance such expenditures, a public school fund was created which was principally supported by state revenue, namely state and county capitation taxes. In addition, the legislature appropriated $100,000 "out of any moneys in the Treasury not appropriated otherwise." This funding was distributed according to a school census. If a township was unable to provide for a four-month term, the county commissioners were permitted to levy local taxes.[45]

Due to limited funding, the Freedmen's Bureau, northern aid societies, and local Black communities continued to support, either fully or in part, most of the Black schools in North Carolina until 1877. In his report for 1869, James Hood noted that over half of the 152 Black schools were privately funded while the remaining were supported by a northern aid or missionary society. In fact, according to Hood, the number of schools operated by denominational aid societies, such as the Presbyterian and Protestant Episcopal churches, more than doubled during this period, predominantly due to the extensive network of Black teacher training institutes that had emerged throughout the state. When the Bureau ceased operations in 1870, a crucial source of funding disappeared. Around the same time, northern aid and missionary associations began withdrawing their support, predominantly due to financial constraints. Consequently, some freedpeople's schools transferred to state control while others remained private institutions and many more ceased to exist. In his last semiannual report, John W. Alvord expressed concern that southern state legislatures had yet to make any considerable investment in Black schools. Shortly before the Bureau finally closed its doors in July 1870, it reported that of the 331 day and night schools in North Carolina, including the third congressional district which was created in 1869 "for the sake of greater convenience," 295 were sustained, wholly or in part, by the freedpeople and 121 buildings were owned by the freedpeople who contributed a total of $9,600 toward the cost of their schooling.[46]

Despite the limitations of the public school system, school attendance rose from 49,000 in 1869 to 65,301 in 1870. School expenditure also increased from approximately $43,000 to over $170,000 during the same period. Nevertheless, the future of North Carolina's system of free and equal public schooling grew uncertain when southern Democrats regained control of the legislature in 1870 and immediately set about undermining the public school system. Although the state constitution forced southern Democrats to retain public schools, they slashed educational funding, cut Ashley's salary, and abolished the position of assistant superintendent. Admittedly, these measures impacted both white and Black schools and it was not until the final decades of the nineteenth century that saw "an ever-widening gap" in the distribution of school funds "for the two races."[47] A direct attack on Black schools occurred when Democratic legislators initiated a plan to replace Black teachers with whites from the South, partly in an effort to exert greater control over the Black community but also to provide employment opportunities to white southerners. Determined to maintain control over their own schools, Black communities vehemently challenged this move and school boards ultimately decided to retain a Black teaching force by rationalizing that they would be cheaper to employ. Such efforts ultimately contributed to the professionalization of Black teachers who, alongside clergymen, constituted 95 percent of North Carolina's Black professional class in 1890.[48]

According to John Bell, the hardest blow to the public school system was the introduction of a law "that required the school taxes to be spent in the county in which they were collected." As Bell concluded, "This restriction destroyed the hope of an equal, state-wide standard of education for Black and white students in all counties." Finally, persistent opposition to tax-supported schools meant that in 1871, the North Carolina Supreme Court decision of *Lane v. Stanley* ruled that the system of levying local taxes when capitation taxes did not cover school costs was unconstitutional without a favorable vote of the people. In November 1871, Ashley resigned from his position as superintendent. According to Daniel J. Whitener, his successor Alexander McIver, "had three attributes that Ashley did not: He was a native, he did not believe in mixed schools, and he was uninterested in Negro education." Indeed, in his first report, McIver explicitly questioned whether the provision of education to those of "the African race" would yield any positive results. Two other native superintendents served until the withdrawal of military forces in 1877; neither exhibited much interest in facilitating the growth and development of Black public schools.[49]

When local public school officials were unable to use the power of the legislature to stymie the development of Black schools, they attempted to subvert Black education in subtler ways. In January 1870, northern Black teacher Robert G. Fitzgerald attempted to incorporate his private school at Woodside Farm into the public school system. To become an official employee of the state, Fitzgerald needed to qualify as a public school teacher, but he encountered numerous obstacles in his attempts to do so. Upon visiting Samuel Hughes, the examiner of teachers for Orange County, Fitzgerald was told that there was not enough funding to support all the children in the region. Instead, Hughes advised Fitzgerald to apply to a northern aid society for financial assistance. Writing in his diary later that evening, Fitzgerald stated, "I told him that I did not want to impose on charity. I would have done so but for the school appropriation made by the Legislature of the state; that I was willing to take my share of that fund though small, rather than apply to a charitable fund, and that he would confer a favor on me if he would assist me in getting my share of the teachers' fund as small as it was." Fitzgerald did not succeed in gaining the support of Hughes until August of that year, and that was only because Fitzgerald purposely intercepted him on the road near Hillsboro and demanded his assistance. Evidently, as Fitzgerald correctly concluded, Hughes was "somewhat biased by prejudice – and he will not put himself to any inconvenience to further the cause of education among the colored people." Later in 1870, when Fitzgerald's school was officially incorporated into the public school system, he was reprimanded for moving it to a more accessible location, in spite of the fact that the schoolhouse previously allocated to him had neither desks nor chairs and many children were unable to attend due to a creek that was obstructing their passage.[50]

As Fitzgerald's experience indicates, the creation of a state-funded public school system ultimately resulted in the professionalization of the teaching force by requiring public school educators to obtain a first-, second-, or third-grade teaching certificate. A first-grade certificate required the completion of a high school or normal school course while the remaining two certificates required an "examination in the studies prescribed for Grammar and High Schools." Due to the slow and haphazard nature of Black schooling during the early stages of Reconstruction, it is not surprising that many prospective teachers initially failed these examinations. Charles Hunter, formerly enslaved in Raleigh, acknowledged that he was chosen to teach in Shoe Hill because of his ability to pass the teaching examination. "Many had been before the Board of County Examiners and had failed," he reflected. "At that time there were only four licensed Negro teachers in the county." The same standards were not always required in the privately funded schools and in his report for 1869, Superintendent of Education L. E. Rice noted that a minority of schools in the new third congressional district of North Carolina were "taught by persons having less merit as teachers than is desirable." [51]

For the new public school system to be a success then, a trained teaching force was absolutely essential. In their reports for 1869, both Samuel S. Ashley and James W. Hood emphasized the need for the establishment of state-funded teacher training institutes for both races. Notably, this had long been a priority for many of the northern aid and missionary societies which gradually began shifting their focus from elementary education to the establishment of Black teacher training institutes, commonly known as normal schools. Acknowledging the challenges of limited funding, waning support, and the continued opposition of white southerners, these organizations recognized the need to train southern Black teachers for southern Black schools.[52] In 1867, the Presbyterian Church established Biddle Institute in Charlotte to educate Black men to become teachers and preachers. Tuition and boarding were free to those who brought "satisfactory testimonials of moral character and talent." At least twenty-nine of the southern Black teachers in North Carolina's schools for the freedpeople attended Biddle Institute. Baptist minister Reverend M. C. Ransome from Franklinton, North Carolina, spent one year at Biddle. In 1867, Ransome taught the freedpeople in Oak Grove, North Carolina, and he continued teaching and preaching to the

Black population for approximately fifty years. Similar institutions in North Carolina included Shaw University in Raleigh, Scotia Seminary in Concord, and Bennett College in Greensboro. Although these schools were chartered as third-level institutions, they were "at first little more than high schools." During the school year 1873–1874, thirty-six students were enrolled in Biddle's classical department. Half of these students were in the lower preparatory class which taught the most rudimentary literacy and numeracy skills.[53]

Due to limited funding, few aid societies were in a position to establish institutions for the explicit purpose of educating teachers. This led many teachers to incorporate normal classes into the regular school system. Comprised of some of the most advanced students, these classes trained Black students to become teachers. In March 1868, while working in Hillsboro under the sponsorship of the FFA, Robert G. Fitzgerald created a normal class of ten students within his school. The following day, this number had risen to fifteen "with the instruction that we are to add to the number such as proved to be of due merit." Similarly, between 1867 and 1877, Robert Harris sent out some of the most promising students at his Fayetteville institution to teach in the rural schools of Cumberland and Moore Counties. When appropriate teacher training opportunities were not available in the South, some agents advocated sending prospective Black teachers to northern institutions. "I think a few of the most promising ought always be sent to the North," wrote freeborn Reverend Francis Lewis Cardozo, "not so much perhaps for the purpose of gaining more knowledge of books, but that they might enjoy the numerous, elevating, moral influences of the North."[54]

By the time federal troops had been withdrawn from the South in 1877, Black and white North Carolinians were being educated in state-funded public schools throughout the state. Although the system was far from perfect, and many challenges lay ahead, it serves as a testament to the determination of Black North Carolinians to gain access to quality schooling. In this process, Black agency succeeded in enriching the educational opportunities for every child throughout the state, regardless of race, which left a lasting legacy on North Carolina's educational landscape. These gains were not achieved in isolation, though, and Black men and women formed robust partnerships with northern aid and missionary organizations, as well as the Freedmen's Bureau, to achieve their goals. Although Black North Carolinians were happy to accept the support of northern allies and southern partners, they were not willing to compromise on the provision of Black teachers for Black schools. When this was threatened after southern Democrats regained control of the legislature in 1870, they organized and mobilized to protect their institutions and preserve the Black teaching force for decades to come. While this marked a significant achievement for Black North Carolinians who looked to the future with hope in their hearts, the road to educational equality was not straightforward and Black North Carolinians would be required to draw on their networks, resources, and resilience time and time again to protect their right to schooling.

3   A Diverse Group of Educators: Freedpeople's Teachers in North Carolina

Between 1862 and 1877, over 1,400 men and women taught the freedpeople in North Carolina. According to the Freedmen's Teacher Project (FTP), these teachers came from a diverse range of regional and racial backgrounds, representing four distinct groups: northern white, southern white, northern Black, and southern Black. Approximately half of the teachers who worked in North Carolina's schools for the freedpeople were Black. The vast majority of these men and women were from the South, mostly North Carolina, and many were probably former slaves. Contrary to much of the historical literature, white northerners represented just over 26 percent of the entire teaching cohort. Admittedly, most of these teachers were young, single women from the New England states of Connecticut, Massachusetts, Maine, New Hampshire, Rhode Island, and Vermont, so the "Yankee schoolmarm" epithet is not entirely unfounded. Approximately 10 percent of the freedpeople's teachers were white southerners, mostly native North Carolinians, however it is likely that many more worked in freedpeople's schools than can currently be accounted for.[1] Across the entire teaching cohort, men taught more frequently than women. Admittedly, there were variations in gender participation across regional and racial lines; northern white women taught more frequently than northern white men while southern men, both Black and white, taught more frequently than southern women. Northern Black men and women, on the other hand, taught in virtually equal numbers. Consequently, by analyzing the freedpeople's teachers as four distinct groups, this chapter serves to clarify and redress many of the misconceptions previously held about this incredibly diverse group of educators.[2]

The very first teachers to work in North Carolina's schools for the freedpeople were Black North Carolinians. In 1862, Martha Culling, a former slave, opened North Carolina's first known school for the freedpeople on Roanoke Island. Described by Reverend Horace James, a Freedmen's Bureau official, as "a bright, smart mulatto girl," Culling taught on the island for two additional years under the sponsorship of the National Freedman's Relief Association (NFRA). Robert

Morrow, born a slave in Orange County, also began teaching the freedpeople in 1862. During the first year of the Civil War, Morrow served as Confederate General James J. Pettigrew's body servant. Upon escaping to Union lines after the Confederate attack on New Bern, Morrow established the Camp Totten Freedmen's School alongside Mary Ann Burnap, a white teacher from Roxbury, Massachusetts. Described as "an enthusiastic and excellent teacher," Morrow enlisted in Company B of the First North Carolina Heavy Artillery and was transferred to Roanoke Island where he taught until his untimely death in 1864.[3]

Although Culling and Morrow both began teaching in 1862, an analysis of the southern Black teaching cohort indicates that few engaged in freedpeople's education prior to the end of the Civil War. This was predominantly due to practical reasons, such as a lack of basic literacy skills which prevented freedpeople from entering the classroom until they first became literate themselves. During the antebellum period, almost every state in the slaveholding South had outlawed the literacy instruction of slaves. This was primarily done in an effort to curb slave unrest. Following the Stono Rebellion of 1739, an uprising that resulted in the deaths of more than sixty people, South Carolina passed the first anti-literacy law which made it a crime to teach slaves to read or write. Subsequent anti-literacy laws, particularly during the 1830s, were incited by the 1829 publication of David Walker's anti-slavery pamphlet, *Appeal to the Colored Citizens of the World*, as well as Nat Turner's rebellion of 1831.[4] Essentially, southern lawmakers feared that educated slaves would become dissatisfied with their subjugated status and attempt to overthrow the institution of slavery. As the North Carolina anti-literacy law of 1831 read:

> Whereas the teaching of slaves to read and write has a tendency to excite dissatisfaction in their minds and to produce insurrection and rebellion to the manifest injury of the citizens of this state . . . any free person who shall hereafter teach or attempt to teach any slave within this State to read or write, the use of figures excepted, Shall be liable to indictment in any court of record in the State having jurisdiction thereof.[5]

In spite of these laws, some enslaved people, albeit a distinct minority, succeeded in acquiring a degree of literacy. According to W. E. B. Du Bois, about 5 percent of slaves could read by 1860, while Eugene D. Genovese suggested that this number could have been closer to 10 percent. In 1863, Henry Clapp, a Massachusetts soldier in New Bern, observed that about one in fifteen freedpeople could read: "We find that many learned, or began to learn, before they were freed by our army - taking their instruction mostly 'on the sly' and indeed in the face of considerable danger."[6]

As Clapp's words suggest, most of the literate freedpeople in North Carolina gained access to education through surreptitious means. Some slaves learned to read and write by eavesdropping, a skill perfected by many enslaved people during the Civil War. "They keep their eyes and ears open to all that is going on around them," remarked a Union officer stationed in New Bern, "and in this little way often learn much that is not intended for them to know." John Sella Martin, formerly enslaved in North Carolina, Georgia, and Alabama, learned to read and write by watching his master's children complete their homework. Although the white children refused to teach Martin because "the law would not allow it," he was determined to master the most basic literacy skills. As he reflected in 1867, "But though the white boys would not teach me, they could not control or prevent the acquisition of a quick and retentive memory with which I was blessed, and by their bantering one another at spelling, and betting each on his proficiency over the other, I learned to spell by sound before I knew by sight a single letter in the alphabet."[7]

In some instances, slaves were secretly taught by members of the white community—at times, by their own masters or mistresses. As a child, Hannah Crafts was taught by a poor white woman from the North. Likewise, before the Civil War, Adora Rienshaw was taught "on de sly" by a judge's wife while Mary Anngady was taught the alphabet by her mistress's daughter. In a similar fashion, James Curry, who later became a fugitive slave, successfully persuaded his master's son to teach him how to read. Although Curry's master forbade the lessons once they were discovered, the enslaved child continued to learn in secret. "As I had got the start, however, I kept on reading and studying and from that time till I came away, I always had a book somewhere about me and if I got an opportunity, I would be reading in it."[8]

Some slaves were taught by members of the free Black community. Freeborn Robert Harris and Mary Day, who subsequently became freedpeople's teachers, secretly taught slaves in antebellum North Carolina. Southern lawmakers were not oblivious to these surreptitious teaching endeavors and anti-literacy laws typically outlined the penalties that would be imposed upon those who were caught. Unsurprisingly, Blacks, and slaves in particular, often received harsher punishments than whites. According to North Carolina's anti-literacy law of 1831, white men and women would be fined no more than $200 and imprisoned, a freeborn Black person would be "fined, imprisoned, or whipped," and a slave would be "sentenced to receive thirty-nine lashes on his or her bare back." Evidently, the harsher punishments inflicted upon slaves attempted to discourage them from seeking access to education.[9]

Once a slave became somewhat proficient in either reading or writing, they passed their knowledge on to other members of the community. In this way, enslaved people used literacy as "an instrument of resistance." Although Adora Rienshaw confessed that she was not well-educated, she taught young children for several years. This tradition continued during the Civil War and Reconstruction period and "those who could read or write provided schooling for those who could not." As one teacher observed, "the freedman no sooner learns even the first letter of the alphabet than he is teaching them to his fellows." Even young children engaged in this practice and a little boy was observed in the streets of New Bern "pointing a group of boys to the letter T." The boys seemed to be learning from him "as if he had been a college professor."[10] In 1868, Freedmen's Bureau General Superintendent of Education John W. Alvord reiterated these sentiments in his first semiannual report on schools when he wrote:

> Throughout the entire South efforts are being made by the colored people to *"educate themselves."* In the absence of teachers they are determined to be self-taught, and everywhere some elementary book, or fragments of it, may be seen in the hands of negros. They communicate to each other that which they learn and with very little learning, many take to teaching.[11]

Although some slaves succeeded in acquiring a degree of literacy, most of North Carolina's enslaved population never learned to read or write. Few even attempted to gain access to schooling, simply because those who were caught were often severely punished. Freedman Chaney Hews of Raleigh recalled that his mother was whipped because she tried to learn to read and "no books wus allowed [sic]." Sam T. Stewart recalled that although he was treated "unusually well" by his Quaker master, he was never taught to read or write and that "most slaves who got reading and writing certainly stole it." Consequently, it is likely that most of the formerly enslaved teachers in North Carolina gained access to education in some of the first schools for the freedpeople.[12] In 1865, Charles N. Hunter, formerly enslaved in Raleigh, was about twelve years old when he first attended a northern missionary school. Almost a decade later, Hunter began teaching the freedpeople in Wake County and by 1875 he was working as a public school teacher in Shoe Hill, now Maxton, Robeson County. In total, Hunter spent "fifty years of service in the school-room." Former slave Lewis Roulhac experienced a similar trajectory. Shortly after being mustered out of the 37th Regiment of the United States Colored Infantry, Roulhac attended a school for the freedpeople near his home in Bertie County. He later attended Shaw University in Raleigh and Hampton Institute in Virginia for brief periods before obtaining work as a teacher. Roulhac began teaching in 1869 and he continued working in this field for a total of nineteen years.[13]

Like their enslaved counterparts, free Blacks in the antebellum South had few educational opportunities. Although North Carolina did not prohibit the education of free Blacks, public opinion was opposed to their education, particularly in the aftermath of David Walker's *Appeal to the Colored Citizens of the World* and Nat Turner's rebellion. As freeborn Mrs. Colman Freeman reflected, "the laws were all against the colored men: they allowed us no schools or learning. If we got learning, we stole it."[14] John Chavis, a free Black man from Virginia who was widely recognized for his excellence in teaching, operated a school for both whites and Blacks in Raleigh between 1808 and 1832 but was forced to close it down due to the restrictive laws imposed after Turner's rebellion. Although some freeborn southern Black people received an education through the apprenticeship system, in 1838, the North Carolina legislature relieved apprentice masters of the duty to teach free Blacks, but not whites, to read and write. After the Civil War, apprenticeship laws in North Carolina evolved "as another form of forced labor" which not only undermined the parental rights of freedpeople but prevented countless Black children from attending school.[15]

With few educational opportunities available to them in the South, many of the freeborn southern Black teachers examined in this study attended Black or interracial schools in the North. Hiram Rhodes Revels attended the Beech Grove Quaker Seminary in Liberty, Indiana, and Darke County Seminary in Ohio, before finally graduating from Knox College in Illinois, in 1857. Although Revels was born free in Fayetteville, he did not teach the freedpeople in his home state. Instead, Revels spent five years teaching the freedpeople in Missouri and Mississippi. After the fall of the Confederacy, Revels went on to lead an impressive career in politics and he was the first Black man to serve in the United States Congress. Revels continued working in education beyond 1877 as the first president of the historically Black Alcorn University in Mississippi.[16] Reverend Cornelius Max Manning, a free Black man from Edenton, North Carolina, also attended school in the North. Beginning his education in a private school in North Carolina at the age of twelve, Manning later attended Iberia College in Ohio and Lincoln University in Pennsylvania until finally receiving a master's and doctorate of divinity degree from Morris Brown College in Atlanta, Georgia. Manning taught the freedpeople for four years in Hertford, North Carolina, and in his hometown of Edenton.[17]

The Patterson siblings from Raleigh also attended northern schools. Although, like Revels, they did not teach the freedpeople in North Carolina, they actively engaged in southern Black schooling throughout the American South. Born in slavery, the Patterson family either bought their freedom or escaped from slavery around 1852 and relocated to Oberlin, Ohio. Mary Jane Patterson, the oldest of about seven siblings, graduated from Oberlin College with a bachelor of arts degree in 1862 (see Figure 2).[18] In 1869, Mary Jane began teaching the freedpeople at the Preparatory High School for Colored Youth in Washington, D.C., and two years later she was appointed principal. John Eaton Patterson, Mary Jane's younger brother, also graduated from Oberlin College and he taught the freedpeople in Tennessee and Arkansas for three years. Chanie Ann Patterson, the youngest of the three siblings, attended Oberlin Preparatory School between 1862 and 1863 and Oberlin College between 1863 and 1867. In 1867, Chanie Ann began teaching the freedpeople in Virginia and she continued in this work for an impressive forty-two years.[19]

Figure 2 Mary Jane Patterson (Image courtesy of Oberlin College Archives).

According to the FTP, which provides data on the teachers' tenure up to 1875, southern Black teachers typically spent around two and a half years in the classroom. While this may seem like a brief period, it is important to remember that most of the southern Black teachers did not enter the classroom until after 1865 and it is likely that many continued working beyond 1875 in the state's new public school system for which corresponding data is not available. Moreover, southern Black men and women faced barriers to their participation in education that were unmatched by others in the field. Due to their lack of a formal education, Black North Carolinians often struggled to secure employment with an aid or missionary society, and many were compelled to establish self-supporting schools which offered an unreliable and often unsustainable source of income. During the spring of 1868, former slave Lucy Brown was teaching in an independent school that she intended to be supported by private tuition fees. When her students proved too poor to pay, Brown wrote to the Freedmen's Bureau in request for aid. "Rev. sir," she wrote F. A. Fiske, "if you can assist the fatherless in any way please do it." Brown did not resume teaching the following year, so it is unlikely that the aid she received from the Bureau, if any, was enough to support her work in the classroom. White hostility also influenced the participation rates of Black North Carolinian teachers who, as will be explored in Chapter 6, experienced unprecedented levels of violence at the hands of white terrorist organizations such as the Ku Klux Klan.[20]

Regardless of the difficulties they faced, a significant number of southern Black teachers taught in excess of two and a half years, and, like the aforementioned Hunter, many dedicated their life's work to education. Not surprisingly, these men and women had secured the sponsorship of an aid or missionary society and many either attended or advanced beyond secondary education. Greensboro native Grace Ann McLean began teaching the freedpeople in 1868 and according to the FTP, she continued in this work for a total of twenty years. McLean, a graduate of Hampton Institute, spent six of these years teaching under the sponsorship of the Friends' Freedmen's Association (FFA) in various locations throughout North Carolina. In 1878, she and her new husband spent three years touring Europe with the Chautauqua Choir. When they returned to the United States, McLean promptly returned to teaching, ultimately securing the position of matron at Livingstone College. Sidney A. Busbee from Raleigh first began teaching the freedpeople in 1865 under the sponsorship of the New England Freedmen's Aid Society (NEFAS) and continued in this work beyond 1875 as a public school teacher. Described by Sylvester Soper of the Freedmen's Bureau as "a very smart and intelligent man," twenty-four-year-old Busbee ran for local appointment to the Snow Hill Precinct as an election inspector in 1867. "I would earnestly recommend him for appointment as a competent person to fill [this] position," endorsed Soper. In total, Busbee spent a total of ten years in the classroom. Another notable Black North Carolinian who spent a significant length of time in education was Wallace Porter Locker. Born a slave in 1853, Locker learned basic literacy and numeracy skills from his father as a child before attending school in New Bern in 1863. After the Civil War, Locker continued attending school in between farming duties until he ultimately received a qualification to teach in 1873. In total, Locker spent an impressive fifty-five years in education before becoming United States Inspector of Customs.[21]

Most of the southern Black teachers came from North Carolina and these men and women generally taught in schools located throughout their home state. A small minority of southern Black teachers came from the surrounding states of South Carolina, Georgia, Maryland, Mississippi, Virginia, and Tennessee. The vast majority of these teachers were men who began teaching in the late 1860s under the sponsorship of a northern missionary organization and most had achieved a common school education at least. As a group, the southern Black teachers who were not natives of North Carolina were particularly well-educated and many of them gained access to third-level education in some of the South's first Historically Black Colleges and Universities (HBCUs). Benjamin Franklin McDowell from Lancaster, South Carolina, began teaching during the 1869–1870 school year under the sponsorship of the Presbyterian Committee on Missions for Freedmen (PCMF). At this time, McDowell was a student in Biddle Memorial Institute's Theological Department. Upon graduating in 1872, McDowell returned to his home state and spent two years teaching in Laurens and Mount Pisgah before returning to North Carolina. In total, he spent twenty-four years in the classroom. Similarly, Harriet L. Green from Sumter, South Carolina, began her teaching career in Virginia while studying at Hampton Institute. Upon graduating in 1871, she began teaching in Flemington and Whiteville, North Carolina, for a total of four years before turning her attention toward raising a family.[22]

Southern Black men taught more frequently than southern Black women. This may have been because southern Black women often had families to care for which prevented them from securing regular employment. Indeed, it was for this very reason that the NFRA established an industrial school in Washington, D.C., with the intention of teaching freedwomen "the first lessons of domestic thrift." Learning the skill of needlework, in particular, would allow these women to take work home and become "self-sustaining and independent" without neglecting their family duties. Teaching freedwomen and girls practical skills was also a motivating factor in the establishment of an industrial school on Roanoke Island. "The need for such a place . . . is quite plain," wrote Esther A. Williams to C. C. Leigh in 1865. Some of the island's freedwomen learned to sew during slavery, "but the majority of them have no idea of cutting, making, or even mending," practical skills which would allow these women to labor "for their own benefit." Teaching not only lacked such flexibility but also proved to be an unreliable source of income for many Black North Carolinians. Like the aforementioned Lucy Brown who took up teaching "to support and educate [her] little ones," many were forced to relinquish their role due to the absence of a steady income. Ultimately, freedwomen's familial duties required them to find a more sustainable source of income which, according to Thavolia Glymph, also saw them retreat from field and plantation work. Not because they perceived the work as unladylike or beneath them but because they required "immediate resources to help sustain them as crops were being made."[23]

Northern Black men and women also engaged in freedpeople's education, albeit in significantly smaller numbers. Out of the 1,419 teachers included in the North Carolina section of the FTP database, only eighty-five were positively identified as Black northerners. This was predominately due to the employment practices of northern aid and missionary societies which often exhibited a preference for employing white teachers instead of Black teachers. As Samuel S. Ashley, an AMA official, once wrote, "my opinion is that white teachers can do more for the freedmen in this city at present than colored." Horace James, a Freedmen's Bureau official, was of a similar opinion and while he supported the work of "colored preachers who were ordained ministers," he did not believe that Black teachers could contribute the same efficiency "and even Eclat which white teachers can." Attitudes like this placed Black northerners at a significant disadvantage. Unlike southern Black teachers who already lived in the state, unsupported northern Black teachers were required to pay for their transportation to and from the South as well as their lodging and expenses. As Rhode Islander Ellen Jackson Garrison confessed in her application to the AMA, "I would have gone [South] upon my own responsibility but I am not able. I thought it would be safer for me to be employed by some Society. Then, I shall not be troubled about my livelihood, for it cramps ones energies to have to think about the means of living."[24] According to Maxine Jones, the AMA was one of the few organizations that made a concerted effort to send more Black teachers to the South. Yet the FTP indicates that out of a total of eighty-five northern Black teachers, the AMA only sponsored fifteen at one point during their southern teaching careers. Based upon an analysis of the FTP, the FFA was actually more likely to support northern Black teachers in North Carolina and it sponsored a total of twenty-seven Black northerners including Sallie A. Daffin and Robert G. Fitzgerald, both from Pennsylvania. Evidently, as North Carolina's first Black assistant superintendent of education James Walker Hood reported, Quaker organizations were less likely to discriminate on the basis of "sex, sect, section, nativity or complexion."[25]

Occasionally, a Black northerner ventured into the southern missionary field without securing any sponsorship at all. James Edward O'Hara from New York City was one such teacher. Between 1863 and 1867, O'Hara taught the freedpeople in an independently supported school before finding employment with the FFA. In order to support his work in the South, O'Hara charged his students one dollar per month in tuition fees and those who were unable to pay were taught for free. Sometimes, Black students paid their teachers "in kind," either in goods or services such as food, fuel, transportation, or lodging. However, most teachers required a more reliable source of income to sustain their work in the classroom. In 1868, Harriett Allen, a Black Pennsylvanian, was forced to leave her post in Hillsboro because the "committee of citizens" who hired her "proved to be poor." According to the FTP, Allen did not undertake any more work among the freedpeople, and it is likely that she returned home.[26]

Peter Vogelsang, a lieutenant in the 54th Massachusetts Volunteer Infantry Regiment, was the first Black northerner to engage in freedpeople's education and the FTP indicates that he taught the freedpeople on Roanoke Island during the school year 1863–1864. Although scant evidence remains of Vogelsang's work at this time, it appears to have occurred while he was recovering from an injury sustained during the Battle of Fort Wagner. Before the war's end, Vogelsang returned to action and although he went home to Brooklyn after the war, he received a commission with the NFRA shortly thereafter which sent him back to Roanoke Island where he taught until 1870. According to the FTP, ten other northern Black teachers served in the Union army. Another thirty-four were from the South. Most of the northern Black veterans were in their twenties or thirties when the Civil War began. First Sergeant Luther C. Hubbard from Greene County, New York, enlisted in the Union army when he was twenty-two years old and served in the 26th United States Colored Troops Infantry Regiment (see Figure 3). In 1871, Hubbard began teaching the freedpeople in Salisbury, most likely within the new public school system, and he kept this position until 1880 at least. As the oldest serving member of the 54th Massachusetts Volunteer Infantry Regiment, however, Peter Vogelsang was forty-seven years old when he first began teaching the freedpeople.[27]

Figure 3 First Sergeant Luther Hubbard of Co. C, 26th US Colored Troops Infantry Regiment in uniform with sword (Image courtesy of Library of Congress, Prints and Photographs Division [LC-DIG-ppmsca-69306]).

On average, northern Black teachers typically spent four and a half years working in the South. Some taught for even longer. Brothers William, Robert, and Cicero Harris spent a considerable length of time in the South. Born free in North Carolina, the Harris family relocated to Cleveland, Ohio, in 1850 and shortly before the end of the Civil War, both William and Robert applied to work for the AMA which sent them to Virginia. Although Robert initially applied to work for a period of six months, he wrote to the AMA in 1865 requesting to be reappointed so that he could "continue in this good work." By 1866, Robert was teaching the freedpeople in Fayetteville alongside his younger brother Cicero who also secured a commission with the AMA. Robert ultimately taught the freedpeople until his death in 1879 while Cicero, who first began teaching in 1866, continued until 1888.[28]

Lydia, Louisa, Charles, and William Warrick from Philadelphia were another group of northern Black siblings who engaged in freedpeople's education. In 1865, Lydia was the first to come South, having received a commission from the NFRA. Her siblings followed suit sometime between 1867 and 1868, each of them having secured the sponsorship of the Pennsylvania Freedmen's Relief Association (PFRA). Between 1866 and 1870, Lydia worked without the sponsorship of a northern aid or missionary association. According to one observer, the town in which she was working at the time, Murfreesboro, had "not been favored by the benevolence of Northern associations." As a result, the freedpeople in this vicinity were forced to rely "upon their own stout hearts and strong arms to educate their children."[29]

As a group, northern Black teachers were generally well-educated which is not surprising considering the aid associations' stringent employment practices in relation to the recruitment of Black teachers. Only one of the northern Black teachers whose education is known did not advance beyond common school. Many attended an advanced secondary institution, such as a normal school, academy, or commercial college. Twelve attended college, eleven graduated from college, and one engaged in postgraduate studies, although he did not obtain a degree. These teachers attended a diverse range of educational institutions, totaling nine different schools in all. Most of these schools were in the North. Some, such as Shaw University in Raleigh and Hampton Institute in Virginia, were in the South which indicates that these men and women gained access to higher education after the Civil War in some of the region's first HBCUs.[30]

Almost 40 percent of the northern Black teachers whose education is known attended Lincoln University in Pennsylvania. Founded as the Ashmun Institute in 1854, Lincoln University was the first institution to provide bachelor's degrees in the arts and sciences for Black men. Robert G. Fitzgerald from Hinsonville, Pennsylvania, attended Lincoln University for a brief period before enlisting in the Union navy in 1863. Between 1866 and 1867, he taught the freedpeople in Virginia before returning home to resume his studies. Fitzgerald's desire to continue working among the freedpeople proved too strong and in 1868 he returned to the southern missionary field without completing the course. Some northern Black teachers attended Philadelphia's Institute for Colored Youth. Founded in 1837, this school is the oldest institute of higher education for Black people in the United States. Others attended the interracial, coeducational Oberlin College which is known for educating "more Black students before the Civil War than all other

American colleges *combined*." Blanche Virginia Harris from Monroe, Michigan, was an Oberlin graduate. Described by James Walker Hood as one of the best teachers in the state, Harris taught the freedpeople alongside her sisters Elizabeth and Frankie Emma for a combined total of more than one hundred years.[31]

In spite of these teachers' impressive educational accomplishments, it is worth bearing in mind that access to education was limited and restricted for most northern Blacks during the antebellum period. Although the mid-century common school movement increased educational opportunities for northern white children, Black children were often prevented from attending these schools. Moreover, increased opposition to Black education, particularly in the wake of Nat Turner's rebellion, meant that access to institutes of higher education was often out of bounds. Consequently, the well-educated northern Black men and women who found work in North Carolina's schools for the freedpeople were the exception, rather than the rule.[32]

Given that many of the educational institutions which admitted Black students in the nineteenth century charged tuition fees, it is also highly likely that these men and women came from middle-class backgrounds. In 1857, for instance, students at Lincoln University were required to pay $110 per session in order to cover "all expenses for tuition, boarding and incidentals." Theological students at the university's predecessor, Ashmun Institute, were not charged tuition fees but they were required to pay eighty-five dollars per session for "board and incidentals." Ashmun's Board of Trustees were aware that these fees were out of reach for many northern Black individuals, so they appealed to the churches "to furnish both the students and the means to educate them." Although Oberlin College initially forfeited tuition fees in exchange for labor, fees of twenty dollars per annum were introduced in 1843 to offset the costs of paying the teachers' salaries.[33]

Some northern Black teachers worked in education before entering the southern missionary field. Husband and wife Laura J. and Thomas W. Cardozo from Brooklyn, New York, were both teachers before securing the sponsorship of the AMA in 1865. Over a period of six years, the Cardozos worked in a total of four different states with the support of four organizations, including the Freedmen's Bureau. Thomas Cardozo was actually born free in Charleston, South Carolina, but relocated to the North shortly after his father's death in 1855. His white father, Isaac Nunez Cardozo, was a member of one of Charleston's most prominent Jewish families while his mixed-race mother was once formerly enslaved. Cardozo met his wife Laura while they were both teaching in New York. Not long after securing the sponsorship of the AMA in 1865, the organization became aware of an extramarital affair between Cardozo and one of his female students in New York and he was accused of misappropriating school funds for her benefit. In spite of his pleas and objections, Cardozo was promptly dismissed and replaced by his brother Francis. After trying his hand as a grocer, Thomas and Laura moved to Baltimore to operate an industrial school on behalf of the Freedmen's Bureau. He subsequently found work with the NFRA and NEFAS before embarking on a political career as Mississippi's first Black superintendent of education but was forced to leave the state in 1876 amidst charges relating to corruption, fraud, and embezzlement which left him "ruined, disgraced and in danger."[34]

Like Cardozo, several other northern Black teachers used their positions in the South to gain a foothold in public office. The aforementioned James Walker Hood came to North Carolina during the Civil War as a missionary with the African Methodist Episcopal Zion Church. In 1865 he was elected president of the Freedmen's Convention of North Carolina and two years later he served as a delegate at the state's constitutional convention. In 1868, Hood was made assistant superintendent of Public Instruction, a position which he held for three years. James Edward O'Hara, the son of an Irish American father and West Indian mother, shared a similar experience. Between 1863 and 1878, O'Hara taught the freedpeople in New Bern and Goldsboro, North Carolina. He was secretary of North Carolina's Freedmen's Convention and, like Hood, also served as a delegate to the state's constitutional convention. Shortly after passing the bar in 1873, O'Hara moved to Enfield, North Carolina, to practice law. In 1882, on his fourth attempt, O'Hara was elected to Congress from North Carolina's "Black Second" district which had a sizable Black majority. He was the second Black candidate from North Carolina to serve in the United States Congress, the first being John Adams Hyman, a former slave. After serving in Congress for four years, O'Hara returned to North Carolina to practice law with his son. Stories like this ultimately attest to the opportunities created for Black political leadership in post–Civil War North Carolina, however short-lived these opportunities actually were. As W. E. B. Du Bois candidly observed, "the slave went free, stood a brief moment in the sun, then moved back toward slavery."[35]

Susan A. Hosmer, Antoinette L. Etheridge, Mary Ann Burnap, and George N. Greene were the pioneer northern white teachers in the state and together they taught for a combined total of twenty-eight years across seven different southern states. Hosmer, a single twenty-eight-year-old woman from Ashby, Massachusetts, taught for twelve consecutive years in New Bern, North Carolina, and Augusta, Georgia, before finally returning home in 1874. Etheridge, a thirty-year-old native of Montrose, Pennsylvania, taught the freedpeople intermittently for a total of ten years and served as the principal of a Black teacher training institute in Charleston, South Carolina. Burnap, a native of Roxbury, Massachusetts, and Greene, a Yale-educated minister, both spent three years teaching formerly enslaved men, women, and children along North Carolina's eastern seaboard. Each of these teachers were employed, either fully or in part, by the AMA and all began their southern teaching careers in the coastal towns of New Bern and Beaufort shortly after the Union army gained control of the region in 1862.[36]

Few northern white teachers were sponsored by just one aid or missionary society for the duration of their southern teaching careers. This was usually because the organization could no longer afford to support a teacher or because the school had shut down or relocated. In 1864, twenty-two-year-old Margaret R. Smith from Beverly, Massachusetts, was sponsored by the Beverly branch of the NEFAS to work in North Carolina. Smith spent one year working in New Bern under the auspices of the NEFAS before moving on to Tennessee, presumably because the Beverly branch lacked the funds to sponsor her for an additional year. There she remained for a further nine years under the sponsorship of the PFRA and another unidentified organization.[37] Similarly, in 1864, forty-year-old Lucelia Electa Williams from Deerfield, Massachusetts, began teaching under the sponsorship of the NFRA. By 1867 she was teaching for the AMA and five years later she was working in the newly established Stanton Normal School in Jacksonville, Florida, which was funded by the local board of public instruction. During the eleven long years that Williams spent in the South, she worked in a total of six different states. Although some northern white teachers spent their entire southern teaching careers in North Carolina, this was generally uncommon.[38]

Like their Black counterparts, some northern white teachers went South without first securing employment, although this was generally quite rare. Between 1863 and 1870, Jennie S. Bell from New Bedford, Massachusetts, worked in schools throughout North Carolina and Virginia, mostly at her own expense. Writing to the Freedmen's Bureau in August 1867 for financial assistance, Bell explained that she had been "laboring in this field 4 years gratuitously." Petitioning the Peabody Education Fund, a philanthropic financial aid organization, on her behalf, F. A. Fiske told trustee William Alexander Graham that Bell "has been a faithful & efficient laborer in this work and has received no salary from any Benevolent Society."[39] Eliza P. Perkins from Norwich, Connecticut, also traveled to North Carolina without securing the sponsorship of a northern organization. During the war, Perkins occupied a managerial role in the Soldiers' Aid Society which was responsible for providing supplies, such as food, bedding, and clothing, and medical assistance to soldiers on the battlefield. As the Civil War progressed, the Soldiers' Aid Society began extending its efforts to the freedpeople in the occupied South and it is possible that Perkins was introduced to teaching by engaging in this work. As Horace James wrote in his 1864 report, "The gratuitous distribution of clothing during the whole winter and spring, was made in person by Miss Eliza P. Perkins, of Norwich, Ct., a lady whose cheerful benevolence of heart led her to devote her energies, without compensation, and most untiringly, to this perplexing and difficult work." According to the FTP, Perkins taught the freedpeople in North Carolina for one year before returning home to work as a visiting nurse.[40]

During the early years of the Civil War and Reconstruction period, northern white teachers dominated North Carolina's missionary field until they gradually became outnumbered by Black North Carolinians (see Table 2). Accounting for 90 percent of the northern white teaching cohort, most of these teachers were young, single women when they first began working in a southern Black school. One of the youngest female teachers, Miranda C. Owen from Wyoming, New York, was just sixteen years old when she began teaching the freedpeople in Alexandria, Virginia. Over a period of eight years, Owen taught the freedpeople across three southern states and when she finally left her post in Beaufort, North Carolina, she was twenty-six years old.[41]

Table 2

Years	Northern Black Teachers	Southern Black Teachers	Northern White Teachers	Southern White Teachers	Total
1861–1862	0	0	0	0	0
1862–1863	1	2	4	0	7
1863–1864	1	7	39	0	47
1864–1865	3	7	53	2	65
1865–1866	13	22	117	23	175
1866–1867	20	57	109	35	221
1867–1868	35	130	106	63	334
1868–1869	43	221	83	58	405
1869–1870	33	262	67	42	404
1870–1871	28	140	57	11	236
1871–1872	22	134	53	6	215
1872–1873	15	128	37	10	190
1873–1874	18	121	40	6	185
1874–1875	16	151	44	5	216

Butchart et al., "The Freedmen's Teacher Project" (2022)

The overrepresentation of women in the northern white teaching cohort stems from multiple factors directly relating to social and cultural changes in the antebellum North. This includes the feminization of teaching which dramatically increased the number of female teachers, the proliferation of sentimental literature which rallied many, mainly women, to the anti-slavery cause, and a growing acceptance of the ideology of domesticity which extended the boundaries of the domestic sphere by facilitating women's participation in education, social reform, and missionary work. The introduction of the common school movement in the early 1830s by educational reformer Horace Mann was a major catalyst for the feminization of teaching. Although a diverse range of elementary schools, including public schools, private schools, church schools, and charity schools, were available to most northern white children by the early 1830s, there was no unified school system. In addition, growing immigration and rapid urbanization had given rise to a number of social issues which educational reformers believed could be rectified through the provision of moral instruction. Consequently, the northern common school movement was initiated to educate white children from diverse ethnic, social, and denominational backgrounds in the fundamental principles of a "native Protestant ideology" which "centered on republicanism, Protestantism, and capitalism." Rooted in the fear that growing immigration and rapid urbanization were destroying the moral fabric of American society, such schools were particularly focused upon molding nineteenth-century children into self-sufficient, law-abiding, disciplined workers.[42]

In an effort to create a "unified and improved school system," northern educational reformers called for nonsectarian, tax-supported elementary schools, increased school spending, longer school terms, and the establishment of teacher training institutions. Predictably, the prospect of increased taxation was met with resistance among many northern residents while the concept of nonsectarian schools was a source of consternation for several religious organizations, most notably the Roman Catholic Church. In an effort to limit the upset caused by increases in taxation, school reformers promoted the use of female teachers on the grounds that they were cheaper to employ. As Alison Prentice and Marjorie R. Theobald found, female teachers could be paid as little as half a male teacher's wage. This trend continued during the Reconstruction period and in 1867, the PCMF justified their use of female teachers on the grounds that they were not only cheaper to employ but also better suited to the work. Samuel S. Ashley, an AMA teacher, missionary, and Freedmen's Bureau officer in North Carolina, reiterated this view in 1869 when he proclaimed that "Teaching is pre-eminently women's sphere and prerogative."[43]

Women's increased participation in the educational workforce resulted in increased participation in higher education and the number of female academies, seminaries, and teacher training institutes, commonly known as normal schools, rose dramatically during the antebellum period.[44] Although few qualifications were necessary to teach the freedpeople, save a common school education in some cases, it is interesting to note that several of the northern white female teachers who worked in North Carolina's schools for the freedpeople attended an advanced, second-level institution such as a high school, normal school, academy, commercial college, or female seminary. Only three women whose education is known did not advance beyond common school. Anne Shaw Fernald and Josephine C. Field both attended a third-level institution, although there is no record of either having graduated. Field, who worked as a teacher before venturing into the southern missionary field, attended Oberlin College, an interracial, coeducational institution established in Ohio in 1833. Known as "a hotbed of abolitionism," eight other northern white female teachers examined in this study attended either Oberlin College or Oberlin Academy, the college's preparatory school.[45]

Mount Holyoke Female Seminary in South Hadley, Massachusetts, was the alma matter of more than 25 percent of the northern white female teachers whose educational institution is known. Typically, these women spent just under five years in the South. Of course, some women taught for even longer. Martha Hale Clary was twenty-four years old when she first began teaching the freedpeople in Beaufort, South Carolina, under the auspices of the AMA. In 1873, Clary moved to Concord, North Carolina, after accepting a position with the PCMF to teach freedwomen at the recently established Scotia Seminary. After spending twenty-five years in the South, Clary finally returned to her Massachusetts home in 1880.[46]

Although teaching became increasingly perceived as an appropriate female occupation during the nineteenth century, northern aid and missionary societies worked hard to justify sending young, white women into the southern missionary field, particularly during the turbulent, and often dangerous, wartime period. Drawing upon the prescribed female virtues of piety and domesticity, the AMA argued that northern white women were needed in the South:

> The question which, just now, is exciting a good deal of inquiry and debate, and which is likely to excite more in the future, is "Woman's sphere and work." She feels, to a degree, the degradation of enforced idleness, and asks for work,

as she has a right to, in all proper ways and places. This feeling led her into the hospitals during the war; where, on a limited scale, she won a good name as a nurse. But this was exceptional. Her work properly began after the war. The rough work of camp, and march, and field, was man's. Hers was that of education and religion; bringing in the ameliorating and purifying influences of church and school and Christian home, to close the wounds of war, and smooth the level furrows of battle.[47]

In particular, the AMA perceived northern white female teachers as central to the elevation of formerly enslaved Black women who were considered degraded by slavery and entirely at odds with the domestic ideals of nineteenth-century American society. Through the work of northern white teachers, both educational and missionary, AMA officials believed that they could facilitate the reformation of Black womanhood and ultimately, the Black household.[48]

Over half of the northern white teachers who worked in North Carolina's schools for the freedpeople came from New England. The remaining teachers came from the surrounding Northeastern or Midwestern states of New York, New Jersey, Pennsylvania, Ohio, Indiana, Illinois, Iowa, Wisconsin, and Michigan. Massachusetts was the dominant source of teachers while New York produced the second largest number. Only one teacher, sixty-three-year-old Thomas Judkins from Oregon, came from the Northwest. So, while it can no longer be said that most of the freedpeople's teachers were northern white women, it is true that most of the northern white teachers were young, unmarried New England females.[49]

Unlike their female counterparts, most of the northern white men were in their forties, fifties, or sixties when they first began teaching the freedpeople. Daniel T. Bachelor from New York was sixty-seven years old when he first entered a southern Black classroom. When the Civil War ended in 1865, Bachelor and his sixteen-year-old daughter Ella secured the sponsorship of the NFRA and together they spent three years in schools throughout the South. Unlike the northern white women, most of these male teachers were married when they first began teaching the freedpeople and many worked in the South alongside a family member. Some, like Bachelor, worked with a son or daughter while others taught alongside their spouse. Samuel Nickerson from Massachusetts came to the South in 1863 and sent for his wife one year later. Together, the Nickersons taught the freedpeople for a total of three years across three southern states.[50]

There were, of course, exceptions and those who did not conform to the dominant profile are equally important to the study of freedpeople's education. The oldest northern white female teachers, Jane M. Cock and Abby H. Horton, were both fifty-five years old when they first ventured into the southern missionary field. Cock, a Quaker, spent two years in the South while Horton spent one year in Beaufort, North Carolina, alongside her husband Francis. While their brief tenures may suggest that older teachers were less likely to spend an extended period of time in the South, the opposite was often true. Forty-seven-year-old Anna Gardner from Nantucket, Massachusetts, taught for twelve years under the auspices of the NEFAS. She was fifty-nine years old when she finally left the South in 1875. Tellingly, Gardner was a Quaker who was also active in the prewar abolitionist movement.[51]

Likewise, the youngest northern white teacher to engage in freedpeople's education was fourteen-year-old William Gardner Dorland. In 1868, William began teaching formerly enslaved women at Scotia Seminary in Concord, North Carolina. Established by his father, Reverend Luke Dorland, in 1867, Scotia Seminary was the first HBCU for Black women in the southern United States. William taught for a total of two years alongside his father, mother, and older brother Charles, once between 1868 and 1869 and again between 1871 and 1872. This suggests that rather than engaging in freedpeople's education for altruistic purposes, William was simply assisting his family. Luke Dorland, on the other hand, dedicated his life's work to the educational advancement of southern Black Americans and remained president of the institution until 1885.[52]

Almost 20 percent of the northern white male teachers fought in the Union army prior to working in a southern Black school. In 1865, Henry Martin Tupper, a Baptist minister and Union veteran from Monson, Massachusetts, began teaching the freedpeople in Raleigh. What began as a small school for freedmen gradually evolved into Shaw University, the oldest HBCU in the South. Tupper served as president of the university until his death in 1893. Other Union veterans, such as Albion W. Tourgée, taught briefly in the state's first freedpeople's schools before moving onto other professions. Between 1865 and 1868, Tourgée taught Black students in Greensboro, North Carolina, before being appointed as a judge in the North Carolina Superior Court. In 1873, Tourgée founded Bennett College, a private HBCU for women in Greensboro that first began as a teacher training institute for Black men and women. Although Black and southern white educators contributed to the development of some of North Carolina's oldest HBCUs, such as Johnson C. Smith University in Charlotte and Livingston College in Salisbury, northern white educators' role in this arena undoubtedly left a lasting legacy on North Carolina's educational landscape.[53]

An analysis of the northern white teachers' educational attainment, previous occupation, and parents' occupation suggests that many came from middle-class backgrounds. During the antebellum period, access to higher education was generally limited to those of the middle and upper classes or, as Mary Kelley suggested, those who had sufficient access to economic, social, and cultural capital. Of the teachers whose prior occupation is known, the majority worked in professions such as education, the ministry, business, or administration. While some occupations may not have required an education, such as skilled laborer or farmer, these professions nonetheless possessed a degree of occupational prestige during the early nineteenth century. The data relating to the teachers' parents' occupations is also highly indicative of their social status. Most were listed as farmers, business professionals, or skilled laborers. Other parents' occupations, in order of commonality, included minister, white-collar worker, teacher, domestic servant, and manual laborer.[54]

White southerners, it would appear, were more cautious about engaging in freedpeople's education. In 1864, John T. Phillips and John C. Hiatt, both Quakers, were the first white North Carolinian teachers in the state. After the Civil War, the number of white North Carolinian teachers gradually increased and peaked during the school year 1867–1868. Even at their peak, though, southern white teachers were significantly outnumbered by northern whites and southern Blacks, and by 1875, only five white North Carolinians remained in the classroom. As a group, southern white teachers represented just 10 percent of the entire teaching force. Admittedly, the race for a significant number of teachers has not yet been identified and as new information comes to light, it is possible that this data could change.[55]

The slow rate of participation among the southern white teaching cohort stemmed from multiple factors ranging from deep-rooted racial prejudice to the immense poverty of the people. During the early days of the Civil War, white North Carolinians also faced many practical obstacles which impeded their participation in education. In 1862, for instance, Edward W. Stanley, the military governor of eastern North Carolina, ordered the closing of two freedpeople's schools in New Bern on the grounds that they were contrary to the laws of the state. Both of these schools were established by Union Army Chaplain and Superintendent of the Poor Vincent Colyer and endorsed by Union General John G. Foster. In an address to the freedpeople, Colyer explained that the schools were closed by Governor Stanley because they violated North Carolina's anti-literacy slave law. Like many of his contemporaries, Stanley, a native of North Carolina, was unhappy with the prospect of emancipation and he attempted to use legal technicalities to preserve the antebellum hierarchical southern social order. His actions did not go without criticism, however, and the northern press condemned his blatant disregard for both the rights of the freedpeople and the orders of the Union army.[56]

Increased poverty in the aftermath of the Civil War may also have contributed to the low number of southern white teachers who engaged in freedpeople's education during the early stages of southern Black schooling. Rather than focusing on the freedpeople's educational needs, white North Carolinians were more concerned about rebuilding their lives. Indeed, Francis King of the Baltimore Association for the Moral and Educational Improvement of the Colored People admitted that he even struggled to find teachers among the Quaker community during the early stages of Reconstruction because people were "so very poor since the war" and "had not the means to organize." Later, persistent poverty actually prompted white North Carolinians to engaged in freedpeople's education as teaching presented a viable source of income for many families whose livelihood had been destroyed during the Civil War.[57]

As the Reconstruction era progressed, white hostility towards freedpeople's education undoubtedly discouraged many white North Carolinians from engaging in the work. Often, teachers experienced this hostility from within their own families. Between 1867 and 1868, white North Carolinian Sarah Elvira Pearson taught sixteen students in her hometown of Morganton, Burke County. Described by a Freedmen's Bureau agent as a "middle aged lady, of good education," Pearson worked independently of a northern aid or missionary association and her school was primarily supported by aid from the Bureau. Her role in education has "not been appreciated by her relatives and friends," reported Assistant Commissioner Hannibal D. Norton, "and she is now 'under a ban,' in consequence." These sentiments were reiterated by Pearson's neighbor, Martha C. Avery, who confirmed that there was "a general feeling of indignation against her in the community particularly in her own family." Reflecting the racial prejudice inherent in the thinking of many southern white men and women at the time, Avery wondered how willing Pearson would be to continue in this work once she found herself surrounded by fifty "negro men" in a classroom at night. "The school in Greensboro had ruined" the freedpeople, continued Avery, "and put notions of equality into their heads." [58]

On average, white North Carolinians spent just over one and a half years teaching the freedpeople. For comparison, northern white teachers typically spent three and a half years in the South while northern and southern Black teachers spent almost three years in the classroom. There were, of course, exceptions and Judith Jemima Mendenhall and William C. Welborn, both Quakers, taught for nine and eleven years, respectively. Jointly supported by the FFA and the Freedmen's Bureau, Mendenhall taught for the duration of her career in her home in Jamestown, even during the vacation period, while Welborn worked in his hometown of Hopewell, Randolph County.[59] Like Mendenhall and Welborn, most of the Quaker teachers in North Carolina taught under the auspices of the FFA. Others were sponsored by individual Quaker churches. In 1869, for instance, the North Carolina Yearly Meeting of Friends established a freedmen's aid organization under the direction of Dr. Tomlinson which was the only southern organization identified in this study. Similarly, most of the Presbyterian and Episcopalian teachers were sponsored by their churches' respective aid societies, the PCMF or the Protestant Episcopal Freedman's Commission (PEFC). In general, however, the majority of white North Carolinians taught in self-supporting schools that were financed by the Freedmen's Bureau, tuition from the freedpeople, or a combination of both. This was partly because northern aid and missionary societies lacked the means to support a significant number of schools and teachers in the state, particularly when the demand for education was in the more rural or remote areas. Moreover, organizations dedicated to freedpeople's education were limited in the South. This meant that southern teachers and missionaries who wished to secure the sponsorship of a denominational organization were required to apply through northern church organizations which could sever their relationship with their own church community. When North Carolinian ministers Reverends Willis L. Miller and Samuel C. Alexander accepted commissions with the PCMF, for instance, they were forced to leave their presbytery, the Presbytery of Concord, and establish a new presbytery that was associated with the northern faction of the church to aid their work.[60]

Although North Carolinian Quakers represented a minority of the state's religious population, accounting for less than 2 percent of the total membership in 1860 and 1870, over 70 percent of the southern white teachers whose religion is known were members of a Quaker church. Five members of the extended Mendenhall family from Guilford County, including the aforementioned Judith Mendenhall and her aunt Delphina (née Gardner–see Figure 4), labored in North Carolina's schools for the freedpeople. Together they taught for a combined total of seventeen years. Like many other Quakers, the Mendenhalls had a long history of racial activism and Judith's father Richard once led the North Carolina Manumission Society. Speaking of Judith and her family, fellow teacher A. H. Jones wrote, "She and her family have been for years the friends of the colored people running much risk both before and since the war on their account."[61]

Figure 4 Delphina E. Mendenhall, Quaker teacher of the freedpeople (Image courtesy of the Quaker Archives, Guilford College, Greensboro, NC).

Native North Carolinian Quaker, Levi Coffin, often known as the "President of the Underground Railroad," was also active in freedpeople's education. When the Civil War broke out in 1861, Coffin was living in Cincinnati, Ohio. During the war, federal forces sent some of the self-emancipated slaves to Cairo, Illinois, in order to alleviate the burden that was being placed upon the Union camps in the South. In 1862, Coffin visited these former slaves and immediately helped them to establish a school. On his return to Cincinnati, Coffin helped to establish the Western Freedmen's Aid Commission (WFAC). Acting as the association's general agent, Coffin was tasked with the job of sponsoring teachers to go South. He also promoted the work of the WFAC around Indiana and Ohio in the hope of soliciting aid and donations. "I was successful in making collections wherever I went," he reflected, "and this enabled us to extend our labors; to send more teachers, and more relief to the sufferers." Occasionally, Coffin traveled to the former Confederate states in order to survey the southern missionary field and ascertain the freedpeople's primary wants and needs.[62]

In 1864, Coffin traveled to England, Scotland, Ireland, and France to solicit aid for the former slaves. He was particularly focused on assisting the freedpeople who were situated west of the Allegheny Mountains since most of the aid and missionary societies were focusing their efforts on the eastern towns and cities. None of the 1,419 teachers examined in this study were employed by the WFAC. According to William P. Vaughn, most of the teachers connected to this organization worked in Tennessee. Coffin's European expedition, which lasted over twelve months, was immensely successful. During this time, "Over a hundred thousand dollars in money, clothing, and other articles" had been forwarded to the WFAC's headquarters with the prospect that more would follow. In addition, freedmen's aid societies had been established in London, Dublin, Belfast, and Glasgow, as well as a number of other "principal towns." These aid societies would continue sending aid and donations to the freedpeople once Coffin returned to the United States.[63]

Nathan H. Hill, a Quaker from High Point, North Carolina, taught the freedpeople between 1865 and 1867 under the sponsorship of the FFA. Although Hill rarely reflected upon his work as a teacher, his family regularly expressed their support. Indeed, Hill's brother, Aaron Orlando, also taught the freedpeople for one year in a private school that was partly supported by the Freedmen's Bureau. During the summer of 1867, Hill's sister Asenath commended her brother's efforts in educating "these degraded people." Like her brother, Asenath had opposed secession from the outset and was fundamentally opposed to racial slavery. As she wrote of the freedpeople, "No wonder they offer praise & thanksgiving night and day to Almighty God that flesh and blood of human beings can no longer be bought & sold in this long boasted land of liberty – if these rebs could only have been willing to acknowledge the inequity of slavery & set them free without the expenditure of so much blood what a blessing it would have been to our dispatched country."[64]

In terms of gender participation, southern white men taught more frequently than southern white women. This partly stems from the fact that teaching in antebellum North Carolina was a male-dominated profession so there were fewer trained female teachers who had the skills or qualifications to work in the classroom; in 1860, women made up just 7 percent of North Carolina's teaching force. Although the Civil War propelled women into the paid workforce, including education, teaching the freedpeople, as Ronald E. Butchart explained, entailed "crossing a double boundary" between women's domestic responsibilities and paid work and the social barrier that restricted interracial contact, particularly when that contact contributed to Black educational advancement.[65]

Over 20 percent of white North Carolinian teachers fought in the Confederate army. Across the entire American South, Butchart found that just over 30 percent of the southern white teachers were Confederate veterans. However, he equally acknowledged that "due to the paucity of school records after the early 1870s" and incomplete southern military records, "it is likely that three to six times" more southern white teachers "fought for the Confederacy" than can be definitively accounted for. Most of the ex-Confederate teachers in North Carolina taught for one year. None taught for more than three. This suggests that postwar poverty and economic hardships influenced their decision to enter the classroom.[66] Over 10 percent of the teachers were former slaveholders or from a slaveholding family. Typically, these men and women spent just over one and a half years teaching the former slaves. Only one ex-slaveholding teacher, Edward Payson Hall, spent any considerable length of time in a Black school. Tellingly, Hall converted to Quakerism during the Civil War, and he spent five years teaching the freedpeople under the auspices of the FFA. In his analysis of such teachers, Butchart concluded that the ex-slaveholding educators "were not drawn from the ranks of the South's elite slave owners." One exception was the aforementioned Willis L. Miller. Although Miller owned fewer than ten slaves in 1860 and, therefore, cannot be considered a planter (someone who typically owned twenty slaves or more), he came from a privileged planter family. "He was the son of a most worthy ancestry," wrote his teaching companion in 1870, "his parents were in prosperous circumstances and he was reared amid the refining influences of the best Southern families."[67]

Although southern white teachers represented a distinct minority of the freedpeople's teaching force, their work had no less of an impact, particularly in North Carolina where a significant number of teachers, being Quakers, were genuinely committed to the education and elevation of the former slaves. Moreover, due to the paucity of records which support their work, either in the form of personal letters or state archives, it is worth considering that the actual number of southern white teachers was greater than can be definitively accounted for. While white northerners left a lasting legacy in the southern missionary field, particularly in relation to the extensive network of HBCUs that were established throughout the state, the real protagonists in this history were the Black men and women who represented almost half of North Carolina's teaching force.

Although the FTP has provided some clues as to their motivations, the juxtaposition of this data alongside traditional archival sources, as outlined in the next chapter, provides a clearer insight into the reasons why these men and women elected to teach the freedpeople during and after the tumultuous Civil War.

4 Answering the Call to Teach: Interrogating Teacher Motivations

The men and women who engaged in freedpeople's education did so for a variety of reasons, each of which were ultimately as unique as the teachers themselves. Although the teachers of the freedpeople can be categorized into four distinct groups–northern white, southern white, northern Black, and southern Black–it is not possible to neatly categorize their motives in much the same way. This is partly because the teachers were rarely guided by just one motivating factor but also because motivations often changed or evolved over time. Moreover, many teachers were motivated by factors that stemmed from shared experiences within the broader social, political, and cultural landscape, as opposed to regional identities or racial backgrounds. The religious revivalism of the antebellum period, for instance, inspired many northern and southern teachers to perceive their work in the South as a means of spreading religion among the former slaves. Similarly, northern Black and white teachers were often influenced by the didactic principles of the common school system to use education as a means of inculcating the former slaves with middle-class ideals and values. Mounting poverty resulting from the postwar economic climate drove many North Carolinians, both Black and white, to enter the classroom as a means of securing an income. Consequently, the complex and multifaceted nature of the teachers' motivations transcends simplistic categorizations by reflecting the dynamic interplay of social, political, and cultural factors that influenced their work among the freedpeople.

Whether they were Black or white, male or female, northern or southern, many teachers perceived their work among the freedpeople as a form of religious duty. Although the Christianization of enslaved people had occurred on a widescale basis during the mid- to late eighteenth century in what Jon Butler termed the "African spiritual holocaust," several teachers took it upon themselves to spread religion among the formerly enslaved community. "I shall not be satisfied so long as there is *one* that has not a song of praise in the mouth for my Savior," reported Mary Ann Burnap, a northern white teacher, in early 1865. One year later, northern Black teacher Robert Harris expressed a similar sentiment and rejoiced when two of his Sabbath school students "embraced religion." "I am laboring for their conversion as well as their enlightenment," he concluded. While teaching in Hillsboro, North Carolina, Black northerner Robert G. Fitzgerald spent much of his free time visiting local freedpeople, distributing tracts and bibles, and encouraging them to attend Sabbath school. "I hope I have done something good for my Savior," he reflected.[1]

Other teachers engaged in a more overt form of proselytization. While working at the Baptist Institute in Raleigh, which later became Shaw University, white northerner Harriet M. Buss wrote home about efforts to convert one of her most promising students, an Episcopalian: "I think he is wheeling around slowly, and will yet be a Baptist, if we let him alone, let him study and investigate for himself." In return for the provision of education, as well as many other basic necessities, many former slaves did indeed convert to a particular religious denomination. These conversions were not always genuine, though, and predominantly stemmed from the freedpeople's desire to acquire both the material and intellectual possessions they needed to extend the boundaries of their newfound freedom. Observing this in his role as a commissioner for the Presbyterian Committee on Missions for Freedmen (PCMF), Reverend Willis L. Miller, a white North Carolinian, advised the Presbyterian Church to stop sending missionaries to the Baptist and Methodist congregations "as they would welcome teachers and preachers and still retain their connection with their own denomination." Evidently, aiding the freedpeople, in this case at least, was only worthwhile if it facilitated religious conversions within the Presbyterian church.[2]

When the teachers were not attempting to convert the freedpeople to a particular religious denomination, they actively attempted to reform the former slaves' unique style of worship which was described by two northern white teachers as "rude" and "excessive." While stationed in Beaufort during the 1866–1867 school year, white northerner Samuel J. Whiton was pleased to report that the local freedpeople were "quiet and orderly in their religious meetings, giving evidence of much improvement in this respect." Such efforts ultimately amounted to a form of cultural colonialism, as discussed in Chapter 2. Black teachers were not indifferent toward the freedpeople's unique style of worship, which northern-born Robert Harris considered extravagant. However, rather than attempting to reform this practice, Harris conceded that it "was better than coldness" which suggests that he was more understanding of the freedpeople's cultural and religious practices than his northern white counterparts.[3]

The desire to facilitate religious conversions was undoubtedly influenced by the Second Great Awakening which was marked by fervent religious enthusiasm and increased church membership, particularly within the evangelical churches. During the Civil War, the South presented as a new opportunity for northern churches to extend their reach and many actively called on their congregants to labor among the freedpeople on their behalf. In 1867, the Baptist church called for more volunteers to go South because their denominational rivals were gaining a worrying number of Black converts. Four years later, in 1871, the Presbyterian Church appealed to its congregants' sense of moral compassion by informing them that 14,000 southern Black Presbyterians were in need of aid and benevolence: "These scattered poor are of *her own* fold, look to *her* for care, and by *her* should be gathered and fed." Although these churches were actively seeking missionaries, the work of teachers and missionaries often went hand in hand. As explained in Chapter 2, denominational aid societies typically preferred sponsoring teachers who were members of their churches because they viewed their work among the freedpeople as both spiritual and educational. As the PCMF explained, "it was useless to attempt to build up a church without teaching the people, at least, to read the Bible."[4]

Some southern churches also pressed their members to engage in freedpeople's education. Not long after the end of the Civil War, North Carolina Superintendent of Education F. A. Fiske reported that two of the state's churches had recently "urged upon their constituency the duty of laboring for the religious instruction of the colored people." Although Fiske did not identify either of these churches by name, it is likely that he was referring to the Presbyterian and Protestant Episcopal churches because the southern factions of both of these churches actively advocated white participation in freedpeople's education. On August 29, 1866, for instance, an article in *The North Carolina Presbyterian* called for more southern white people to engage in freedpeople's education. While the writer acknowledged that hostility toward freedpeople's schools posed a very real threat, they argued that Black schools could be used to maintain social control. Moreover, with or without the assistance of the southern white community, they warned, the freedpeople were determined to gain access to education: "Our unwillingness to see the negro educated . . . will not prevent that consummation. Our refusal to do the work, will not insure his continuance in ignorance, even if that was desirable."[5]

Presbyterian ministers Willis L. Miller and Samuel C. Alexander both accepted the call to educate the freedpeople and in 1867 they cofounded the Henry J. Biddle Memorial Institute in Charlotte, North Carolina. Now known as Johnson C. Smith University, Biddle Institute was established to educate Black men to become teachers and preachers. Although Alexander was born in Pennsylvania, he had been living and working in North Carolina before the Civil War broke out. This is why he is included in the Freedmen's Teacher Project (FTP) as a southern white teacher. As Ronald E. Butchart explained, any teacher living in the South for five years or longer, especially those who married a southerner (which Alexander did), "are presumed to have imbibed enough southern culture to generally identify with southern values and southern racial attitudes." Interestingly, the FTP indicates that Alexander may have been involved in the prewar abolitionist movement. Miller, on the other hand, was a native of North Carolina. He was also a former slaveholder and ex-Confederate soldier.[6]

So why would a southern white slaveholder who had fought to preserve the institution of slavery establish a school for the freedpeople? In the main, Miller's primary motive was to sustain the Presbyterian Church in the South. When the Civil War ended in 1865, the former slaves asserted their freedom by demanding access to the two institutions that were fundamentally denied to them during slavery: the church and the school. In North Carolina, Black congregations descended from the galleries of the churches they attended during slavery and sought to be ministered to by members of their own race. This was particularly problematic for the Presbyterian denomination because there were no Black ministers in the southern Presbyterian Church. Consequently, many southern Black Presbyterians left their former places of worship for the leadership of Black preachers, some of whom were uneducated and inexperienced Presbyterians but many of whom were members of other denominations. Speaking of the disgruntled white ministers in his locality, James Sinclair, an ex-slaveholding Presbyterian minister from Scotland, remarked that "not one of the negroes who formally attended their churches will go to them now." As a result, Biddle Institute's primary function was to furnish Black Presbyterian preachers for the Black community. These preachers would not only work to keep Black Presbyterians within the church's fold, but they would also serve to attract new Black members. In 1867, forty-three students were enrolled in Biddle Institute, twenty-two of whom were candidates for the ministry. On weekends and during the summer vacation, these trainee ministers preached in local Black churches, taught in local Black schools, held prayer meetings, distributed Bibles, and superintended Sabbath schools. "The success of the plan has been truly remarkable," wrote the editors of Biddle's first annual catalog in 1868. "The congregations served by these catechists are strongly attached to them, and much evidence of the usefulness of their humble labors has come before the faculty, who, in the character of evangelists, superintend the field."[7]

In addition to Biddle Institute, Miller also helped to establish Black elementary schools throughout North Carolina. By 1868, he had seven Black schools, including Biddle, under his care. Although, as a commissioner for the PCMF, Miller's primary goal was to establish Black churches throughout the Carolinas, he knew that the provision of education would not only win back the Black Presbyterians who had left the church at the time of their emancipation but also attract other southern Blacks into the denomination. A similar approach was adopted by the Episcopalians who also experienced a mass exodus from their churches after the fall of the Confederacy. Interestingly, although the southern Presbyterian Church claimed to support freedpeople's education, it did not establish an aid or missionary society explicitly for that purpose. This caused some issues when southern church members attempted to engage in freedpeople's education. In 1867, Miller and Alexander were forced to leave their presbytery, the Presbytery of Concord, for accepting commissions with the PCMF. Together with Sidney S. Murkland they established the Catawba Presbytery, and two churches quickly followed, the Freedom Church near Statesville and McClintock Church near Charlotte. Black churches were formed "in the bounds of every white Presbyterian church" and before long, Miller and Alexander had organized "ten or twelve churches" that were "supplied by students studying for the ministry."[8]

Although Biddle's primary function was to educate Black teachers and preachers, it was designed to furnish a particular type of teacher and preacher. Indeed, Biddle Institute did not indiscriminately admit just anyone to the school. In order to be considered for a place, Black men first had to bring "satisfactory testimonials of moral character." They also had to serve a probationary period of one month, at their own expense, before being formally enrolled into the school. Such a stringent enrollment policy suggests that Miller regarded Biddle Institute as a means of training Black men to become the leadership class of the next generation of southern Blacks. As he wrote to F. A. Fiske in 1868, "The Lord has a great work to be done among the freedmen and colored ministers must do it. It will have to be done principally by men who will *support themselves* while they preach."[9]

Charles Phillips, a Presbyterian minister and professor of mathematics at the University of North Carolina, Chapel Hill, also engaged in freedpeople's education to spread religion among the former slaves. Described as a man who was deeply committed to the ministry, in 1867 Phillips established a Black Sunday school which he taught alongside his wife Laura. He also assisted local Black residents to establish their own schools. Petitioning the Freedmen's Bureau for seventy dollars in 1867, Phillips wrote, "The Freedmen who have asked me to get them some help (for they are very poor) are very respectable persons of that class of society. I would like to help them become still more respectable."[10]

An analysis of Phillips's personal correspondence reveals that his educational efforts did not stem from a desire to move the freedpeople toward equality with whites. On the contrary, Phillips was opposed to racial equality. Although he was often sympathetic to the freedpeople's destitution, he was unhappy with many of the measures taken during Congressional Reconstruction, not least because the necessitated reorganization of the University of North Carolina resulted in the loss of his position. Phillips was particularly aggrieved with the ratification of North Carolina's new state constitution in April 1868, principally because the University of North Carolina now held "an inseparable connection with the Free Public School System of the State" and no provision was made for segregated schooling. Thus, at least theoretically, Black students could be admitted to the university. Writing less than one month after the constitution was adopted, Phillips's frustration showed when he wrote: "There is no more facility for negroes getting into the Univ. now than there ever has been here & at every college in N.C. that is – facility afforded by new wording of charter or bye laws – In none there is any distinction between white and blacks. But I am not cool enough to comment on what seems to us to be a great disaster – the results of the late election." Phillips need not have worried. In 1873, North Carolina's Democratically controlled legislature passed an amendment which removed the "inseparable connection" between the university and public schools.[11]

Stemming from the highly charged religious atmosphere of the pre–Civil War period, the promise of spiritual salvation also motivated many northern white teachers, in particular, to engage in freedpeople's education. Inspired by Charles G. Finney's theology of disinterested benevolence which entailed "the rejection of one's own interests and its replacement by benevolence, usefulness and good works," many northern evangelicals believed that salvation could be achieved for both themselves and others through religious conversion and social reform. This goal is particularly evident in the teachers' frequent characterization of freedpeople's education as a "field of usefulness," a term that gained prominence during the revivalist period when Finney preached about the significance of "being useful in the highest degree possible." Writing to her parents from her school in Raleigh, Harriet Buss rejoiced that she was "so fully satisfied" in her work. "There is such a wide field of usefulness," she continued, "so many ways of doing good, that not a moment be lost." Similarly, in her letter of application to the American Missionary Association (AMA), Elizabeth James wrote that her previous teaching experience would prepare her "for a large amount of usefulness in this department of the Lord's Vineyard." James, from Medford, Massachusetts, had been a teacher for seventeen years prior to seeking work in the South. She was forty years old when she first ventured into the southern missionary field and spent a total of ten years teaching former slaves across North Carolina and Virginia. Having turned down five teaching offers from northern schools, James was particularly inspired to work with the freedpeople. According to her cousin, Freedmen's Bureau official Reverend Horace James, Elizabeth was profoundly anti-slavery and this, coupled with her desire to serve God and spread religion among the former slaves, motivated her work in the South.[12]

Joanna P. R. Hanly, the widow of a Methodist minister, circuit rider, and former missionary to China, similarly described her work in terms of fulfilling a religious duty. Writing to Freedmen's Bureau Commissioner General O. O. Howard during the spring of 1869, Hanly explained that she had been inspired by her bereaved husband's missionary work to seek work in the South. "Thus moved I went forward," she explained, "not to the mission fields of China, for broad and useful ones were opened up in our own land, in every State throughout the South where the unfettered slave, lifted their unbound hands to heaven and cried for help." By this time, Hanly had been working in North Carolina for three years, mostly at her own expense, and indeed at a considerable cost to herself. As she explained to Howard, she had spent over $3,000 building a school for the freedpeople and "a very pleasant dwelling house" for the teachers which she now hoped the Freedmen's Bureau could recompense. "What I have expended has not been for my own benefit," she assured Howard, "and not a dollar of it to my own earthly advantage, higher and holier motives prompted every act in the matter." According to Butchart, the teachers who engaged in southern Black schooling explicitly for the purpose of seeking salvation were typically not concerned about extending or securing the boundaries of Black freedom. This motivation was "self-referential, fastening attention on the one providing the service as much as the one presumably being served." This is certainly reflected in the work of Hanly and others like her who, while professing a desire to lighten the freedpeople's "suffering and sorrows," notably omit any discussion in their correspondence of the privileges or opportunities that education could provide the freedpeople in their new lives after slavery.[13]

In spite of her efforts, Howard decided not to reimburse Hanly for her expenses. According to James O. Whittemore, who was asked to advise on the matter, the building was not worth the $2,500 that Hanly was requesting. Due to prejudice toward freedpeople's education, Hanly was overcharged for the building materials and labor and he maintained that he could have a better building erected for a fraction of the cost. "With every consideration for Mrs Hanly and my best wishes for her success," wrote Whittemore, "I must say it would be an extravagant use of the public money to pay the sum of $2500 for Mrs Hanleys property [sic]." In total, Hanly spent six years working in North Carolina. Her daughter Maggie and son John worked alongside her for some of those years. Unable to secure the support of the Freedmen's Bureau, the Hanlys returned home to Philadelphia at the end of the school year in 1869.[14]

According to Butchart, the teachers who attended Mount Holyoke Female Seminary in South Hadley, Massachusetts, were particularly inspired to "'move the world' through disinterested benevolence in the interest of salvation." Influencing this goal was the words of a minister who implored Mount Holyoke's female students to seek work in southern Black schools, "not in solidarity with freed slaves" but "to be in the service of the republic." Acquiescence in the concept of disinterested benevolence is certainly reflected in the words of Ella Roper, a Massachusetts native and graduate of Mount Holyoke, who declared how much more blessed it was "to give than to receive." In her letter of application for a teaching position, Roper expressed her desire to be a "self-denying teacher" and perceived her work as a form of religious vocation. In total, Roper spent twelve years teaching the freedpeople across Georgia and North Carolina under the auspices of the AMA and the National Freedman's Relief Association (NFRA).[15]

For many teachers, the desire to spread religion among the former slaves was reflected in their efforts to provide them with a Christian education. To this end, schools often opened with prayer and a reading from the scriptures. Students learned religious songs and the Bible frequently served as a supplementary textbook. In addition to their regular school duties, many teachers conducted Sunday or Sabbath schools while others distributed tracts and bibles in the local community. Prayer meetings were regularly held after school hours. A typical Sunday for Harriet Buss involved superintending Sabbath schools in the morning and afternoon, teaching bible classes before and after lunch, and attending morning, afternoon, and evening services.[16]

In the main, religious instruction was viewed as a means of ameliorating the degrading effects of slavery by providing the former slaves with a moral compass of sorts that would guide their interactions in freedom. Sarah P. Freeman, a white northerner, was a firm believer in the importance of Sabbath schools and she regularly appealed to her sponsoring organization for aid to support them. "Whatever else is withheld from this people," she wrote in a letter to the NFRA, "*I feel that the bread of life must not be.*" Although Freeman did not elucidate why she believed religious education was more important than everything else, her beliefs about the freedpeople were betrayed by other comments she made in letters that were published by *The National Freedman*, the NFRA's monthly organ. As she wrote in 1866, "The educating and elevating of this people must go forward, or they will become a curse to our nation, and their freedom a curse rather than a blessing to themselves." From this extract, it is clear that Freeman was concerned about the implications of Black freedom and believed that religious education was one of the primary means through which the former slaves could be successfully integrated into American society.[17] Presbyterian minister Reverend Willis L. Miller shared a similar thought process and in a conversation with an ex-slaveholding neighbor, Miller explained the value of providing former slaves with religious instruction: "If the negros are taught that they have no souls they will steal from you, and if angry will burn your barns. Let them have churches, think they have souls, make Christians of them, they will not steal from you and when you hire one of them he will do you honest work." Undoubtedly influenced by the prevailing racial stereotypes, Miller explicitly linked the provision of religious instruction to the development of moral behavior which reflected a paternalistic mindset rooted in discriminatory assumptions about Black people's character and conduct. Tellingly, Miller's final words suggest that his vision of Black freedom was at odds with that of the Black community. In his view, the former slaves were going to continue occupying a social position below that of whites while working for whites.[18]

Freeman and Miller were not the only teachers who were influenced by the prevailing racial stereotypes that portrayed Black people, and Black men in particular, as dangerous, immoral, and predisposed to criminality. As James D. Anderson explained, "Most northern missionaries went south with the preconceived notion that the slave regime was so brutal and dehumanizing that blacks were little more than uncivilized victims who needed to be taught the values and rules of civil society." To this end, many teachers used their work in the South as a means of inculcating the former slaves with northern middle-class ideals and values. "I have aimed to instruct [the freedpeople] in the practical duties of life," wrote a teacher in Elizabeth City, "not only of judgement, but of temperance, of love, and of purity."[19] Indeed, the promotion of temperance was a goal shared by many teachers, regardless of their regional or racial identity. Northern Black teacher Robert Harris explicitly intended to facilitate the freedpeople's development in "Education, Morality, Temperance [and] Religion" while white northerner Mary Ann Burnap actively encouraged Black soldiers on Roanoke Island to take the pledge. "It is wonderful to see what the Lord is doing on this island," she wrote in 1865, "I can do nothing but praise him." One year later, a northern white teacher in Elizabeth City convinced a Black shopkeeper to stop selling alcohol while H. S. Beals, an AMA superintendent stationed in Beaufort, openly rejoiced when eighty children joined the temperance organization Band of Hope, promising to abstain from alcohol and "that curse of North Carolina, tobacco." Charles N. Hunter, a former slave who taught the freedpeople for more than fifty years, was also actively involved in the temperance movement and in 1871 he helped to organize a juvenile temperance society called the Howard Band of Hope, so named after Freedmen's Bureau commissioner General Oliver O. Howard. According to John Haley, Hunter's biographer, Hunter's involvement in the temperance movement may have stemmed from his desire for public recognition and prestige rather than from a moral objection to alcohol. Indeed, Haley argued that Black men often engaged in such organizations because it was a way for them to "sublimate their desires for political involvement and to exercise their leadership abilities in a way that was acceptable to whites."[20]

Recognizing that many northern teachers worked in education before seeking work in a southern Black school, it is highly likely that the didactic ideals of the northern common school movement influenced their efforts to inculcate the freedpeople with middle-class ideals and values. Reflecting similar efforts and practices in the North, Frances Graves and Annie P. Merriam took it upon themselves to improve their students' "manners, appearance, and faces" and perceived any change in the former slaves' demeanor or deportment as proof of the civilizing influence of education. "We are rejoiced to see that education has already produced a decided change for the better, that can be perceived in the bright, intelligent countenance," they wrote from their post in New Bern. "We are more than ever satisfied that our labors are not in vain, and that the seed we are now sowing is already springing up to be a blessing to future generations." Some white northerners perceived these changes as proof of the former slaves' educability and General Saxton was pleasantly surprised to find that "efforts to teach [the freedpeople] good habits of housekeeping are responded to more quickly than we had expected." As Saxton's words suggest, efforts to inculcate the freedpeople with domestic ideals and values were included in the curriculum as part of a deliberate attempt to reform the Black household, and Black women in particular. George Newcomb, a white Massachusetts native, took it upon himself to teach the freedpeople about the sanctity of marriage, presumably in response to the prevalence of informal unions between freedmen and women which will be discussed more thoroughly in Chapter 5. Although Newcomb claimed that these lessons were "well received" and produced "favorable results," they were rooted in the paternalistic viewpoint that formerly enslaved men and women needed the guidance and assistance of white northerners to navigate their newfound freedom.[21]

Once in the South, the teachers' preconceived notions of the freedpeople often shifted or evolved over time and many began to question what they thought they knew about the former slaves and their supposed degradation. "I can sometimes scarcely realize that I am teaching among these ignorant, uncultivated children so pleasantly does everything go on from day to day," confessed a somewhat surprised Frances Bonnell in 1865, whose words reveal the extent to which prewar racial conditioning influenced her perception of the former slaves. While stationed at Hilton Head, South Carolina, Martha L. Kellogg's expectation of the former slaves' intellect was also challenged and she acknowledged that while her students differed "like others in mental capacity . . . they are much more intelligent than I supposed."[22] The life and work of Harriet M. Buss effectively illuminates the way in which teachers often changed their perspectives of the former slaves. Initially referring to her students as "darkey children" who did not learn as quickly as northern students, Buss's attitude toward the freedpeople shifted over time and she developed genuine affection for many of her students in Raleigh. Reflecting on a scholarly debate that she was asked to observe during the winter of 1869, Buss praised the students for the respect and politeness that they afforded her, questioning whether she would have had a similar experience with "the same number of white students."[23]

Committed to free-labor ideology, a pressing goal for many teachers was to mold the freedpeople into self-reliant and self-supporting laborers. To this end, Sarah P. Freeman taught the freedwomen on Roanoke Island how to refashion unwanted clothing into "good serviceable garments" so that they could become "thrifty housewives." She was also actively involved in the development of Roanoke Island's industrial school which, due to her efforts, was "in successful operation" by January 1866. Although the school closed its doors less than one year later, it trained over 130 formerly enslaved women to sew, knit, braid straw, and quilt, skills which Horace James argued were necessary in order to transform the South from a slave to a free-labor society. While efforts such as this undoubtedly enabled freedwomen to secure employment in the post-emancipation South, it ultimately stemmed from the belief that benevolence enabled dependency and that if left unchecked, the former slaves would resort to a life of idleness in freedom. Thus, it was with great satisfaction when Freeman reported that she had employed a group of old men to tie yards of fishing net so that they could "have the satisfaction of feeling that they had paid for a pair of pants or a jacket, and that they are thus living like freemen."[24]

Efforts to engage the freedpeople in labor, which the NEFAS termed "the organization of industry," were ultimately encouraged by northern aid and missionary societies which perceived their work in the South as a means of stabilizing the workforce, rebuilding the southern economy, restoring economic prosperity, and protecting American society. As Reverend Francis Wharton of the Protestant Episcopal Freedman's Commission (PEFC) argued in 1866, "No industrial class is now ready to take [the freedpeople's] place; yet, without some competent industrial class, not merely will the South be permanently desolated, but the prosperity, the peace, the solvency of the whole country will be seriously shocked." As such, organizations such as the NFRA sent teachers South not only for the purpose of teaching the freedpeople "the rudiments of learning," but also "to systematize their labor, to encourage them in habits of regular industry, and to prepare them for civilization and the freedom to which the nation has called them."[25]

Interestingly, not long after the end of the Civil War, the NEFAS attempted to challenge the preconception that formerly enslaved men and women posed a threat to the reconstruction of the South. Rather than concerning themselves with the place of newly freed slaves in southern society, writers of *The Freedmen's Record* urged readers to consider the fate of former slaveowners instead. Without slaves to work for them, southern whites "are left more dependent upon charity than those they consider their inferiors." Moreover, the writers also attempted to challenge prevailing racial stereotypes that former slaves were "unthinking, unthrifty, dull machines" by praising their enterprising efforts to generate an income in the aftermath of war. This view appeared to change in 1867 when the secretary of the organization argued that both whites and Blacks were "in some sense responsible" for the labor scarcity that permeated the postwar South. Although he acknowledged that the freedpeople were often reluctant to work for southern white employers because they had been cheated out of their wages, he also suggested that freedmen were attempting to take advantage of their newfound freedom by resorting to idleness and enjoying the privileges of free travel "in the spirit of adventure." Ultimately, these conflicting positions not only reflect the complexities surrounding the perception of Black freedom during Reconstruction, but also how views of the freedpeople were shaped by wider socioeconomic factors, such as labor shortages and economic instability in this case.[26]

Although the stabilization of the workforce was an explicit goal for many northern aid and missionary societies, there is little evidence in the teachers' letters or diaries to suggest that they deliberately attempted to push the freedpeople back into the fields and onto the plantations as a subservient workforce. In fact, Sarah P. Freeman was genuinely concerned when many former slaves were forced to return "to their old homes" in January 1866 due to severe destitution. While she was determined to ensure that the freedpeople would not become dependent upon northern largesse, she believed that they would have greater opportunity working in the new northern enterprises that were developing in places like Plymouth and New Bern. This is undoubtedly why she devoted so much of her time and energy into growing and sustaining the industrial school on Roanoke Island.[27]

The Freedmen's Bureau, on the other hand, was less concerned about enabling the freedpeople to secure fair and equitable employment. In 1866, Lieutenant George O. Sanderson, a former Union officer, claimed that some government officials on Roanoke Island actively attempted to drive the freedpeople back onto the plantations. In his report to the Joint Committee on Reconstruction, a Congressional organization established to investigate the condition of the former Confederate states, Sanderson reported that some Freedmen's Bureau officials purposely withheld rations from the freedpeople in an effort to compel them to seek wage labor. "The whole object seems to be at present out there to drive them back into the employ of their masters – at any rate, to get them off from the government as fast as they can." Although Sanderson agreed that the freedpeople should be encouraged to become self-sufficient, he did not believe in "making them suffer."[28]

During military occupation, some freedpeople secured employment with the federal government. However, in many cases, the former slaves were treated no less favorably than had they returned to their former masters. In 1865, a news article in *The Freedman* praised the work of approximately 700 freedmen who were now working for the government. The writer was particularly pleased to report that the formerly enslaved men continued to display the same humble and subdued characteristics "of yore" while working under the surveillance of a "gangman" which, in this context, was a term synonymous with "overseer." What is particularly striking about this observation is that the writer did not appear to see anything wrong with the fact that freedmen were laboring under a system that so closely resembled slavery. In fact, they commended the government's decision to deduct pay from those who demonstrated "a lack of duty" or a "shirking of industry."[29]

Such efforts undoubtedly stemmed from the words of Major General Oliver O. Howard who, in 1865, called on Freedmen's Bureau officers to "introduce practical systems of compensated labor." "While a generous provision should be made for the aged, infirm, and sick," he wrote, "the able-bodied should be encouraged, and, if necessary, compelled to labor for their own support." In order to reduce relief efforts and "make the people self-supporting," Howard instructed Bureau agents to limit the distribution of government supplies, to keep precise records of those who received them, and to consider any supplies issued "as a lien upon the crops." Like many of his contemporaries, Howard was preoccupied with the fear that the former slaves would become a permanent dependent class. While he believed that the freedpeople "must be free to choose their own employers, and be paid for their labor," they were not necessarily free to choose not to work and he also advocated for "the use of the vagrant laws which applied to whites." Thus, whether intended or not, his words often served to drive the freedpeople back into the hands of their prejudiced former masters.[30]

Not unlike the northern common school movement which, as discussed in Chapter 3, was intended to ameliorate many of the social issues that emerged from the rapid urbanization and industrialization of the antebellum period, freedpeople's schools were similarly viewed as a mechanism for social control. This goal was made explicit by Samuel Ashley who, in a letter to a prominent North Carolina planter, outlined the role of the teachers under his care:

> Their business is not only to teach the knowledge of letters, but to instruct [the freedpeople] in the duties which now devolve upon them in their new relations – to make clear to their understanding the principles by which they must be guided in all their intercourse with their fellowmen – to inculcate obedience to law and respect for the rights and property of others, and reverence for those in authority; enforcing honesty, industry and economy, guarding them against fostering animosities and prejudices, and against all unjust and indecorous assumptions, above all indoctrinating them in the Gospel of our Lord and Savior Jesus Christ.[31]

Although Ashley's words are not a direct reflection of the teachers' motivations, he suggests that their primary role was to prepare the former slaves for responsible citizenship by teaching them their duties and responsibilities as freedmen and women. However, it is also worth pointing out that Ashley was a shrewd diplomat who knew that support from the southern white community, particularly members of the planter class, could be gained by framing freedpeople's education as a positive initiative that would ultimately benefit the ruling classes by serving to maintain the antebellum status quo. While not without his shortcomings, Ashley, a Congregational minister from Northborough, Massachusetts, worked tirelessly to implement an equitable system of public schooling in North Carolina for both Black and white children as the state's first postwar superintendent of Public Instruction. As a Republican delegate to North Carolina's constitutional convention in 1868 and as chairman of the convention's Committee on Education, Ashley was responsible for drafting Article IX of North Carolina's new state constitution which established a system of free public schooling for all children, regardless of race, between the ages of six and twenty-one. Although many conservative delegates opposed the new constitution's article on education, principally because it did not provide for segregated schools, Ashley refused to make a provision for separate schools. As he argued, the United States Constitution made no mention of race in terms of education so neither should the state constitution. Despite rising opposition, Ashley remained steadfast because he feared that the provision of racial segregation within the constitution would only serve to undermine Black schools and fuel racial prejudice. Unsurprisingly, Ashley's position meant that he was not well-regarded in southern society and in 1919, North Carolina historian J. G. de Roulhac Hamilton described him as "a carpetbagger from Massachusetts who was probably himself of mixed blood."[32]

In April 1868, North Carolina's constitution was ratified by a vote of 93,086 to 74,014 and Ashley was appointed superintendent of Public Instruction. However, when southern Democrats regained control of the legislature in 1870, they slashed educational funding as well as Ashley's salary. Fearing that the legislature would continue to undermine the public school system while he was in control, Ashley resigned in 1871. As he wrote to George Whipple of the AMA one year earlier, "If I resign some Southern man can be appointed who is not so obnoxious to the ruling class as myself, and who can secure better than I can, the attention of the people, white people, I mean." Although Ashley did not actively support social equality, he made a significant contribution to the growth and development of southern Black schooling. As John Bell observed, in spite of his shortcomings, "Ashley bequeathed a positive educational legacy to North Carolina. Seeing that the legislature could abolish the school system by law in 1866, he insisted that the guarantee of a public school education for all of North Carolina's children be embedded in the constitution beyond the reach of legislative majorities."[33]

As the Reconstruction period progressed, southern white men and women, particularly those of the "better and more intelligent class," grew more accepting of freedpeople's education. According to Samuel Ashley, several North Carolinian planters were beginning to recognize that plantation schools would help to retain a stable labor force. As he reported to Fiske in 1866, schools were established by them "as a matter of self defense . . . i.e. the Freedmen insist on coming to the City because by so doing their children can attend schools. Therefore, plantation schools are a necessity if the Farmers would retain their hands." Freedmen's Bureau General Superintendent of Education John W. Alvord confirmed Ashley's claim and found that the provision of schooling was often incorporated into the freedpeople's labor contracts. Other members of the southern white community recognized that schooling could be used as "a powerful agent" to preserve the antebellum status quo and contribute toward the creation of a more productive workforce. As *The Fayetteville News* reported in 1866, controlled and regulated education would enable the freedpeople to more fully "understand and appreciate the difference of caste and social position existing between themselves and the whites" and "the necessity of laboring earnestly."[34] This particular viewpoint is reflective of the way in which attitudes toward freedpeople's education changed or evolved over time. In a letter to the Freedmen's Convention of North Carolina one year earlier, former state senator and governor of North Carolina, William Alexander Graham, acknowledged that while the freedpeople should receive "instruction in morals and virtue," this kind of education could be received at home, in church, or at Sunday school. Viewing the former slaves as a "people who must live by labor," Graham believed that the freedman's most pressing goal "should be to obtain an honest livelihood for himself and his family, by labor." This, he argued, was more necessary "at present than the knowledge of letters and books."[35]

Although North Carolinian planters were becoming more receptive to freedpeople's education, few actually taught the freedpeople themselves. Instead, most applied to a northern aid society to send a teacher to their plantation. Finding a teacher who was willing to work on a plantation was not always an easy task, however, particularly because northern aid societies were reluctant to send teachers to the more rural and remote areas of the state. During the summer of 1866, W. H. Worden asked Fiske to send a teacher to his plantation in Rowan County. Worden, "a northern gentleman who has either purchased or leased the plantation," offered to board the teacher and pay all expenses except for the teacher's salary. Nevertheless, Fiske found it extremely difficult to find someone to take on the school. This was partly because the school was located 150 miles west of Raleigh and northern aid societies preferred sending teachers to the more populated areas of the state. However, a lack of funding may have also contributed to the problem. As Fiske informed Worden, "it is more difficult to obtain teachers [now] than last year."[36]

In an attempt to find a teacher for Worden's plantation, Fiske first applied to a northern aid society. When this proved unsuccessful, he contacted Miss A. Thurston, a minister's daughter from Fall River, Massachusetts, who was eager to obtain work in the South. This attempt also proved unsuccessful. Although Fiske reported that Thurston was "ready and very anxious" to leave, she was unable to secure employment with any of the aid societies that she applied to, largely due to a lack of funding. Finally, Fiske contacted Eunice S. Leland, the wife of a northern teacher in Raleigh, who was "anxious to return to N.C. and enter again into the same service." Although the FTP confirms that Leland was teaching between 1866 and 1867, the location of her school has been identified as Raleigh, so it is not clear if Fiske was successful in securing a teacher for the plantation in Rowan County. Although Fiske was usually hesitant about sending white women to teach in the plantation schools, he admitted that Worden and his wife "seem to be very pleasant people." Indeed, Worden had also served with the Freedmen's Bureau, and this may have helped to subside Fiske's fears about sending a white woman to this remote area.[37]

If white southerners wanted to use education as a means of preserving the antebellum social order, teachers who would not challenge the racial hierarchy or, as one local North Carolinian charged, "put notions of equality into [the freedpeople's] heads," were required. Hostility toward teachers who did not conform to these expectations is exemplified by an incident which occurred in 1866 when thirty-nine white residents and the mayor of Franklinton signed a petition to remove James Crawford, a Black Pennsylvanian, from his teaching position in a local school. According to the white residents, Crawford regularly held noisy religious meetings that were "demoralizing in their effects upon the Freedmen." In addition, local whites charged that these meetings made the former slaves unfit for the "fruitful discharge of their duties as laborers" and resulted "in an increase of vice among them." Crawford was also accused of being "under the influence" as well as the leader of a "certain clique of colored persons." When Fiske investigated these claims, he found that the religious meetings were no different to those being held by white people and that they never lasted later than ten o'clock in the evening. As he reported to Freedmen's Bureau Assistant Commissioner in North Carolina Jacob F. Chur: "Mr. Crawford repeatedly and faithfully cautioned and warned the attendants to retire with quietness, promptness and good order." Consequently, Fiske deemed it unjust to dismiss Crawford. Nevertheless, he cautioned the freedpeople to "refrain from extravagance and boisterousness in the evening meetings, and for the present at least to hold those meetings less frequently."[38] Although Fiske attempted to aid the freedpeople in their transition from slavery to freedom, he also attempted to appease southern whites. Rather than condemning whites for their attempts to subvert Black education by defaming Crawford, he advised Black residents to avoid aggravating whites.

Not surprisingly, a sense of racial solidarity moved many Black teachers to engage in freedpeople's education. As Sallie Daffin wrote in 1865:

> I presume my interest in the freedmen, and the motive that induces me to leave my home to labor for them, will not be questioned, when it is remembered that they are my people. And how much soever those of other races may sympathize with them, yet none can fully experience the strength of their needs, nor understand the means necessary to relieve them as we are who identified with them. And while we fully appreciate every effort on the part of our friends for the elevation of our race, yet it is my desire to contribute something to our cause.[39]

Sallie, or Sarah Louise, Daffin was a native of Philadelphia and as her words suggest, she believed that Black people were best placed to educate the former slaves. Other motivations also moved her work, some of which were influenced by her well-educated background and prior experience as a northern common schoolteacher. As a devout member of the African Methodist Episcopal Church, Daffin was particularly eager to facilitate the "Christianization of [her] long oppressed race" and viewed moral instruction as central to the education of freedpeople. Over the course of her southern teaching career, Daffin taught the freedpeople for thirteen consecutive years in four different states before accepting a public school position in Washington, D.C.[40]

Like Daffin, many other Black people felt that they were best suited to teach the freedpeople. As Ellen Garrison Jackson from Newport, Rhode Island, wrote in her letter of application for a teaching position: "I have a great desire to go and labor among the Freedmen of the South. I think it is our duty as a people to spend our lives in trying to elevate our own race.... And who can feel the sympathy that we can who are identified with them?" Jackson taught the freedpeople for nine years between 1864 and 1875 across three different states. Sara G. Stanley expressed a similar sentiment and in 1864 she wrote the AMA, "My reasons for asking to engage in the work of instructing the Freedpeople of the South are few and simple. I am myself a colored woman, bound to that ignorant, degraded, long enslaved race, by ties of love and consanguinity; they are socially and politically, 'my people.'" Although she was born free in North Carolina, Stanley did not teach the freedpeople in her home state. Born to a prominent slaveholding family of mixed-race ancestry, Stanley studied at Oberlin College and while she was there her family relocated to Delaware first, then to Ohio. After graduating from Oberlin in 1857, Stanley taught in a northern common school. Upon applying to the AMA for a position in the South, Stanley was sent to Virginia. She later taught the freedpeople in Missouri, Kentucky, and Alabama.[41] It is also important to note that freedmen and women wanted to be educated by Black teachers, a point made explicit during the Freedmen's Convention of North Carolina in 1865. Although delegates to the convention appreciated the work of white teachers, they believed that Black teachers were better suited to the work. Reiterating the words of Daffin, Jackson, and Stanley, formerly enslaved James Henry Harris declared that "no one can enter so fully into the sympathy of the negro's condition as the negro himself."[42]

Several other Black teachers spoke of their work in terms of racial elevation. In his letter of application for a teaching position, twenty-four-year-old Robert Harris wrote that he wanted to assist "in the noble work of elevating and evangelizing our oppressed and long abused race." Likewise, in a letter to North Carolina Governor William W. Holden, Mary A. Best from Duplin County wrote: "I feel it is my duty to try to elevate the mindes of my color," before continuing that she hoped "to elevate the poor colored children so they would not always be troden underfoot [sic]." Former slave Robert Martin also viewed his work as a form of racial uplift and in an application to the Freedmen's Bureau for aid, he wrote, "without help we can't begin to be elevated and prepared for the duties that seem to await us."[43]

Some white northerners engaged in freedpeople's education to elevate the Black race. Albion W. Tourgée, a native of Ohio, was one such teacher. Between 1865 and 1868 Tourgée and his wife Emma taught the freedpeople just outside Greensboro in North Carolina. Described by Mark Elliott as "a pioneer of civil rights activism," Tourgée dedicated his life's work to securing equal rights for the newly freed slaves. After serving as a delegate to North Carolina's constitutional convention in 1868, Tourgée served as a superior court judge and used this position to challenge Ku Klux Klan activity in the war-torn South. Tourgée's most powerful fight for Black justice occurred in 1896 when he served as attorney for Homer A. Plessy in the renowned *Plessy v. Ferguson* Supreme Court case. Although this case resulted in Tourgée's defeat by upholding the constitutionality of racial segregation under the doctrine of "separate but equal," it clearly demonstrates his commitment to racial advancement. Unsurprisingly, Tourgée's campaign for racial equality was viewed with contempt by many local whites and he frequently faced death threats and intimidation.[44]

Although Tourgée was committed to racial advancement, he equally sought to benefit from the South's unstable postwar economic conditions. Often branded a "carpetbagger," Tourgée infuriated the local white community by attempting to buy and sell plantation land. In 1867, Tourgée wrote to Nathan Hill, a local Quaker teacher in Lincolnton, North Carolina, requesting descriptions of plots of land which he hoped to sell. "I am ready to convince people here that it is policy to sell," he wrote, "and people North that it is policy to buy." Ultimately, as Elliott found, "Though he hoped his entrepreneurial ventures would benefit the freedpeople, Tourgée also intended to make a profit." Nevertheless, Tourgée's primary commitment was to the freedpeople, and he was one of the few northern white teachers who actively promoted racial equality. "The inherent inferiority of the African of the United States" he argued, "has been shown by irrefrangible evidence of experience to be false."[45]

In the end, Tourgée was deeply unhappy with the course of Reconstruction, and he blamed his party, the Republican Party, for its ultimate failure. Reflecting upon the successes and failures of the Republican Party in 1884, Tourgée concluded that formerly enslaved Black men and women made very few gains during the tumultuous Reconstruction period, particularly in terms of education but also in relation to the franchise:

> Those whom we made free in law, we have yet to make free in fact. Those whom we gave the sword of power, we have yet to teach to wield it; those upon whom we laid the burden of American citizenship, we have yet to give an opportunity to learn the duties of the American citizen; those whom we found oppressed with legal servitude, we have yet to free, not from formal fetters, but from the actual and more terrible enslavement of ignorance.[46]

As far as Tourgée was concerned, the Republican Party had failed to secure Black equal rights and until every free man had the right to vote and attend school, he believed that southern Blacks remained "enchained."[47]

Tourgée was not the only northern white teacher committed to Black educational advancement. Yardley Warner, a Quaker from Pennsylvania, was also deeply committed to growing and sustaining a system of schools for the freedpeople. Arriving in North Carolina in 1864 under the auspices of the Friends' Freedmen's Association (FFA), Warner was actively involved in the creation of schools throughout North Carolina, Virginia, Tennessee, and Alabama. On two occasions in 1873 and 1876, he traveled to England and Ireland to raise funds for freedpeople's education and upon his return to the South, Warner used this money to help create a network of teacher training institutes for Black men and women.[48]

The teachers who have been identified as antebellum abolitionists in the FTP were often staunch proponents of civil, political, and economic equality. Martha Kellogg openly endorsed land redistribution among the former slaves and frequently pleaded with northern benefactors to help them acquire land. "To one living among them, amid their continued and ever present distress," she wrote in 1868, "the indispensableness of some such provision is constantly evident, and induces the belief that their friends must have the purpose to deliver them from the remains of their oppression, by some beneficent land appropriation." Kellogg spent a total of seven years in the South, and it is likely that she would have continued teaching the freedpeople had it not been for her untimely death in March 1869. Indeed, the abolitionist teachers' commitment to freedpeople's education is further illustrated by the length of time they spent in the South. Collectively, these men and women spent a total of 139 years teaching the freedpeople, averaging at just over five and a half years per teacher. For comparison, a typical northern white teacher spent three and a half years working in a southern Black school.[49]

Being a prewar abolitionist did not necessarily mean being devoid of racial prejudice. Freedmen's Bureau Superintendent of Negro Affairs Horace James is a prime example of this. Drawing upon the stereotype that Black men and women were physically stronger than their white counterparts, James determined that miscegenation would be detrimental to the Black race because it would diminish their "vitality and force" and shorten their life. Although, like Kellogg, James believed that the freedpeople deserved the right to own their own property, he drew sharp distinctions between granting the freedpeople political and social equality. "Give the colored man equality," he wrote, "not of social condition, but equality before the law."[50]

Although only a minority of the northern white teachers have been identified as prewar abolitionists, the remainder were arguably anti-slavery. The proliferation of sentimental literature, the anti-slavery novel in particular, during the antebellum period certainly contributed to this. Essentially, this literary genre was designed to evoke an emotional response in the reader in an effort to incite social reform. Although northern abolitionists used newspapers, pamphlets, slave narratives, and other forms of literature to mobilize readers against slavery, anti-slavery fiction was one of the most powerful forces in winning white northerners to the abolitionist cause. Harriet Beecher Stowe's *Uncle Tom's Cabin* is undeniably one of the best-known examples of anti-slavery fiction. Written in response to the controversial Fugitive Slave Act of 1850 and subsequently published in 1852, this work of fiction was the best-selling novel of the entire nineteenth century. Although it has been heavily criticized for its racist undertones, support for colonization, and perpetuation of Black stereotypes, *Uncle Tom's Cabin* had a profound impact upon its worldwide readership and rallied many to anti-slavery activism.[51]

Recognizing that sentimental fiction was a fundamentally female genre whereby women readers and writers formed the majority, it is not surprising that anti-slavery sentiment rose rapidly among antebellum women. However, the social limitations imposed upon women readers and writers meant that female authors were often prevented from exploring the harsh realities of slavery, including the separation of families, the sexual exploitation of female slaves, and the inhumane cruelty often inflicted upon enslaved people. Accordingly, works of anti-slavery fiction often depicted enslaved people as childlike, humble, docile, and submissive. This meant that many women went South with a skewed image of southern Black people. Indeed, many northern white teachers were perplexed, and occasionally offended, when they encountered assertive Black people who were eager to take control of their own educational institutions.[52]

Like their northern counterparts, some southern white men and women also engaged in freedpeople's education because they wanted to contribute to the education and elevation of the Black race. The number of teachers who were driven by this motivation was relatively high in North Carolina, principally because the state was home to a large Quaker population. Edward Payson Hall, a Quaker teacher from Mount Vernon, was committed to facilitating Black educational advancement. Upon petitioning the Freedmen's Bureau for $150 to build a Black school, Hall wrote, "my desire to serve [the freedpeople] is great – knowing the field for usefulness there would be wider than any other now unoccupied." To assist the freedpeople even further, Hall gratuitously pledged them one acre of land as well as logs from his woods. The freedmen, he promised F. A. Fiske, would provide the labor. They will "cut and hew the logs," he wrote, "and put up said building and will do all they can in labor – they are so poor they could not raise but a very little money." Although Hall's petition was successful, he and his wife were forced to flee their home in 1870 due to rising hostility and opposition to their work.[53]

Mary Bowers from Chapel Hill also expressed an interest in elevating the former slaves. However, based upon her interactions with the local Black community, it appears as though this motive was mostly guided by a sense of racial paternalism. In particular, Bowers did not value the freedpeople's right to take charge of their own educational institutions. This became evident during the spring of 1866 when the FFA threatened to close Bowers's school down because it was in poor condition and could not accommodate many students. After much debate,

Bowers successfully persuaded the association to keep the school open because local freedpeople were in the process of constructing a new schoolhouse. However, this schoolhouse was not being constructed as quickly as Bowers would have liked. Taking matters into her own hands, Bowers asked the Freedmen's Bureau for permission to let the schoolhouse in its current, unfinished condition to the lowest bidder. She also asked the Bureau for financial aid to hire someone to complete the building. As she wrote in March 1866, "I am going to see if I can get it in my hands I *know* I can have it completed and keep up our school I do hate to see it go down after all the trouble and sacrifices I have made for it."[54]

The Chapel Hill freedpeople were not pleased when they heard of Bowers's plans. As Jordan Swain, a local Black resident, explained, "Suppose the white people had some business on hand and some old *nigger wence* was to come in and try to take it out of their hands, she would be drummed out of town and it ought to be so [sic]." According to Bowers, Swain argued that "it was for *them* to say whether those logs should lay there and rot or even be made a home of." Bowers was perplexed by Swain's reaction because she believed that she was acting in the freedpeople's best interests. Ultimately, however, Bowers completely disregarded the freedpeople's right to take charge of their school and her failure to consult them regarding her plans suggests that she was blinded by a sense of her own cultural superiority.[55]

Not surprisingly, a lack of funds prevented the freedpeople in Chapel Hill from constructing the schoolhouse in a timely manner. After Bowers attempted to take charge of the school, Jordan Swain wrote to Fiske requesting aid. "The collard friends will not or cand not pay the expenses – to finish the hous – so i have undertaken to finish the hous with the help of God i am Determen to finish it," he wrote in November 1866. "Dear sir with a little help from our northen friends I cand git a long – i must have a little help from some whers [sic]." Contrary to what Bowers argued during the spring of 1866, Swain was not indifferent to education. He was simply frustrated that a white person attempted to take control of a project that the Black community was working on. As he explained in his letter to Fiske, Swain was still more than willing for Bowers to teach the freedpeople in the new schoolhouse once it was constructed.[56]

Bowers was not the only southern white teacher whose desire to aid the former slaves was driven by a sense of racial paternalism. Like their northern counterparts, many southern whites viewed the former slaves as an ignorant, childlike, and submissive race who lacked the ability to live as autonomous free men and women, much less the knowledge and skills to control their own schools. James Sinclair's reasons for supporting freedpeople's education were arguably shaped by paternalistic notions of Black inferiority and he steadfastly believed that any northern man whom the freedpeople trusted could manipulate and control them. Although Sinclair, a Presbyterian minister, did not directly teach the former slaves, he established a Black Sabbath school and unsuccessfully applied for a northern teacher to conduct a day school in his home. Sinclair did not support Black suffrage though, most likely because he did not believe that Black men were capable of exercising intelligent use of the franchise.[57]

Other motivating factors were influenced by the teachers' personal backgrounds or wider social and political contexts. Some northern white men and women, for instance, were moved to engage in freedpeople's education out of a sense of patriotism and many saw their work in the South as a means of contributing to the Union war effort. According to Horace James, the bereavements of war influenced many northern white women to seek work in North Carolina's schools for the freedpeople, not least because war widows sought to continue the patriotic work their deceased husbands had been doing for the preservation of the Union. In 1865, Carrie E. Croome began working in a Black school in Clumfort's Creek, North Carolina, under the auspices of the NEFAS. Her motivation for seeking work in the South, James observed, was due to her husband's wartime death. "The rebels had slain her noble husband while in command of his battery at South Mountain; and she would avenge his untimely death by teaching the ignorant negroes how to throw off the yoke which those dastardly rebels had put upon their necks."[58]

Some southern Black people began teaching the former slaves incidentally, particularly as the demand for Black teachers grew. Shortly after enrolling in a school during the spring of 1864, former slave London R. Ferebee's progress "was so rapid" that his northern white teacher, Ella Roper, made him her assistant. At this time, Ferebee was fifteen years old. When the Civil War ended, Ferebee moved to Elizabeth City with his father, enrolled in a school, and was soon asked to teach the freedpeople in Nixonton. After teaching there for three years, Ferebee attended normal school in Mississippi and Virginia. He taught the freedpeople for a total of six years.[59] Charles N. Hunter, formerly enslaved in Raleigh, had a similar experience. In 1875, he was asked by Reverend W. W. Morgan of the Methodist Episcopal Church to teach the freedpeople in Shoe Hill, Robeson County. According to Hunter, Morgan had been "requested by the school committee to secure for them a teacher who could meet the requirements," namely his ability to pass the teaching examinations. Described by John Haley as "a passive accommodationist," Hunter adopted a conservative approach to race relations throughout much of the Reconstruction period. Although committed to elevating and uplifting the Black race, Hunter did not aggressively call for civil, social, or political equality with whites. Instead, he supported a separate but equal doctrine which envisioned whites and Blacks living amicably side by side. According to Haley, this approach was not uncommon among many of North Carolina's most prominent Black leaders, which often included teachers. Hiram Rhodes Revels, a freeborn teacher and politician from North Carolina, was described by one scholar as having a "moderate political orientation" while James Henry Harris, born enslaved in North Carolina, was also described by Haley as conservative. Of course, this did not mean that such teachers did not steadfastly press for Black civil rights. Although not particularly aggressive in his approach, Congressman James Edward O'Hara did not shy away from controversy during his political career, and he actively advocated for the rights of southern Black people as well as other underrepresented groups including women, Native Americans, and poor whites.[60] Like other Black educators, Hunter recognized that education could be used to elevate the Black race. Writing in 1877, he declared, "our only hope, and the only hope of our many friends for us is in our education. Without this we must ever remain dependent, helpless and poor. We must ever be subject to oppression and insult. But knowledge will devise a means of relief for us from all our present ills, and place us beyond their influence for the future." In total, Hunter spent fifty years in the classroom.[61]

For many freedpeople, teaching was a respectable occupation. Alongside Black ministers, teachers were held in high esteem by members of the Black community, and many were seen as the leaders of their race. "The school, in the freedmen's estimation," concluded F. A. Fiske, "stands next in importance to the church and the preaching of the gospel, and the teacher next to the preacher." Evidence of this can be clearly seen in northern Black teacher Robert Fitzgerald's nomination as delegate to Virginia's constitutional convention in 1867. As his nominators explained, "we believe you are the most reliable we can send to represent our interests in that important Body. We therefore beg that you accept this nomination." Although the Black community obviously thought very highly of Fitzgerald, he was reluctant to accept the nomination, partly because he did not feel qualified for the role, and he attempted to convince the freedpeople to select another candidate. His attempts were futile, however, and he served as delegate to the state's constitutional convention between July and August.[62]

Due to the harsh economic climate in Reconstruction North Carolina, several southern white teachers engaged in freedpeople's education for financial reasons. In 1868, Sophia Groner began teaching formerly enslaved children near her home in Dallas, Gaston County. Married to an ex-Confederate grocer, Sophia began teaching the freedpeople in order to support her family. Although her husband was worth a total of $300 in 1860, a decade later he could only report half that amount. In spite of only teaching for two years, the Freedmen's Bureau was pleased with her work and one agent described her as "the only Southern woman of proper respect & character I have met, who would take a school." "From all I can learn," he continued, "she does very well for a School of young children such as she has."[63] Francis Flake undoubtedly taught for financial reasons also. Three years after the war's end, Flake began teaching the freedpeople in his hometown of Lanesboro, Anson County. Prior to enlisting in the Confederate army, Flake owned four slaves, and his net worth was approximately $2,600. However, emancipation and the fall of the Confederacy rendered Flake virtually worthless and by 1870 he "owned no land and could report no net worth." After teaching the freedpeople for just one year, Flake resumed farming on rented land.[64] Noah Hancock, a nonslaveholding farmer from Asheboro, experienced a similar trajectory. When the Civil War broke out in 1861, Hancock was worth a total of $375. In 1862, at age thirty, he enlisted in the Confederate army as a private in Company F of North Carolina's 46th Infantry Regiment but was injured and subsequently lost the use of his leg. Confined to the use of a crutch and relegated to "light labor," as described by a physician in his application for a Confederate pension, it appears as though Hancock was no longer able to make a living from the farm and during the 1866–1867 school year, he taught the freedpeople in a self-supporting school in Fork Creek, Randolph County. After teaching the freedpeople for one year, Hancock returned to work on the farm, but by 1870, he was still struggling to make ends meet and was worth just $170.[65]

Financial necessity also drove Mary A. Chambers, a former slaveowner from Montgomery County, into the classroom. As she explained to H. C. Vogell in 1869, "I have always been in good circumstances & being now reduced to do something to help make A Support & so many colored children near by I thought probably it would be best to try & get a colored school if I could get a compensation for it." In a letter to Vogell one month later, she added, "we have always had a plenty but the War has ruined us." As Chambers's words suggest, teaching the freedpeople was often viewed as a viable source of income due to the proliferation of schools throughout the state. Notably absent from her words, though, was any indication that Chambers was committed to elevating the former slaves or assisting their transition from slavery to freedom. Evidently, for Chambers and others like her, teaching the freedpeople presented itself as nothing more than a practical means of securing an income in the face of rising economic hardships. Tellingly, Chambers only taught the freedpeople for one year between 1869 and 1870 in an independent, self-supporting school.[66]

In August 1867, twenty-one-year-old William R. Ashworth, an ex-Confederate soldier from Randolph County, sought the support of Nathan Hill to help him find work in a freedpeople's school. One month previously, Ashworth wrote to the Freedmen's Bureau requesting information on the salary he could expect, which suggests that financial considerations were, at the very least, a factor in his application. Ultimately, Ashworth was told that "The Bureau has no authority to expend money for the pay of teachers. Rents repairs &c. are the only charges allowed against the School Fund." Although Ashworth is not included in the FTP, various archival records indicate that he worked as a teacher until his death in 1927. In Randolph County's 1894 business directory, for instance, Ashworth is listed as a teacher in Asheboro. As the race of the school is not explicitly identified as "colored," it is likely that he was teaching in a white school.[67]

Although little else is known about Ashworth's role in freedpeople's education, if he played any role at all, his father Joel Ashworth was "a new Republican voter" who Mark Elliot argues became a true believer in "the principal of racial equality." As Ashworth wrote to Hill in 1867, "I never had much prejudice against the negro and what I had I have laid aside." He continued, "I visited several of their schools last winter and I heard several of them speak in the Convention and my opinion is that there is but little if any difference in the talents of the two races and I am willing to give them all an even start in the race. I am for 'Liberty, Union, and political equality.'" It is possible that his son shared these viewpoints and simply did not mind if he taught in a white or Black school. Like Chambers, he may have recognized that freedpeople's schools offered greater employment opportunities. In August 1867, H. C. Talley also asked Nathan Hill for a teaching position, and he explicitly stated that he did not mind working in a white or Black school. "Having attended, school pretty closely the two last summers and having had a considerable start before," he wrote, "I now consider my ability sufficient to conduct a common school."[68]

As each of these cases demonstrate, the reasons why so many men and women elected to become teachers is complex and multifaceted. While the teachers can be organized into neat groups according to their regional and racial identities, their motives transcend such simplistic categorizations. Regardless of their regional backgrounds or racial identities, many educators were motivated by factors that stemmed from shared experiences in the broader social, political, and cultural landscape. The antebellum common school movement, for instance, played a pivotal role in shaping the ideals of northern Black and white teachers while postwar economic hardships served as the impetus for the work of white and Black North Carolinians. The evolving nature of the teachers' motivations combined with the inherent bias in much of their writings adds another layer of complexity to this already complex history. However, by providing some initial clues to their motivations, data from the FTP combined with traditional archival sources proved to be particularly useful in providing another insight into the reasons why these men and women chose to engage in this very important work.

5

The Textbooks Used in North Carolina's Schools for the Freedpeople

The textbooks used in North Carolina's schools for the freedpeople ranged from donations of northern common school textbooks to those that were explicitly created for the newly emancipated people, otherwise known as freedmen's texts or textbooks. Due to a lack of financial resources, the Bible and religious pamphlets were often used as supplementary textbooks because they were widely available and usually distributed for free. Although textbook analyses tell us little about what was actually taught or learned in schools, they provide useful insights into the dominant ideologies of those who created them. "Textbooks are political instruments," wrote Heather A. Williams, "aimed at transmitting particular ways of looking at the world" and while students may accept, reject, or forget what they read in a textbook, if they read them at all, they reflect prevailing social values, perspectives, and norms, particularly in relation to concepts such as race, class, and gender. Consequently, this chapter analyzes the textbooks that were used in North Carolina's schools for the freedpeople, not as a record of what North Carolinian freedpeople were actually taught or learned, but as a means of identifying how Black people and their projected place in nineteenth-century American society was perceived, both before and after the Civil War period.[1]

During the antebellum period, the northern common school system was perceived as a mechanism for social control. Consequently, the textbooks produced during this era were profoundly didactic and explicit in their intention to influence readers and shape society by infusing practical lessons in literacy, numeracy, and other curricular areas with religious and moral content. As Noah Webster wrote in the preface to his best-selling *Blue-Backed Speller*, his textbook would not only instruct children in "the first rudiments of the language" but also "some just ideas of religion, morals and domestic economy."[2] The northern common school textbooks that were donated to southern Black schools consisted of an array of readers, spellers, arithmetic, geography, and history textbooks. In their letters, diaries, and reports, teachers often referred to using a first, second, or third reader while arithmetic and geography textbooks were often recorded as "small" or "large" to differentiate between higher and lower levels. Occasionally, teachers specifically named the books they were using in their classroom. In New Bern, Betsey L. Canedy reported that she was using *Willson's Third Reader* with her students. Similarly, when reporting on North Carolinian schools between July 1 and December 31, 1869, State Superintendent of Education H. C. Vogell made reference to students who were using "Mitchell's Intermediate," "Greenleaf's Elementary Arithmetic," and "Brown's First Lines of Grammar."[3]

Given the limitations on funding that persisted throughout the Civil War and Reconstruction period, it is highly likely that most of the textbooks used in North Carolina's schools for the freedpeople were donations of those that were being used in the North. During the 1869–1870 school year, northern publishers donated more than 50,000 textbooks to the South. Some of the major textbooks used in northern common schools included readers from the McGuffey and Willson series, Webster's *Blue-Backed Speller,* and geography textbooks from the Mitchell and Monteith series. Although content relating to race was absent from the northern common school readers and spellers examined in this study, it was a persistent theme in the geography textbooks, all of which were created during the antebellum period. Typically, such lessons were directed toward Native Americans and other racial groups on European and African continents, rather than southern Black men and women specifically, and all were explicit in their intent to promote white supremacy and justify European and American imperialism.[4]

The textbooks produced for southern Black students during the Civil War and Reconstruction era were equally didactic in tone. Between 1864 and 1866, the Boston branch of the American Tract Society (ATS), an evangelical organization focused on the distribution of religious material, published a series of textbooks explicitly created for the freedpeople. Such texts included conventional readers and spellers, such as *The Freedman's Spelling Book* and *The Freedman's First, Second,* and *Third Reader,* as well as advice manuals like *Advice to Freedmen* by Isaac W. Brinckerhoff and *Friendly Counsels for Freedmen* by Jared Bell Waterbury. Other textbooks were published by the American Baptist Publication Society which supplemented the work of the American Baptist Home Mission Society by "preparing and supplying" the freedpeople with "elementary religious publications," the Presbyterian Publication Committee, and individual authors like Lydia Maria Child and Lucy Evelyn Sparhawk Brown. Only one publication examined in this study, *The Freedman's Torchlight,* was published by a Black organization.[5]

Although the primary goal of the freedmen's textbooks was to provide the former slaves with basic literacy skills, they also attempted to inculcate the freedpeople with northern ideals and values. While this was a feature of the northern common school textbooks also, the ideals and values promoted by the freedmen's texts were rarely intended to facilitate upward mobility and economic progression. On the contrary, freedmen's textbooks often encouraged the former slaves to accept their subjugated status and return to work in the fields and on the plantations for their former masters, if necessary.[6] Lydia Maria Child's *The Freedmen's Book* and the African Civilization Society's *The Freedman's Torchlight* were two outliers in this respect and while Child's publication was occasionally conservative in tone, particularly in relation to the freedpeople's relationship with white southerners, both publications attempted to foster a sense of racial pride and uplift.

Shortly after the publication of *The Freedman's First Reader*, the American Freedmen's Union Commission (AFUC) challenged the decision to name the textbooks "freedmen's" books:

> But why have a *Freedman's* Primer any more than a Dutchman's Primer or an Irishman's Primer? Are not the so-called freedmen to learn the same language, spell the same words, and read the same literature as the rest of us? Then why in the name of common sense not learn out of the same primers? If we want to abolish these odious caste distinctions from our laws, why ingrain it in our educational systems by the very titles of our book.[7]

The ATS justified its decision by arguing that the freedpeople were degraded by slavery and while it acknowledged that immoral behavior relating to "theft, falsehood, and chastity" were vices found among many members of society, they argued that they were "particularly rife among those long held in slavery." As such, the ATS maintained that the freedpeople required "instruction which is not found in ordinary school-books." Although northern common school textbooks were already profoundly didactic and explicit in their intent to shape the ideals and morals of nineteenth-century children, the ATS maintained that freedpeople needed an education that went beyond what was provided in these curricular materials.

Consequently, lessons in morality were a common feature of the freedmen's textbooks and southern Black students were frequently taught not to lie, steal, or swear. Although northern common school textbooks warned against similar vices, lessons on temperance were a particularly pervasive feature of the textbooks created for the freedpeople which reflected the misconception that formerly enslaved men and women would resort to a life of drunken idleness if left to their own devices. In a lesson in *The Freedman,* an instructional newspaper published by the ATS between 1864 and 1868, Black students were warned that smoking tobacco "causes an unnatural expectoration, and consequent loss of the fluids of the system through the salivary glands." The thirst that this produces can only be satisfied with alcohol "and he who drinks at all is almost sure to become a drunkard." While lessons such as this were explicit in their intention to ward the freedpeople from the vices of alcohol and tobacco, others were more implicit in nature. A math lesson in *The Freedman,* for example, asked students to calculate how long it would take a man "to drink up an acre of ground worth a hundred dollars" if he drank "thirty cents' worth of liquor in a day." Although lessons on temperance were also included in northern common school textbooks, the former slaves were considered to be particularly susceptible to the vices of alcohol and tobacco, "not because they are black, or a different race from whites," the ATS attempted to justify, "but because they are peculiarly ignorant of what they just now peculiarly need to know." The American Missionary Association (AMA), which sponsored a significant number of teachers in North Carolina, was equally concerned about the freedpeople's potential susceptibility to the vices of alcohol and in 1867, it vowed "to promote everywhere among [the freedpeople] the cause of Temperance," a goal which was ultimately reflected in the work of several educators as discussed in Chapter 4.[8]

Unlike the northern common school textbooks examined in this study, freedmen's textbooks placed a significant emphasis on teaching the freedpeople the value of chastity and the sanctity of marriage. Having been denied the right to legally marry, enslaved people often conceived children out of wedlock and, when slaveowners permitted it, many informally lived together as husband and wife. Due to restrictive slave codes which did not honor these relationships, families were frequently separated, and it was not uncommon for an enslaved person to have multiple partners over their lifetime. This behavior ultimately served as an affront to the nineteenth-century ideals of purity and female domesticity. However, rather than viewing these practices as the result of oppressive laws and the dehumanizing institution of slavery, textbook authors placed the blame upon the formerly enslaved community and tasked them with rectifying these perceived wrongs.[9] Referring to the practice of "taking up" or "sweethearting" which according to Katherine M. Franke were "open-ended and non-exclusive" types of relationships formed in slavery, Clinton B. Fisk chastised the former slaves for their past behavior and encouraged those who were living together out of wedlock to legalize their unions as soon as possible:

> When you were slaves you "took up" with each other and were not taught what a bad thing it was to break God's law of marriage. But now you can only be sorry for the past and begin life anew, and on a pure foundation. You who have been and are now living together as husband and wife and have had children born to you, should be married according to law, as soon as possible.[10]

When the Civil War ended, the former slaves were not just permitted the right to legally marry, they were obliged to. In August 1865, the Freedmen's Bureau issued General Order No. 8 which stated that freedmen and women were "not allowed to live together as husband and wife until their marriage has been legally solemnized." In a similar vein, North Carolina's General Assembly gave formerly enslaved cohabitating couples less than six months to register their marriages with the county clerk. Failure to do so, as Franke found, "constituted a distinct and separately prosecutable criminal offense."[11]

The enforcement of marriage laws was problematic for several reasons. First, due to the restrictions imposed upon them in slavery, formerly enslaved men and women had developed their own interpretations of marriage and adult relationships. Although many freedpeople embraced the opportunity to legalize their unions in freedom, others were not willing to immediately abandon the practices they had formed in slavery. From the federal government's perspective, marriage was viewed as a necessary precursor to citizenship and, on a practical level, it served to reduce their responsibility to provide financial support for the former slaves by imposing a legal obligation upon freedmen to support their families. This message was reinforced in the textbooks created for the freedpeople which attempted to impose a patriarchal family culture upon the formerly enslaved community. "Husbands must provide for their families," wrote Fisk in *Plain Counsels for Freedmen*. "Your wives will not love you if you do not provide bread and clothes for them." J. B. Waterbury made a similar claim in *Friendly Counsels for Freedmen* and urged his male readers to purchase a home as soon as possible. "Move your family into it," he wrote, "and begin to live as one who is responsible to God and who is determined to show that slavery has not robbed him of all his manhood." Freedwomen were equally expected to adhere to gendered norms and expectations and a lesson in *Friendly Counsels for Freedmen* advised female readers to learn how to manage the domestic space before getting married.[12]

Although lessons on chastity were directed toward both men and women, freedwomen received special instruction on navigating the advances of white men. Largely stemming from the perception of formerly enslaved Black women as hypersexualized seducers, Fisk advised freedwomen to hate white men "as you hate the devil." "You had better hang yourself by the neck until you are dead than to yield to them," he morbidly warned. In another lesson, Fisk accused freedwomen of being "careless of [their] morals" during slavery and now that they were free, it was their responsibility to "live as becomes a free Christian woman." Not only did these lessons reaffirm and perpetuate the damaging racial stereotype of the "oversexed Jezebel" but they also completely overlooked the rape and sexual exploitation of female slaves, a fact which Fisk either failed to recognize or chose to ignore. Perhaps unsurprisingly, lessons such as this were completely absent from any of the northern common school textbooks examined in this study.[13]

Lessons on industry were frequently incorporated into both northern common school textbooks and those that were specifically created for the freedpeople. However, unlike the northern common school textbooks which frequently linked work with economic prosperity, the textbooks created for the freedpeople actively promoted the value of industry in an attempt to mold the former slaves into a reliable workforce. As one lesson in *The Freedman* illustrates:

> I wonder why Susan does not work, and earn an honest living. It is, I think, because she is lazy. I can think of no other reason; for there is surely work enough to be done, if one has a will to do it. She could wash and iron, or sew, or clean house, or go errands, or bake cakes, or hoe corn, or sell fruit. She could not do nice work; but plain, coarse work she could have in plenty.[14]

One questions the value of education if Susan could not do "nice work." As Christopher Span argued, southern Blacks "were in school to become something more than a cotton picker or menial laborer for another's profit." Lessons such as this were ultimately grounded in the misconception that former slaves must be induced to labor. "I know that it is quite natural that you should associate work with slavery. . ." wrote Fisk in *Plain Counsels for Freedmen*. "But let me explain. . . . A free man works for himself – that is, he gets pay for his labor." J. B. Waterbury reiterated Fisk's sentiments in *Friendly Counsels for Freedmen*: "Don't fall into the mistake of some, that freedom means idleness," he wrote. "Free people have to work, and some of them have to work very hard even to get their bread." Some freedmen's textbooks even encouraged the freedpeople to continue working for their former masters. "Do not think, that in order to be free, you must fall out with your old master, gather off your bundles and trudge off to a strange city," wrote Fisk. "This is a great mistake. As a general rule, you can be as free and as happy in your old home, for the present, as anywhere else in the world." Due to mounting poverty, financial hardships, and pressure from the Freedmen's Bureau, many freedpeople had little choice but to return to work on the plantations, a move which ultimately served to benefit former masters and plantation owners who engineered an exploitative labor system that was deeply reminiscent of slavery.[15]

In addition to the conflicting interpretations of the value of industry, northern and freedmen's textbooks promoted alternate messages on the relationship between wealth and happiness. In the textbooks created for the freedpeople, Black students were advised that money "won't buy off sickness; it won't buy off sorrow, it won't buy off death." Northern common school textbooks, on the other hand, explicitly equated poverty with misery and prosperity with happiness. "The idle boy is almost invariably poor and miserable," read a lesson in *Willson's Third Reader*. "The industrious boy is happy and prosperous." Interestingly, and not surprisingly considering the pervasiveness of capitalist ideology in the antebellum North, *Willson's Second Reader* discouraged young learners from saving the fruits of their labor. Money is meant to be spent, advised Marcius Willson, "to buy clothes with, and to buy food with." "It is foolish to get money just to keep it, to be proud of, and to tell how rich you are," he continued. Lessons such as this were ultimately designed to prepare northern common school students for their place in the free-labor marketplace while freedpeople were encouraged to accept the status quo. In *The Freedman*, the ATS went a step further by using religious messaging to encourage formerly enslaved men and women to endure hardships, physical suffering, and a lack of material possessions in the name of religious devotion. "Are we willing to sacrifice all that we have of earthly good for Jesus' sake?" posed a question in *The Freedman*, "and can we wear with joy the crown of thorns, enduring the scorn and contempt of the world, in hope of the crown of life which he will give to his faithful followers at the last day." In this sense, freedmen's textbooks represented a strategic attempt to perpetuate the racial subordination of southern Blacks. Although northern common school textbooks were also replete with religious content, its purpose was to foster values such as temperance, thrift, honesty, generosity, parental obedience, a sense of duty to God, and, in the case of northern geography textbooks, to justify imperialism by positioning Christian nations as "much superior in knowledge and power to all others."[16]

Racial undertones were prevalent in both sets of textbooks which consistently portrayed whites as the superior race. In the fictional tale of *John Freeman and His Family*, the white characters of Miss Horton and Lieutenant Hall were characterized as intelligent, industrious, pious, and generous while the Black characters of Prince and Clarissa Freeman were portrayed as lazy, ignorant, and degraded by slavery. Prince, who served as a coachman during times of slavery, was stereotypically portrayed as a man who preferred to spend his days "lounging under the shade of a tree smoking his pipe," rather than working. Clarissa, on the other hand, was more than willing to engage in paid labor and she earnestly conveyed this willingness to Miss Horton. Despite her childlike eagerness to please the white teacher, Clarissa was unable to keep a clean and tidy home, the hallmark of nineteenth-century female domesticity. Although Miss Horton happily shared her homemaking tips with Clarissa, this lesson attempted to reinforce the notion that formerly enslaved Black women were degraded by slavery and unable to live up to the domestic ideals prescribed for white women.[17]

Other freedmen's texts attempted to foster white supremacy by positioning northern white men as saviors of the Black race. A lesson in *The Freedman's Spelling Book*, for instance, included a short story about a white Union soldier who had just returned from war. "It was sad to see men die in battle," read one lesson, "but it was to make us free." Similarly, in *Advice to Freedmen*, Black learners were informed that their freedom came at a huge cost to the white population. "With treasure and precious blood your freedom has been purchased," wrote Isaac W. Brinkerhoff. "Let these sufferings and sacrifices never be forgotten when you remember that you are not now a slave but a freedman." In contrast, *The Freedman* celebrated the achievements of Black soldiers who served in both the Revolutionary and Civil Wars, idealistically heralding their involvement as signaling the beginning of racial equality.[18]

Although representations of race and racism were not particularly prevalent in northern common school readers or spellers, geography textbooks frequently included lessons which served to promote the notion of white supremacy. While the African continent was often described in favorable terms due to its fertile land and plentiful natural resources, the African people were invariably described as uncivilized and uneducated. "Africa is the least civilized of the great divisions of the earth," read a lesson in Mitchell's *An Easy Introduction to the Study of Geography*. "The chief part of its inhabitants are ignorant of books and learning and destitute of true religion." In other lessons, Africans were described as simple and childlike or barbaric and violent. The inhabitants of Abyssinia (present-day Ethiopia), Mitchell instructed, "are very rude and brutal in their manners. At their feasts they eat raw flesh, streaming with blood, cut from the animal while yet warm."[19]

White people, on the other hand, were frequently described as civilized, industrious, and intelligent. In *A System of Modern Geography*, Samuel Mitchell divided mankind into five racial categories: "European or Caucasian, Asiatic or Mongolian, American, Malay, and African or negro." In this instance, the term

"American" was used to describe Native Americans. "The European or Caucasian is the most noble of the five races," wrote Mitchell. "It excels all others in learning and the arts, and includes the most powerful nations of ancient and modern times. The most valuable institutions of society, and the most important and useful inventions have originated with the people of this race." The same textbook included a frontispiece illustration entitled "Stages of Society" which divided the races into four stages of civilization: barbarous, savage, civilized and enlightened, and half-civilized. Unsurprisingly, whites were placed in the "civilized and enlightened" category while Blacks were placed in the "barbarous" category and Native Americans were considered "savage."[20]

Although lessons on race and civilization were primarily used to promote white supremacy, they were also used to justify European and American imperialism. Thus, it comes as no surprise that nineteenth-century geography textbooks portrayed the United States as a distinctly superior nation and its inhabitants as "the most intelligent, industrious, and enterprising people in the world." Equally favorable qualities were attributed to American and European colonies in Africa. Liberia was described as "a fertile country" which "contains about 5000 civilized inhabitants" while readers learned that Sierra Leone "was established for the purpose of teaching the natives to read and write, and instructing them in Christian religion."[21]

A critique of racial slavery was notably absent from both sets of textbooks. In *Plain Counsels for Freedmen,* Fisk briefly acknowledged the hardships of slavery by referring to the practice of buying and selling enslaved people and separating children from their parents. "You were owned, bought, and sold like cattle and horses," he wrote, ". . . your children were not yours, but were the property of your masters, and they had the power to take them from you and to sell them to whomsoever they pleased." Lydia Maria Child, the abolitionist author of *The Freedmen's Book,* also addressed some controversial issues associated with slavery, namely miscegenation, the use of literacy as an act of resistance, and the coordination of a slave rebellion. In the same texts, however, both authors encouraged their readers to remain respectful toward members of the southern white community. Although Fisk acknowledged that some white southerners were prejudiced toward Blacks, the former slaves were advised to "avoid everything you can which will inflame those prejudices." "If you are bent on being good and kind," he wrote, "and return soft answers to hard words and good for evil, you will have few troubles with white men." Child attempted to impart a similar message in *The Freedmen's Book* by encouraging Black students to always be "respectful and polite," especially to those who consider them "an inferior race." This is "one of the best ways to prove you are not inferior," she concluded. Messages such as this were ultimately grounded in the mistaken belief that racial prejudices would dissipate if the freedpeople could prove that they were worthy of freedom. This was the subject of another lesson in Child's book which featured an extract from a speech delivered by Judge Henry Wilson to South Carolinian freedpeople in Charleston. "The great lesson for you in the future is to prove that we were right," he admonished, "to prove that you were worthy of liberty." Consequently, the onus was placed upon the freedpeople rather than the southern white population to eliminate racial prejudice.[22]

Admittedly, Child's textbook also featured lessons which directly contradicted some of the more conservative messages. Published by Ticknor and Fields in 1865, and at a cost of $600 to herself, a total of twenty-four writers contributed to the production of *The Freedmen's Book,* eleven of whom were Black. Essentially, Child hoped that from the inclusion of authors such as Frederick Douglass, Harriett Jacobs, Charlotte Forten, and George Moses Horton, the freedpeople would "derive fresh strength and courage from this true record of what colored men have accomplished under great disadvantages." According to Jessica Enoch, the conflicting messages contained within *The Freedmen's Book* partly stemmed from the fact that, as a nineteenth-century woman, Child was expected to conform to certain "gendered expectations" which often prevented female writers from examining the harsh realities of slavery or calling for radical social change. Indeed, Child's 1833 publication of the abolitionist tract, *An Appeal in Favor of That Class of Americans Called Africans,* resulted in her dismissal from the Boston Athenaeum, of which she was only the second female member, as well as cancelled subscriptions to her children's magazine, *The Juvenile Miscellany.* Although she was widely recognized in abolitionist circles, even Lewis Tappan, cofounder of the AMA, refused to help Child publish *The Freedmen's Book* unless certain sections were omitted. So, while *The Freedmen's Book* often imparted conservative messages about Black freedom, the limitations imposed upon Child cannot be discounted and the multiple voices contained within her textbook offered readers alternative perspectives, thus enabling them to critically assess their role as a free people and their place in American society.[23]

Recognizing the limitations imposed upon nineteenth-century authors, particularly those who wrote about divisive issues such as race and freedom, it is equally possible that the conservative messages contained within ATS publications stemmed from a desire to appease the southern white population. If textbooks are to be successful, "they must appeal to a large number of people." Consequently, textbook publishers "deliberately tend to avoid controversy." Isaac W.

Brinkerhoff, a Baptist minister and Freedmen's Bureau agent from New York, published two versions of *Advice to Freedmen* in an effort to appease the southern white community which was growing increasingly hostile toward northern efforts to educate southern Blacks. *The Freedman*, it would appear, was less concerned about white southerners' feelings and one arithmetic lesson asked, "if the freedmen should kill, or take prisoners, 394 of the rebels who numbered 462, how many would be left to run away after the battle?"[24]

Other than Child's *The Freedmen's Book*, only one other textbook examined in this study made any attempt to foster racial pride. Unsurprisingly, this textbook was the only publication created for and by Black people. Published by the African Civilization Society (ACS) in 1866, *The Freedman's Torchlight* was an instructional newspaper that combined academic lessons with news articles on current affairs and other contemporary issues relevant to the lives of freedpeople. Like the ATS, the ACS was founded during the antebellum period. Unlike the ATS, it was "an organization officered and managed entirely by colored men." Originally established to aid the repatriation of Black people to Africa, the society reorganized itself into a freedmen's aid society during the Civil War and by 1866 it had twenty-two schools in operation in four southern states. Operating under the assumption that Black teachers could best instruct their own people, ACS schools were staffed and managed entirely by members of the Black community. As Reverend Dr. Bellows wrote in the first issue of *The Freedman's Torchlight*, "The peculiarity of our Society is its being an enterprise managed by negros for the elevation of themselves as a race. We ourselves must elevate our own race to the status of self reliance, the fundamental element of which is Education."[25]

Although *The Freedman's Torchlight* equally sought to imbue the freedpeople with the duties and responsibilities of freedom, the overarching message was one of racial uplift rather than racial subordination. This was particularly evident in the choice of vocabulary used to teach literacy. In contrast to the first issue of *The Freedman* which taught basic literacy skills through simple two- and three-letter words, the first issue of *The Freedman's Torchlight* included reading and spelling vocabulary such as "free," "life," "live," "now," "thank," "God," "good," "right," "learn," "land," "made," and "slaves." For the more advanced readers, these words were used in sentences such as "I am free and well," "I will love God," "God made all men free," "We should learn to read and write and be good," "We will stand up for the union, now and forever." Due to financial difficulties, it seems as though *The Freedman's Torchlight* ceased publication after just a few issues and only one copy of it has been located. Nevertheless, given that this copy is the very first issue, it gives the reader a clear insight into the ACS's aims and expectations of Black education.[26]

Racial slavery was rarely mentioned in any of the textbooks examined in this study. In some instances, when it was referred to, an idyllic image of slavery was presented. In *John Freeman and His Family,* Helen E. Brown described Prince and Hattie Freeman's life in slavery as "easy" and "happy." "Their work was light, their master and mistress kind, and at dusk they were usually at liberty to lead the dance on the green, to sit and chat lovingly by the fireside." Lessons such as this were also incorporated into the textbooks created by the Confederacy during the Civil War. Miranda Branson Moore, a North Carolinian teacher from Randolph County, wrote several textbooks which presented an idealized image of slavery. One lesson in the *First Dixie Reader,* for instance, intimated that slavery was better than freedom because masters assumed responsibility for their slaves' care in old age. "Old aunt Ann" was too old to work anymore but she knew that "Miss, as she calls her, will take care as long as she lives." "Ma-ny poor white folks would be glad to live in her house and eat what Miss Kate sends out for din-ner," the lesson concluded. Although there is no evidence to suggest that Confederate textbooks were used in North Carolina's schools for the freedpeople, they represent a deliberate attempt to skew the reality of slavery, a tactic which lived on for decades after the Civil War and Reconstruction period. Northern common school textbooks, on the other hand, rarely made any reference to racial slavery. However, on the few occasions that it was mentioned, the issue was presented as a distinctly southern problem. Similarly, while the slave trade received some discussion in northern geography textbooks, the blame was placed on Africans and white Europeans.[27]

Although there is no denying that textbooks can and have been used as political instruments, that is to say, to further a particular social, cultural, or economic agenda, there is much debate surrounding the extent to which students may or may not be influenced by textbook content. Nevertheless, for centuries, educators, politicians, and concerned members of the public have debated over textbook content, leading Ruth Elson to conclude that "popular opinion still accepts without question the importance of schoolbooks in forming public opinion." Although Elson agreed that the extent to which students may or may not be influenced by textbooks needs further examination, she argued that nineteenth-century textbooks were probably more influential than contemporary curricular materials, not just because the nineteenth-century child "read little beside his schoolbooks" but also because they were the primary instructional materials in most schools. Another study reiterated Elson's sentiments and argued that nineteenth-century textbooks "were more reflective of mainstream attitudes as well as influential in reinforcing these attitudes and beliefs" because they "did not compete with television, movies, and other twentieth-century forms of popular culture." Given that southern Black students had limited access to reading materials, before, during, and after the Civil War, and recognizing that textbooks were often the only available resources in freedpeople's schools, it would be easy to argue that the textbooks used in southern Black schools were powerful forces in helping to shape the former slaves' attitudes, beliefs, and values. Like many learners, however, the freedpeople were not passive consumers of the knowledge and information imparted to them. This is particularly evident in the way in which southern Blacks selectively interpreted the proslavery messages preached to them from the pulpit during times of slavery.[28]

At the same time, it would be naïve to think that lessons about race or civilization did not influence the thinking and ideology of the students who engaged with them, especially considering that nineteenth-century common school students were "generally required to memorize [racial] characteristics and the rank of each race in the accepted racial hierarchy." In her guide for third-level instructors, Helen Fox confessed that much of her understanding about race were shaped by college textbooks. Referring to an anthropology lesson that divided mankind into five races, much like the lesson in Mitchell's geography textbook, Fox wrote, "I was certain that this idea was correct . . . because it was presented to us as scientific, and therefore unassailable." So, while we may never fully understand how the freedpeople interpreted the racial messages contained within nineteenth-century textbooks, it is important to keep in mind that, like all students, some former slaves may have internalized what they learned while others may have forgotten, ignored, or completely rejected it. "But," as one study surmised, "even if students forget, ignore, or reject what they encounter in textbooks, textbook content is still important because it withholds, obscures, and renders unimportant many ideas and areas of knowledge."[29]

Ultimately, an analysis of the textbooks examined in this study not only reflects prevailing racial attitudes before and after the Civil War period, but also how curricular materials can be used to perpetuate and reinforce these attitudes, regardless of how effective they may or may not have been in shaping the views of those who engaged with them. Moreover, the textbooks specifically created for the freedpeople exemplify how white northerners attempted to shape the post-emancipation landscape in a way that aligned with their own perspectives and interests. By encouraging former slaves to accept their subjugated status and return to work in the fields and on the plantations, for their former masters, if necessary, these curricular materials serve as a testament to the way in which freedpeople's education was perceived as a mechanism for social control in the war-torn South.

6

Life in Reconstruction North Carolina

In 1865, northern white teacher Sarah P. Freeman met with a group of freedpeople in Edenton, North Carolina, to discuss the possibility of opening a school there. After consulting with the freedpeople who agreed to provide the building for the schoolhouse, rent a house for the teacher's home, and furnish both with fuel and provisions, Freeman wrote to the National Freedman's Relief Association (NFRA) to send a teacher. Acknowledging that the local white residents were very much opposed to freedpeople's education, Freeman advised the organization to send someone who was physically, mentally, and morally strong. Although this teacher should have some classroom experience, it was more important to find someone who was not "afraid or ashamed to labor." This teacher should not expect "the most luxurious living," she wrote. Instead, they should be "capable of making themselves comfortable and happy under all circumstances [and] willing to enter the field to labor for the good of the human race, rather than for honor or profit pecuniarily."[1]

As Freeman's words suggest, teaching the freedpeople was a challenging occupation that required the utmost strength and resilience. Long and arduous working hours, insufficient resources, and white paramilitary violence were just some of the challenges these men and women faced. Those who were brave enough to labor during the Civil War period also faced the threat of military invasion. After the fall of Plymouth to Confederate forces in April 1864, teachers were forced to evacuate to Roanoke Island. Two months earlier, Confederate troops threatened to invade the Carteret-Craven region of eastern North Carolina which was home to a significant number of both teachers and freedpeople. Although they were unsuccessful, many teachers began to question their decision to work in the war-torn South. "However light a matter the Northern papers may make of it," wrote Emily Gill in 1864, "we were in great danger of being captured that first week of February, as New Bern was defended by an insufficient number of troops." Tellingly, Gill did not return to North Carolina for a second year of teaching.[2]

During the early days of freedom, the freedpeople's destitution was so great that education was often secondary to the myriads of humanitarian activities that the teachers performed on a daily basis. On Roanoke Island, where Freeman worked alongside her daughter Kate, a typical day often included visiting the old and infirm, administering to the sick and needy, conducting prayer meetings, sorting, unpacking and distributing aid, petitioning northern organizations for donations, organizing labor, establishing schools and, when time allowed, classroom teaching.[3] The distribution of aid, described by Elizabeth Havard James as "a most laborious duty," took up much of the teachers' time and crowds gathered "from before sunrise until nearly nine at night to buy, beg, or to look on." "It exhausts my strength," admitted James, "but there is great need, and I volunteered to do this." In an effort to prevent dependency, northern aid and missionary organizations encouraged teachers to sell donated material to those who were able to pay. This added to the teachers' workload who, according to Eliza Perkins, were "now required to keep an account of the value of everything given." It also put the teachers in a difficult position as they were compelled to ascertain who had the means to support themselves and who did not. On one occasion, James followed a freedwoman more than three miles home, on horseback, to establish if she really needed a flannel for her sick child. "She seemed honest," admitted James, "but there is so much wrong-doing that I am compelled to ascertain always." Although the freedpeople were eager and willing to contribute toward their newfound freedom, few possessed the capacity to do so, particularly during the early years of the Civil War and Reconstruction period. "They are not wanting in interest or enthusiasm but in means," concluded Freedmen's Bureau Superintendent of Education F. A. Fiske.[4]

After the Civil War, the freedpeople's teachers were able to focus more of their attention on educational matters. In general, teachers taught both day and night school while many also taught Sunday school. Although some teachers were fortunate enough to walk into a ready-made school and begin teaching immediately, particularly during the latter stages of Reconstruction when freedpeople's education was more well-established, others were required to build a school from the ground up. In the main, this required finding a suitable location, organizing books, resources and other classroom material, raising the requisite funds, and, of course, enrolling students from the local community. The teachers' duties were not always limited to elementary education, and on Roanoke Island Sarah Freeman led the establishment of an industrial school which, during its short lifespan, was responsible for teaching 130 women to sew, knit, braid straw, and quilt.[5]

Due to the shortage of teachers that persisted throughout the Civil War and Reconstruction period, class sizes were understandably large. In 1867, Robert Fitzgerald reported that he had 150 students enrolled in his day school and 130 in his Sabbath school. Robert Harris reported similar numbers and used "the more advanced pupils as assistants." However, he confessed, "The room is not large enough for two teachers." In addition, the students often ranged in age. Betsey L. Canedy, a northern white woman employed by the Friends' Freedmen's Association (FFA), had students ranging from age five to forty-five in her classroom while Esther Warren's school was attended by a sixty-year-old woman. "She washes and irons the first two days in the week," reported Warren, "comes punctually the rest of the week, and is making considerable progress."[6]

Given the large class sizes and diverse age groups, it is not surprising that the freedpeople's teachers occasionally experienced unruly behavior and some did not hesitate to use corporal punishment. In a diary entry from July 16, 1867, Robert Fitzgerald confessed that he "punished a boy severely for stubbornness," but that he was "Sorry to do so." Less than a week later, Fitzgerald wrote that he sent a girl home for talking in class and on September 1, 1870, Fitzgerald whipped a girl "for lying and carrying tales."[7] Speaking of his school in Shoe Hill, Charles Hunter claimed that his students were no different from those who could be found in any other classroom. "I would not convey the impression that these children were very much different from other children," he wrote. "They were not. They were average boys and girls full of vigor, bursting with energy, brimming with life and artful in mischievous enterprise. I would not have it believed that there were not times when corrective measures had to be applied." Robert Harris painted a slightly different picture of his schoolhouse in Virginia, although he equally admitted to using corporal punishment from time to time. "I find but little difficulty in governing," he wrote. "The pupils are generally docile and obedient. I have had no case of insubordination thus far. I have only had to inflict punishment for bad behavior *out* of school, for tardiness, imperfect recitations, whispering &ce." The punishments Harris generally meted out for such behavior included "the use of the birch, depriving them of recess" and "compelling them to stand a long time." Ridicule, such as calling a child "tardy," he claimed, was one of the most effective classroom management techniques.[8]

In spite of the long and arduous working hours, teaching the freedpeople was not well paid and educators could often earn double in northern schools. In 1865, the NEFAS reported that its male principals received sixty dollars a month while the female principals received half that amount. Similarly, male assistants were paid forty-five dollars a month while females received twenty dollars. In spite of the obvious gender pay inequality, these salaries were quite generous in comparison to those offered by the religious organizations. During the initial stages of southern Black schooling, the American Missionary Association (AMA) paid its female teachers between nine and ten dollars per month, although this amount increased to approximately fifteen dollars for both sexes after the war in an effort to attract more teachers. In a letter to the AMA, Robert Harris admitted that although he did not think highly of the southern Black teachers who were hired to assist him, they were inadequately paid. "We cannot complain," he wrote, "when we only pay them $15 per month. It is 'poor teach' and 'poor pay.'" Nonetheless, Harris still requested the AMA to send him "two competent teachers from the North."[9]

In 1869, the AMA offered Michael P. Jerkins, a Black North Carolinian from Beaufort, twenty dollars per month to continue teaching during the summer period. However, this money was to be shared between himself and two assistants. "You can make whatever bargain you want to with your assistants," wrote Edward Smith of the AMA, "you can have the house rent free, and can retain any money you may collect from tuition." Even if the freedpeople were in a position to pay tuition, which in this case they were not, twenty dollars per month was barely enough to support one teacher, let alone three. Nevertheless, Jerkins accepted the offer.[10] By November 1869, Jerkins had still not been paid for the work he did during the summer, and he was in constant correspondence with the AMA regarding this payment. Although he finally received his wages for the summer period on November 10, he was still awaiting payment for September, October, and November, something that the AMA was attempting to dispute. Fortunately, Jerkins kept a record of all the payments he had received and in December 1869 he wrote in exasperation, "I have been paid all you owe for last year. I *ask* for *money* for *this year*." To add to the indignation of not being paid on time, as well as having to repeatedly ask for his wages, Jerkins was advised by the AMA that if he wanted schoolbooks, he should purchase them himself and then sell them to his students. Knowing how poor the freedpeople were, Jerkins responded that this was not an option. "I do not see how I can pay for them," he wrote. "If I should get them I could not sell but a very few of them. . . . I see a very few able to buy books. As you know my salary is very low. I cannot afford to pay for them myself." Ultimately, inadequate wages forced Jerkins's resignation and although he initially returned to work as a barber, he later became one of the founding trustees of the AMA's Washburn Seminary in Beaufort, North Carolina. Jerkins's experience was by no means unique, and several other educators complained to the Bureau because they did not receive payment, either from their sponsoring organization or from the Bureau itself. This not only reflects the significant funding issues that plagued the growth of freedpeople's schools in North Carolina, but also the way in which the Bureau could be used as a mediator between teachers and their employers.[11]

Financial limitations and white hostility also meant that appropriate housing for the freedpeople's teachers was often difficult to source. According to Colonel E. Whittlesey, it was "utterly impossible" to find northern white teachers a place to live in Raleigh, even though many local white families were anxious for boarders to help offset the increasing cost of living. "When it was frankly stated to them that these were young ladies from the north who were there for the purpose of teaching colored schools," he recalled, "they turned their backs upon them."[12] As a result, many teachers were required to board in uncomfortable, makeshift homes. Although Elizabeth James secured suitable accommodation on Roanoke Island when she first arrived in 1863, she was forced to give it up the following year to Sarah and Kate Freeman who subsequently shared the premises with Ella Roper and Mary Ann Burnap. Elizabeth's cousin, Freedmen's Bureau officer Horace James, promised to build her a new house, but in the meantime, she was required to live in a small cabin which she described as a "little filthy vermin filled shanty." It was not until July 1865 that James moved into a comfortable home in the "freedmen's village" section of the island.[13]

Of course, some teachers were fortunate enough to secure comfortable living quarters. In letters to her parents from her post at the present-day Shaw University, Harriet M. Buss frequently commented on her "nice and cozy" living arrangements. "I am feeling fully at home," she wrote one month after her arrival in 1869, "and see nothing why I am not just as pleasantly comfortable and happily situated as I was in Norfolk." Other teachers, like white northerners Margaret Thorpe and Elizabeth Pennock, found accommodation with a local Black family. This interracial housing arrangement initially concerned Thorpe who did not want it to appear as though she was living "with uncle Albert and his family as one family, not with him as servants!" Nevertheless, her fears were allayed when a visit from an Episcopalian clergyman bore witness to Thorpe and Pennock dining alone "with a man waiter," thereby maintaining the prewar racial hierarchy.[14]

While every effort was made to secure accommodations for northern white teachers, northern Black teachers were often required to source their own accommodations. When Blanche Harris was first sent to Mississippi, she complained that the AMA did not assist any of the Black teachers in finding accommodations or pay for their board. "The distinction between the two classes of teachers [white and black] is so marked that it is the topic of conversation among the better class of colored people," she wrote. Harris spent just two years working for the AMA before securing the sponsorship of the FFA and moving to Goldsboro, North Carolina. Occasionally, northern Black teachers were permitted to board in the mission house. However, in 1866 a controversy arose within the AMA regarding the housing arrangements of Sallie Daffin from Philadelphia. AMA Superintendent of Schools Samuel Ashley decided that Daffin should board with a local Black family rather than in the mission house with other white teachers because he was worried that an interracial housing situation would intensify white hostility. However, he was also aware that some white teachers were "uncomfortable living with Blacks."[15] In an attempt to justify his decision, Ashley wrote the AMA:

> Colored teachers are needed at the South – they must come South. But then, it does not seem to me to be wise to send them in company and to board in company, with white teachers. There are very few places in the North where it would be wise to do this. Such a course at the South brings your white teachers out and in such sharp contact with prejudices of the southern people that their (the teachers) situation is made almost intolerable. We are charged with endeavouring to bring about a condition of social equality between Blacks and whites – we are charged with teaching the Blacks that they have a right to demand from the whites social equality – now. If they can point to mission families or teachers homes where there is complete social equality between colored and white, they have proved to their own satisfaction at least, their assertion. They can say that if not in theory, we do in practice, teach social equality.[16]

Ashley's response to the AMA illuminates the constraints of working in the South at this time. While Blacks demanded freedom, southern whites called for their political re-enslavement and school officials such as Ashley were often required to mediate between each group in the hope of maintaining support and reducing friction. Unfortunately, this mediation often undermined Black peoples' educational endeavors and southern Blacks were offered a limited and restricted equality instead. In the end, Daffin refused to board outside of the mission house, and she began working for the FFA in 1867.[17]

Black teachers also experienced racism in their daily lives. While traveling to his post in Shoe Hill, and before the introduction of Jim Crow segregation laws, Charles Hunter was instructed to sit in the front of the stagecoach with the driver so that the only remaining passenger, a white man, would not have to share the carriage with him. During a brief stop on route, the driver and passenger were invited into the home of a white woman and served coffee while Hunter was left standing by the fireside and ignored. Robert Fitzgerald also experienced racial discrimination. On a boat journey from Washington, D.C., to Richmond, Virginia, on route to his post in North Carolina, Fitzgerald realized that he had misplaced his transportation papers. The captain of the boat did not permit Fitzgerald to search for the documents and ordered him to pitch coal in the fire room instead. Enraged at this treatment Fitzgerald refused, so he was instructed to hand over his watch or be removed from the boat. "Captain, you have treated me like a dog," fumed Fitzgerald, "you have ordered me from the saloon; you will not have an enquiry made for the papers which I am sure some of your passengers must have; you treat me as though I am not a man because I am colored. And now sir, you can put me ashore, I will not pay my passage twice." When the tension escalated and the threat of violence became more imminent, Fitzgerald jumped ashore. "I regret the whole affair," he wrote in his diary later that evening, "but more sincerely that vessels are allowed to leave and return daily to the national Capital commanded by men who delight to insult and maltreat passengers merely because they are colored." Fitzgerald, who was of mixed-race ancestry, was raised by his white mother to be proud of his Black heritage. Hunter, on the other hand, was raised to respect the prewar racial hierarchy, so his lack of indignance is not entirely surprising.[18]

During times of difficulty, teachers relied on each other for comfort and support. While stationed in Raleigh, Harriet Buss became very close with her fellow teachers and roommates. "Miss Haley is full of life," she told her parents, "she keeps us laughing so at home, that we shall not be likely to suffer from dyspepsia."[19] Nevertheless, personalities occasionally clashed, and conflicts arose, much to the perplexity of the superintendents who were tasked with keeping the peace. In 1865, Nellie F. Stearns from Bedford, Massachusetts, complained to a friend about a fellow teacher who developed a relationship with a government clerk. "He came in the other night and had a regular romp with one of the girls," complained Stearns. "They made a great noise and I have just heard there have been remarks about it by people who passed. This young lady is very lively and rather coarse and rude, and I suspect she will get us all into trouble." Worried that this particular woman would bring the entire teaching force into disrepute, Stearns concluded, "A few thoughtless girls bring scandal on the rest of us, and I declare it makes me *provoked*. There are abominable stories about the teachers circulated and believed too even by sensible *Northern* people." In spite of this drawback, Stearns claimed that she enjoyed living and working in North Carolina. In her spare time, which she admitted was not too often, Stearns planned to go horseback riding to see the countryside, especially the cotton fields which were somewhat of a novelty. "We have very pleasant social times and I enjoy my life here much," she concluded.[20]

Margaret Newbold Thorpe, a white woman from Salem, New Jersey, had a different experience. While working in Warrenton, North Carolina, Thorpe and her teaching companion Elizabeth Pennock were socially ostracized by the white community who, according to one resident, "did not approve of their work or of their coming." "You can imagine how strange it seems never to speak to a white person and have absolutely no social life, not one visitor," wrote Thorpe in 1869. "The Southern women will not notice us at all, and we will not allow the men to call on us, though we have received several notes requesting permission to do so; we always reply that if they will bring either their mother or their sisters with them, we will be glad to receive them." Admittedly, Harriet Buss had a very different experience in Raleigh, and it was not uncommon for her and her teaching companions to receive visits from both northern and southern women. Evidently, while the teachers' experiences were similar in many respects, they cannot be overgeneralized and multiple factors, which will be examined shortly, impacted the lives of those who elected to teach the freedpeople, particularly in relation to the level of hostility they encountered.[21]

In Warrenton, Thorpe and Pennock liked to sew, read, and go horseback riding in their spare time. Having been ostracized by the white community, they also occasionally attended Black social gatherings. However, at these events, Thorpe was reluctant to interact with the Black guests as social equals. Upon attending a neighbor's wedding, for instance, Thorpe was pleased to be seated separately from the Black guests who never annoyed her with "the slightest attempt at social equality." On another occasion, Thorpe and Pennock were invited to dinner at the home "of one of the leading colored men," the daughter of whom was a student in Thorpe's school. Impressed with the house and surrounding farm, Thorpe was pleased to report that they had a delicious meal with "four waiters, father, mother, son, and daughter to watch and anticipate our every want."[22] Thorpe's reluctance to socialize with members of the Black community was not uncommon and many teachers refrained from engaging with their students or other Black individuals outside of normal school hours. As one teacher remarked, "It is one thing to sit in one's office or drawing room and weave fine spun theories in regard to the Negro character, but it is quite another to come into actual contact with him. I fail to see those beauties and excellencies [of black people] that some do."[23] Evidently, the northern white teachers were not egalitarians in the modern sense of the word and many harbored deep racial prejudices. However, their work should be situated within the national context. As C. Vann Woodward pointed out, racism was just as pervasive in the antebellum North. In this sense, the teachers of the freedpeople were ahead of their time. While few were willing to perceive Black people as their social equals, they nonetheless believed in the educability of the former slaves, something that few white northerners and even fewer white southerners were willing to concede.[24]

Fisk Parsons Brewer, a Yale-educated principal of a Black school in Raleigh, also experienced social ostracism. According to Kemp Battle, a Chapel Hill resident and former president of the University of North Carolina, this was primarily because Brewer and his wife regularly received visits from Black people in their home. Although Brewer was well-respected in northern society, having come from a distinguished family of missionaries, abolitionists, and Supreme Court justices, white North Carolinians could not condone his blatant disregard for the prewar racial hierarchy and southern social norms. According to Battle, northerners like Brewer were treated in this way because they were viewed as "creatures of [the] abolitionists" who "brought on the Civil War."[25] However, southern white teachers also faced social ostracism. Shortly after engaging in freedpeople's education, Reverend Willis L. Miller, a former slaveholder and Confederate soldier, was rendered "poor and not respected only by the colored people." While some former associates privately supported his work, they were reluctant to openly endorse it for fear of reprisal. Margaret S. Clark, a white native of Gaston County, shared a similar experience. Writing to the Freedmen's Bureau in 1868, Clark reported that she had been driven out of her school on two separate occasions by hostile whites and ostracized from the community. "You a wished to know how meny white people was keeping [school] for them," she wrote to F. A. Fiske, "they haint ben nery white person that lived in the South that kept school for them but my self and they rest of the white people disclaimed me very much for keeping for them [sic]."[26]

In spite of the fact that North Carolina has often been described as a racially progressive state, white hostility posed a very real threat to students and teachers alike. However, throughout the Civil War and Reconstruction period, numerous firsthand reports suggest that white North Carolinians were indifferent toward freedpeople's education. In an attempt to extend the reach of southern Black schooling, Freedmen's Bureau Assistant Commissioner in North Carolina Colonel E. Whittlesey asked local white farmers to establish schools for the freedpeople on their land. "In some instances they say they have no objection to a school if a teacher can be found," Whittlesey remarked, "and if such arrangement can be made as not to interrupt the work of the farm." Perceived ambivalence toward freedpeople's education is further reflected in the records of the Freedmen's Bureau during the first quarter of 1867 which saw most of the nineteen agents who submitted questionnaires report that local whites were indifferent to freedpeople's schools.[27]

Actions speak louder than words and while many white North Carolinians claimed indifference toward freedpeople's education, the experiences of teachers and students tell a very different story. Regardless of whether they were northern or southern, Black or white, male or female, freedpeople's teachers were regularly insulted in the street and defamed in the press. Local white residents often refused to board teachers or serve them in their stores while others refused to sell or lease land or property for the purpose of a schoolhouse. In April 1866, William Elliott, a Black North Carolinian teacher from Wake County, reported that he was unable to build or rent a schoolhouse. There is "not one man in This place that is Willing to Let me Build or Rent a House on Theair Land," he wrote to North Carolina Superintendent of Education F. A. Fiske. "They are so much *opposed* To Colard Mens Education that they will do all in thiar power to pull it down [sic]."[28] One month earlier, Robert Harris reported on the difficulty he faced in procuring firewood for his school. "The whites near us refuse to give or sell any wood for school purposes," he wrote Samuel Hunt of the AMA, "and warn us not to cut any on their land."[29]

Admittedly, the geographical location of a school often determined the extent to which teachers and students experienced violence, harassment, or any sort of behavior that could be construed as resistant to the growth of freedpeople's education. In Raleigh, Harriet M. Buss regularly commented on how courteous and polite the storekeepers were. "I don't know how the people of Raleigh feel," she wrote in 1869. "But I was never more politely treated at stores and places of business than I have been here ever since I came." While "not very large," in Buss's estimation at least, Raleigh seemed to exhibit certain characteristics that are more commonly associated with cosmopolitan towns and cities. Similarly, in the busy town of Fayetteville, Mark Andrew Huddle contends that the Black population experienced fewer incidences of racial violence compared to other parts of the state. This may have been because antebellum Fayetteville, like many urban centers in the prewar South, experienced a degree of racial integration where free and enslaved Blacks lived and worked alongside whites of all social classes. However, it is also worth considering that the relatively accepting attitudes toward freedpeople's education in these areas may have emanated more from a strong military presence than a genuine acceptance of Black freedom. Indeed, shortly after the end of the Civil War, Fayetteville whites attempted to reinstate elements of the antebellum slave system, including public whippings, until the town's white leaders were forced to enlist the military protection of the Freedmen's Bureau. It is no wonder, then, that Freedmen's Bureau agents throughout the American South frequently emphasized the necessity for continued military support, especially in the area of education which was viewed as one of the most contentious elements of Black freedom among white North Carolinians.[30]

Localized violence, threats, and intimidation played a key role in suppressing freedpeople's education and in February 1866, F. A. Fiske reported that a school in Nixonton was closed after just six weeks due to "the threatening state of public feeling." Around the same time, "a Union man" had been shot and according to Fiske, schoolteacher Alfred W. Morris, a native of Elizabeth City, "became apprehensive for his safety." Tellingly, Morris did not resume teaching the following year. By 1870, matters had not much improved and Fiske's successor H. C. Vogell reported that several schools temporarily closed due to "the influence of certain lawless bands." "In many sections teachers have become frightened and schools nearly broken up by threats of violence," he continued, "and it has required every effort and influence I could put forth to resuscitate and keep them going." Black students were not exempt from such hostility and in 1866, northern Black teacher Robert Harris reported that two of his students were attacked by "a party of white trash" and were robbed of their books on their way home from school. "The boys said or did nothing to provoke the attack," wrote Harris in a letter to Samuel Hunt of the AMA. "It is by such despicable acts of meanness that they strive to hinder the colored children from attending school."[31]

Incendiarism was a common reaction to southern Black schooling and made all the more possible by the primitive nature of some school buildings. Early in 1866, Colonel Whittlesey reported that an angry mob of whites burned down a building that was being fitted for a schoolhouse in Elizabeth City. Later that year, Fiske also reported that a school in Smithfield "was destroyed by fire." By April 1867, matters had not much improved, and schoolhouses had been burned down in Greene and Chatham Counties. Yet, he concluded, old prejudices against freedpeople's education "are decidedly on the wane." "In a few localities," he continued, "there has been such a complete transformation that former opposers are now willing to give countenance and aid to the work."[32]

Fiske's moderate response to these instances of white hostility was not unusual. As Michael Goldhaber found, "Time after time, Fiske's most emphatic professions of optimism were expressed in the wake of tragedies." According to Goldhaber, Fiske's "startling indifference to white opposition" was grounded in the belief that white southerners, particularly those of the upper-class, would take control of freedpeople's education. Horace James shared Fiske's vision and in 1865 he reported that he was attempting to prepare southern whites to take control of Black schools. "The time is near where negros must look to them for justice or nowhere," he wrote. Ultimately, both Fiske and James recognized that the Freedmen's Bureau was a temporary agency and, reflecting the racial paternalism that often characterized the Bureau's efforts, both agents envisioned southern whites taking control of Black schools once the Bureau ceased operations.[33]

Exactly one year after Fiske concluded that old prejudices were dissipating, he noticed a sudden change in attitude. In his school report for April 1868, Fiske wrote that white hostility had increased "since the election" of Republican nominee William Woods Holden as governor. That same month also saw the ratification of North Carolina's new constitution which authorized the establishment of a public school system for all children, regardless of race, between the ages of six and twenty-one. Increased opposition to Black schooling is well-reflected in the school statistics for the months of May, June, and July 1868 which saw the number of schools, teachers, and students steadily decrease. Finally, in August 1868, the figures started to rise again and in his monthly report for September, Fiske acknowledged that there was "a slight change for the better."[34]

This tumultuous period of Reconstruction coincides with the rise of white supremacist terrorist organizations such as the Ku Klux Klan (KKK), the Red Shirts, and the White League. Established in Pulaski, Tennessee, in 1865 by six former Confederate soldiers, the KKK was the most notorious of these organizations and it made its first appearance in North Carolina in the lead up to the 1868 election. Bent upon restoring southern Democrats to power, Klansmen launched an aggressive campaign to overthrow the Republican Party by terrorizing both white and Black supporters and suppressing the Black vote. Above all, the KKK was committed to preserving the prewar racial hierarchy and some of the atrocities that it committed included beatings, whippings, arson, torture, and murder.[35]

Women and children also fell victim to Klan violence. In 1871, the homes of W. C. Brackin and his brother Alfred in Yancey County were raided and ransacked by the KKK. After dragging Alfred from his home and repeatedly beating him over the head with a pistol "until he was covered with blood from head to foot," Klansmen reentered his house, threw his baby across the room, and raped his wife. This caused considerable outrage in the Republican press which reported the event as a "horrible outrage" against a "respectable woman." Although the Brackins's race was not identified in the newspaper that reported the crime, they were supposedly targeted for being "Radicals" and the description of Brackin's wife as "respectable," as well as the sheer condemnation of the attack, suggests they were white. Predictably, little was done to bring the perpetrators to justice until the United States assistant district attorney was sent to investigate the matter, resulting in the arrest of six men.[36] One year earlier, the Republican *Daily Standard* reported that a young Black boy from Orange County was hanged because he allegedly made "some improper and foolish remark about the white ladies." "His body hung ten days until the vultures partly consumed it and no one during that time dared to take him down." According to the KKK trials, a committee organized by the federal government to investigate Klan violence in the former Confederate states, countless other atrocities were committed across North Carolina during the turbulent Reconstruction period and regrettably persisted well into the twentieth and twenty-first centuries.[37]

The KKK directed much of their aggression toward freedpeople's schools and teachers, principally because Black schools served as an affront to racial assumptions of Black inferiority. On December 19, 1866, Thomas B. Barton, a northern white teacher, was dragged from his bed, taken to the woods, beaten, and robbed by six armed men. According to his report, these men pointed a gun to his head and said, "you damn nigger teacher, we have got you now and will blow your damned yankee brains out." "The niggers were bad enough before you came," his attackers continued, "but since you have been teaching them, they know too much and are a damn sight worse." Although Barton was given five days to leave the state, he reported the incident to AMA Superintendent of Schools Samuel Ashley in Wilmington, twenty miles south of his post in Long Creek. In response, Barton was given a "protection paper" which was intended to protect his school from future attacks. Deeming the protection paper all but useless, Barton armed himself and confessed, "I depend more on my powder and lead than I do on a bit of paper." In 1867, Barton returned to his home in the North after just one year of teaching.[38]

Three years after the attack on Barton, white northerners Alonzo B. Corliss and his wife Francis were driven out of their post in Company Shops (present day Burlington) by the KKK. In the early hours of November 26, 1869, Corliss was dragged from his home and beaten. Klansmen then proceeded to shave half his head and paint it black before warning him to leave the state. Although Corliss identified four of his attackers, none were prosecuted due to insufficient evidence. Upon leaving Company Shops, the Corliss's relocated to Halifax County, Virginia. While the couple appears to have finished their southern teaching careers in 1870, AMA records show that between 1891 and 1892, both Alonzo and Francis worked as a minister and teacher, respectively, in Mississippi.[39]

The aforementioned Robert G. Fitzgerald often reported being subjected to Klan threats and intimidation, partly because of his role in educating the freedpeople but also because of his active support for the Republican Party. Although Fitzgerald reported that race relations were relatively amicable in Orange County during the early stages of Reconstruction, KKK activity increased during the autumn of 1869. "The infamous Ku Klux Klan has visited our post town Hillsboro and kill'd a black man who was supposed to have burned a barn," wrote Fitzgerald in September of that year. "They have also marched or paraded in Chapel Hill & are committing depredations on Union men all around. They are unwilling to be governed by law and should therefore be considered Out Laws and dealt with accordingly." Shortly after their arrival in Hillsboro, the KKK turned their attention to Fitzgerald and he and his new wife were forced to hide out in his family's home for fear of attack.[40]

Contrary to what traditional historians once argued, southern white men and women also fell victim to Klan violence and in his testimony to the Southern Claims Commission, William Bowers from Chapel Hill reported that the Klan had threatened him because of his wife's role in freedpeople's education. "My wife was teaching the colored population and I heard it spoken in the neighborhood several times that it was on that account [the KKK] were going to visit me."[41] Like the aforementioned Brackin families, southern white Republicans who had little connection to Black schools also fell victim to Klan violence. In 1870, Republican State Senator and Union League member John W. Stephens was killed by the KKK near his home in Yanceyville, Caswell County. Described by one newspaper reporter as "a typical scalawag politician," Stephens was accused of supplying local Blacks with matches to burn down the town's hotel as well as a series of other buildings.[42] Although no evidence was ever produced to demonstrate the veracity of this accusation, Stephens was tried in absentia by the KKK, convicted, and sentenced to death. On May 21, 1870, the ex-Confederate senator was lured to the storage room of the Yanceyville courthouse by Frank A. Wiley, former sheriff, and killed by the Klan.[43] No one was ever convicted of the murder and details of his death remained a mystery until the death of John G. Lea in 1935. In 1919, Lea, the Klan's former leader, made an affidavit to the North Carolina Historical Commission outlining the details of Stephens's murder. Released upon his death, this affidavit described Stephens's murder:

> Immediately I rushed into the room with eight or 10 men, found him sitting flat on the floor. He arose and approached me and we went and sat down where the wood had been taken away, in an opening in the wood on the wood-pile, and he asked me not to let them kill him. Captain Mitchell rushed at him with a rope, drew it around his neck, put his feet against his chest and by that time about a half dozen men rushed up: Tom Oliver, Pink Morgan, Dr. Richmond and Joe Fowler. Stevens was then stabbed in the breast and also in

the neck by Tom Oliver, and the knife was thrown at his feet and the rope left around his neck. We all came out, closed the door and locked it on the outside and took the key and threw it into County Line creek.[44]

Stephens was hanged on a hook in the Yanceyville courthouse and found the following morning.

From the time of his death in 1870 to Lea's revelations in 1935, southern newspapers remained unsympathetic to Stephens's murder. "Some called it murder," wrote W. C. Burton in 1870. "Others, doubtless the majority, considered it an execution and an improvement in society." In 1935, one newspaper reporter justified the KKK's actions, claiming that Stephens's death "broke the menace to white supremacy." "One thing of widespread importance revealed by the affidavit is the fact that Stevens was not the victim of spontaneous assassination. He had been tried by a Klansmen's jury of 12 for burning a hotel at Yanceyville, a row of brick buildings and the tobacco crops of at least two worthy Caswell County men." The reporter neglected to reveal that Stephens was not present at the trial nor was there any substantial evidence to support the Klan's claims.[45]

The murder of Stephens and the lynching of Wyatt Outlaw, a Black Republican leader, three months previously in neighboring Alamance County precipitated what became known as the "Kirk-Holden war." Headed by Union army veteran George W. Kirk under the direction of North Carolina Governor William Woods Holden, military forces were sent to both Caswell and Alamance counties to suppress Klan activity. Although over one hundred arrests were made, Holden's decision to deploy military forces proved widely unpopular. Exploiting this resentment, Democrats successfully gained control of North Carolina's legislature in 1870, and charges of impeachment were quickly brought against Holden resulting in his dismissal as governor in March of the following year. Lamenting the Democrats' restoration to power, Samuel Ashley wrote of the newly appointed general assembly, "among them are the leading *Ku-Klux* spirits of the State. The King or Emperor of the 'Invisible Empire' is Clerk of the Senate. The chief of the Ku Klux Klan that decreed the death of a State Senator, the man who issued the order for that murder, is the *leader* of the House of Representatives." Thereafter, North Carolinian Klansmen were able to use extralegal measures as well as the power of the legislature to subvert Black schooling. Known as "Redeemers," Democratic politicians and lawmakers disenfranchised Black men, slashed educational funding for Black schools, and instigated an era of racial oppression through discriminatory Jim Crow laws that would last until the Civil Rights Movement of the 1950s and 1960s.[46]

In the midst of this chaos, teachers and students continued with their work in the classroom. Not surprisingly, the difficult southern lifestyle prompted many educators to withdraw from the work. While white terror undoubtedly played a role in some cases, others left due to practical reasons, such as poor living conditions, homesickness, and illness. According to the Freedman's Teacher Project, a total of fourteen teachers died while working in the South while many others suffered from afflictions which rendered them temporarily unable to work. White northerners Nellie F. Stearns and Sarah P. Freeman both contracted malaria while working in North Carolina. Although Margaret Thorpe dedicated six years of her life to freedpeople's education, she ultimately left because she could not withstand the harsh southern conditions any longer. "We are beaten, not spiritually but physically and cannot stay any longer than to the end of this month," she wrote in April 1871. Citing "hunger, cold, and weariness" as the reasons why she was leaving, Thorpe's words exemplify the struggles many teachers faced in Reconstruction North Carolina and while many were genuinely committed to Black racial advancement, the harsh and often hostile realities of the environment presented very real challenges that circumscribed their work.[47]

Epilogue

The Struggle for
Educational Equality
Continues

By the time the last of the military troops had been withdrawn from North Carolina in 1877, southern Democrats had secured political dominance in the state and the period of "Redemption" was well and truly underway. Yet Black schools experienced little disruption at first and it was not until the late 1880s that white opposition to Black education intensified, marking a pivotal shift in the educational landscape and the struggle for educational equality. When newly elected Democratic Governor Zebulon B. Vance assumed office in January 1877, he urged legislators to "make no discrimination in the matter of public education." The North Carolina General Assembly adhered to his word and some significant legislative measures were introduced which actually contributed to Black educational advancement, such as the 1877 act which provided for the establishment of the first State Colored Normal School and the appropriation of $2,000 in state funds to support it. Having received somewhat of a head start in the realm of public education, the standards in Black schools often surpassed those in the emerging white schools, something a court trial revealed in 1878 when five white boys in Fayetteville were unable to sign their names while six Black boys did so with ease. Due to the local Black community's determination to become self-sufficient, as well as the robust partnerships they had formed with northern philanthropists, Fayetteville's Black school could sustain a full four-month term whereas the white public school could only run for eight weeks. Humiliated that Black children were surpassing their own, the white community in Fayetteville raised $3,000 in voluntary contributions and this, together with funding from the Peabody Education Fund, allowed for the establishment of Fayetteville's first, white, graded school.[1]

Admittedly, stories such as this were the exception rather than the rule. This particular example simply illustrates how *some* Black communities in *some* geographical areas could organize and mobilize to provide a quality education for their children. During the antebellum period, Fayetteville had been a thriving town that boasted a significant community of free people of color, many of whom had the social, cultural, and at times, economic capital to maintain an independent network of post–Civil War schools. Not everyone was as lucky, though, and geographical location played a key role in determining the extent to which Black communities could achieve educational success. Given the rural nature of North Carolina, Black communities were often widely dispersed which hindered the development of schools. In 1873, Black children in Mitchell and Stokes Counties were so widely dispersed that schools could not be organized. In Robeson County, which experienced a significant shortage of Black teachers, only 624 out of a possible 4,484 Black, school-aged children were enrolled. While these dismal figures were undoubtedly due to limitations in funding, which ultimately impacted both white and Black children, the effect of localized violence, threats, and intimidation on Black educational endeavors should not be discounted. Racial violence persisted beyond the restoration of southern Democrats to power. Thousands of Black people were lynched during and after the 1880s and white terrorist organizations like the Ku Klux Klan and the Red Shirts continued to instigate a climate of fear and hostility in many areas of the state until the 1890s, at least. In 1898, the infamous Wilmington massacre further exemplified the continuation of racial violence as white supremacists, fueled by political and racial animosities, violently overthrew the duly elected biracial government in the Black-majority town. This brutal event underscored the persistence of systemic racism in North Carolina as white supremacists sought to suppress Black political and economic progress through intimidation and violence. Consequently, we may never know the number of potential students who did not attend school out of fear of reprisal.[2]

Opposition to Black education intensified in the 1880s when white residents mobilized against the use of their taxes to support Black schools. In 1881, white residents in Goldsboro obtained permission from the legislature to hold an election on the introduction of legislation that would allow for the division of school taxes on a racial basis. The bill passed and Durham secured similar permissive legislation that allowed them to establish white, graded schools with white taxpayers' money and Black, graded schools with Black taxpayers' money. Two years later, the North Carolina legislature enacted a law that recognized the practice of separating school taxes on the basis of race. Although this law was eventually declared unconstitutional, underscoring the significant work completed by the interracial constitutional convention in 1868, it reflected the white community's persistent opposition to Black educational advancement.[3]

Another attack on Black schooling occurred in 1885 when justices of the peace and county commissioners were given the right to elect members to the county boards of education which effectively excluded Black representation. At the time,

Epilogue

school board officials had some control over the distribution of school funds which invariably found their way to white schools instead of Black schools. The unequal distribution of funds ultimately meant that Black schoolhouses were small and in poor condition, facilities were primitive, and resources were inadequate. Due to a lack of space, many Black students were unable to gain access to education as schools were already at capacity. In North Carolina, the average salary for a white teacher was one hundred dollars per year but Black teachers were paid considerably lower. As a result, "only the poorest local talent" would teach.[4]

The defeat of the Blair education bill in 1890 dealt another blow to North Carolina's system of public schooling for both Black and white children. First introduced by Senator Henry W. Blair in 1880, this bill proposed providing $77 million in federal funds to state public schools on the basis of their illiteracy rates. With more than 48 percent of the state's population unable to read or write at the time, North Carolina's public schools served to benefit immensely from the passing of this bill and although there were some divided opinions, North Carolinians were typically in favor of it. Although opposition to tax-supported schools, particularly among the white residents of the state, was evident from the beginning, public opinion gradually began to sway, and federally supported schools were certainly more appealing than levying local taxes on an already overburdened population. North Carolinian taxpayers should not be burdened with the responsibility of educating its "illiterate citizens," argued a writer in the *Goldsboro Messenger* in 1887, especially not the recently enfranchised Black men who they claimed were "utterly unprepared and unfit" for this responsibility. Indeed, it was for this very reason that many white North Carolinians began to gradually accept the provision of free public schooling for the Black race. Uneducated slaves were tolerable, preferable in fact, but uneducated Black voters posed a particular threat to the southern social order. Black North Carolinians were not surprisingly particularly supportive of the bill and many of those who began their educational work in the first schools for the freedpeople, such as James Edward O'Hara and Charles N. Hunter, actively attempted to influence its passage. Although the bill passed the Senate three times in the 1880s, it never passed the House and was ultimately defeated by the Senate in 1890.[5]

Although Black North Carolinians experienced some minor gains when a fusionist coalition of Populists and Republicans assumed control of the state legislature between 1894 and 1898, the Democratic return to power on a white supremacist platform signaled a new era of racial segregation and discriminatory Jim Crow laws. According to Hilary Green, these events, combined with the defeat of the Blair education bill, "signaled the real closure" of Reconstruction "and the opening of another phase of African American education," namely the industrial education model. "One of the inevitable expedients for fastening serfdom on the country Negro was enforced ignorance," wrote W. E. B. DuBois in 1907, and although coercive labor contracts, restrictive vagrancy laws, and debt peonage worked to relegate Black North Carolinian men and women to a predominantly agricultural workforce during the late nineteenth century, an unequal and inadequate system of education equally played a part. Epitomized by Hampton Institute in Virginia and Tuskegee Institute in Alabama, the industrial education model was designed to teach Black students the skills, habits, and value of industry, particularly in relation to agricultural work and trades. Like many of the freedpeople's schools envisioned by white North Carolinians during the Civil War and Reconstruction era, these institutions were equally viewed as a means of producing "efficient and content" laborers who accepted "the southern racial hierarchy."[6] Although Hampton Institute was established by a white Union army veteran, Samuel C. Armstrong, Tuskegee was led by Booker T. Washington, a former slave who had received his first education during the post-emancipation period. While southern Black Americans had decades of practice resisting the limited and restricted models of education often imposed on them by southern whites, in particular, and northern whites at times, "they could not readily overcome this challenge from within the African American community."[7]

During the 1890s, industrial education gained traction in North Carolina as a means of training poor whites and Blacks to become more effective and efficient workers. However, this model of instruction became increasingly perceived as the most appropriate form of education for members of the Black race and those who aspired to become something more than a mechanic, farm laborer, or even teacher encountered numerous obstacles in their attempts to do so. Echoing sentiments similar to those in the textbooks created for the freedpeople decades earlier, Reverend A. D. Mayo advised Black North Carolinians to embrace the industrial education model. Do not believe "that common work is a hardship," he warned, "that the higher education is a short cut out of it." "The price of all enduring success is intelligent and persistent labor," he concluded. In his youth, Charles W. Chesnutt, the son of freeborn parents from Fayetteville, spoke of his aspirations to achieve fame, success, and wealth. In considering his career choices, he toyed with the idea of becoming a doctor, a stenographer, and a writer before conceding that the only opportunity available to him "without capital" was in the field of education. As Chesnutt correctly deduced, teaching was one of the few prospects available to Black men and women who desired a career outside of manual or agricultural work. And while this would not have been possible without the organized and sustained efforts of Black North Carolinians to ensure the provision of Black teachers for Black schools, it was reflective of the limited opportunities available to Black men and women in the decades that followed the Civil War and Reconstruction era. After leading a successful career in Fayetteville as principal of the State Colored Normal School, Chesnutt left North Carolina in 1883 in pursuit of a better life for himself and his new wife. He turned his hand to law and stenography, ultimately embodying DuBois's elusive vision of the "talented tenth."[8]

From the 1890s onward, southern Black schooling entered a new phase of unequal segregated education that persisted until the renowned *Brown v. Board of Education* US Supreme Court case in 1954 which decreed that segregated public schools were unconstitutional. While this was a positive step in the right direction, the implementation of desegregation faced significant resistance in some areas and achieving genuine educational equality remained a complex and ongoing struggle. Marked by challenges such as "white flight" to private schools, disparities in resource allocation, and persisting socioeconomic inequalities, the promises of integration often fell short as Black communities grappled with systemic barriers which hindered the full realization of equitable education. The loss of Black teachers, as numerous historians have shown, dealt a particularly hard blow to Black communities, leading to the concomitant "loss of school traditions, trophies, mascots, and support systems."[9]

Although some of the greatest blows to southern Black schooling came during the late 1890s, the seeds of destruction were laid during the early, relatively positive years of Black freedom. White opposition to freedpeople's education, which ranged from passive aggressive acts of resistance to brutal incidences of white paramilitary violence, was arguably the clearest indicator that white North Carolinians were not willing to accept Black freedom and the privileges it brings. When the last of the federal troops were withdrawn from the state in 1877, Black schools gradually transferred to state control. Yet racial violence persisted, and intensified in many cases, until the doctrine of white supremacy was codified into law. Long before emancipation, though, racial prejudice had become ingrained in American society and Black Americans, regardless of their condition of servitude, were viewed as an inferior race. This was particularly evident in the antebellum northern common school textbooks which repeatedly positioned Black people at the bottom of a prescribed racial hierarchy. The textbooks specifically created for the freedpeople did little to challenge the prevailing racial stereotypes that undermined the Black experience. Although the extent to which textbook content may or may not be influential in shaping the ideas of those who engage with them is widely contested, they offer a revealing insight into the ideologies of those who created them. When the industrial model of education was first introduced in the South, many of the same racial stereotypes emerged in the writings and speeches of those who supported it. Labeled childlike and frivolous, Black men and women continued to be portrayed as unfit for freedom and key proponents of the movement adopted a paternalistic stance when they encouraged this model of schooling in lieu of higher education. Although the freedpeople faced many challenges during the Civil War and Reconstruction period, the future looked bright for Black North Carolinians, particularly in the immediate postwar years when educational opportunities began to expand throughout the state. However, by the close of the nineteenth century, an unequal, segregated school system combined with disenfranchisement, white paramilitary violence, legal segregation, and a variety of discriminatory Jim Crow laws to relegate Black North Carolinians to a position of second-class citizenship. While efforts to overcome these systemic barriers have continued well into the twenty-first century, the recent United States Supreme Court decision to overturn affirmative action in colleges and universities, including the University of North Carolina, effectively unraveled much of the progress that had been made in relation to addressing persistent racial discrimination in higher education.[10]

Nevertheless, the educational advancements made by North Carolinian freedpeople and their allies during the Civil War and Reconstruction period, 1861–1877, should not be underestimated. As the events of the 1880s show, many of the key players during this period had the foresight to protect the Black institution through the letter of the law which served to keep some elements of the public school system envisioned by Radical Republicans intact, at least. Moreover, by 1890, Black teachers, alongside ministers, represented 95 percent of the Black professional class which serves as a testament to Black North Carolinians' commitment to maintain control over their own schools. Throughout the period under examination, 1861–1877, Black North Carolinians consistently proved to be active agents in the construction of freedpeople's education. Faced with a myriad of challenges, including poverty, limited funding, overt hostility, racial prejudice, and conflicting interpretations of Black freedom and the role that education should play, these men and women did what they could with the resources they had in order to continuously move toward a more equitable system of schooling for themselves and their children.

Acknowledgments

This book, born from a dissertation, has reached fruition with the support of numerous individuals to whom I owe immense gratitude. First, my heartfelt thanks go to my doctoral advisor, Una Bromell. Her invaluable insights, guidance, and unwavering encouragement have been instrumental in shaping the trajectory of this work. I would also like to thank Brian Kelly and Enrico Dal Lago who served on my dissertation committee for their insightful comments and feedback during the early stages of this research. I am extremely grateful for the continued support of everyone at Fordham University Press, particularly Andy Slap whose contributions significantly shaped the ideas presented in this book, and Lis Pearson for her copyediting assistance. Thank you also to Hilary Green who, along with Andy, reviewed an earlier draft of this manuscript. Their assistance and feedback played a pivotal role in enhancing the quality and depth of this work. I would like to thank Ronald Butchart for sharing the North Carolina section of the Freedmen's Teacher Project with me and for providing insights on an earlier draft of this research which I presented at the American Educational Research Association conference. Thank you also to Christopher Span for his support and encouragement while I was in the early stages of this research project. I would like to thank my colleagues at Mary Immaculate College for their support and encouragement throughout all stages of the research and writing process, especially my colleagues in the Department of Learning, Society, and Religious Education. A special thanks is owed to Amanda J. Evans for her editorial assistance and to Ashlee Mason-Cleary for generously sharing her unpublished research on the topic of freedpeople's textbooks. Her discoveries have enriched this narrative, and I look forward to learning more about her research. I am grateful to the Gilder Lehrman Institute of American History, the North Caroliniana Society, and the Fulbright Program for the awards and fellowships that facilitated my research trips. I also wish to thank the archivists at Tryon Palace, New Bern, the Wilson Library at the University of North Carolina, Chapel Hill, and North Carolina State Archives. Their assistance in providing me with access to requested documents has been immensely valuable to this project. Finally, my deepest appreciation goes to my husband, Gary, and children, Adam and Daniel, for their unwavering support, enthusiasm, and patience throughout this process. Thank you from the bottom of my heart.

Notes

Introduction

1. Oliver O. Howard, *Autobiography of Oliver Otis Howard, Major General, United States Army: Volume 2* (New York: Baker & Taylor, 1908), 221.

2. Edgar W. Knight, "The 'Messianic' Invasion of the South After 1865," *School and Society* 57, no. 1484 (1943): 645–51; Eric Foner, "Reconstruction Revisited," *Reviews in American History* 10, no. 4 (1982): 82–100. For traditional interpretations of freedpeople's education, see also Wilbur J. Cash, *The Mind of the South* (New York: Knopf, 1941); Henry L. Swint, *The Northern Teacher in the South, 1862–1870* (Nashville, TN: George Peabody College for Teachers, 1941). On the mischaracterization of the freedpeople's teachers as northern white women, see Sandra E. Small, "The Yankee Schoolmarm in Freedmen's Schools: An Analysis of Attitudes," *The Journal of Southern History* 45, no. 3 (1979): 381–402. W. E. B Du Bois was one of the first historians to write about freedpeople's education, but his work was often overshadowed by the vociferous Dunning School. See W. E. B. Du Bois, *The Souls of Black Folk: Essays and Sketches* (Chicago: A.C. McClurg & Co., 1903).

3. Heather Andrea Williams, *Self-Taught: African American Education in Slavery and Freedom* (Chapel Hill: University of North Carolina Press, 2005); Christopher M. Span, *From Cotton Field to Schoolhouse: African American Education in Mississippi, 1862–1875* (Chapel Hill: University of North Carolina Press, 2009); Hilary Green, *Educational Reconstruction: African American Schools in the Urban South, 1865–1890* (New York: Fordham University Press, 2016); Ronald E. Butchart, *Schooling the Freed People: Teaching, Learning, and the Struggle for Black Freedom, 1861–1876* (Chapel Hill: University of North Carolina Press, 2010).

4. By 1860, less than one-third of North Carolina's white population owned slaves. William T. Auman, *Civil War in the North Carolina Quaker Belt: The Confederate Campaign Against Peace Agitators, Deserters, and Draft Dodgers* (Jefferson, NC: McFarland & Company, 2014), 9; John Hope Franklin, *The Free Negro in North Carolina, 1790–1860* (reprint, New York: W. W. Norton, 1971), 9. Although western North Carolina was dominated by nonslaveholding yeoman farmers, approximately 10 percent of the population were slaveowners, many of whom represented the slaveholding elite. John Inscoe, *Mountain Masters: Slavery Sectional Crisis Western North Carolina* (Knoxville: University of Tennessee Press, 1989).

5. Auman, *Civil War*, 9. See also J. Timothy Allen, *North Carolina Quakers: Spring Friends Meeting* (Charleston, SC: Arcadia Publishing, 2011), 9; Butchart, *Schooling*, 63; Damon D. Hickey, "Pioneers of the New South: The Baltimore Association and North Carolina Friends in Reconstruction," *Quaker History* 74, no. 1 (1985): 1–17. For more information on Quaker teachers see Scot Beck, "Friends, Freedmen, Common Schools, and Reconstruction," *The Southern Friend, Journal of Quaker History* 17, no. 1 (1995): 5–31.

6. Auman, *Civil War*, 11; Delphina E. Mendenhall to John L. Ham, February 1, 1869, Paul W. Bean Civil War Papers, University of Maine, accessed August 22, 2024, https://digitalcommons.library.umaine.edu/paul_bean_papers/54.

7. Franklin, *The Free Negro*, 67; Levi Coffin, *Reminiscences of Levi Coffin: The Reputed President of the Underground Railroad*, 2nd ed. (Cincinnati: Robert Clarke & Co., 1880), 71 (first quotation), 190 (second quotation). Coffin's educational efforts during the Reconstruction period are examined more fully in Chapter 4.

8. Franklin, *The Free Negro*, 15 (quotation), 18; Warren Eugene Milteer Jr., *North Carolina's Free People of Color, 1715–1885* (Baton Rouge: Louisiana State University Press, 2020), *Beyond Slavery's Shadow: Free People of Color in the South* (Chapel Hill: University of North Carolina Press, 2021), and "Life in a Great Dismal Swamp Community: Free People of Color in Pre–Civil War Gates County, North Carolina," *The North Carolina Historical Review* 91, no. 2 (2014): 144–70 (quotation p. 153).

9. Butchart, *Schooling*, 58.

10. Ronald E. Butchart et al., "The Freedmen's Teacher Project: Teachers Among the Freed People in the U.S. South, 1861–1877," Harvard Dataverse, V3 (2022), https://doi.org/10.7910/DVN/0HBDZD, hereafter cited as The FTP; Ronald E. Butchart, "Wealth Database" (2013), used with permission. For a more detailed description of the database, see Ronald E. Butchart, "Recruits to the 'Army of Civilization': Gender, Race, Class, and the Freedmen's Teachers, 1862–1875," *Journal of Education* 172 (1990): 76–87.

11. Butchart, *Schooling*, 95; Butchart et al., The FTP. Although the precise state has not been identified for fifty teachers, the database has established whether they were from the North or the South.

12. Out of the 1,419 teachers in the database, 705 have been identified as Black. 613 of these teachers were from a slave state, eighty-five were from the North, and seven came from countries outside of the US, such as Barbados and the West Indies. 563 of the southern Black teachers were from North Carolina. 371 teachers have been positively identified as white northerners and 276 of these were women. A total of 143 teachers have been positively identified as white southerners. Butchart et al., The FTP.

1. The Civil War and Early Reconstruction Period in North Carolina

1. Judkin Browning, "Visions of Freedom and Civilization Opening Before Them: African Americans Search for Autonomy During Military Occupation in North Carolina," in *North Carolinians in the Era of the Civil War and Reconstruction*, ed. Paul D. Escott (Chapel Hill: University of North Carolina Press, 2008), 69–100, see p. 71 specifically; Alex Christopher Meekins, *Elizabeth City, North Carolina and the Civil War: A History of Battle and Occupation* (Charleston, SC: History Press, 2007), 29. For firsthand accounts of events in Elizabeth City see for example, Richard Benbury Creecy, *Grandfather's Tales of North Carolina History* (Raleigh, NC: Edwards & Broughton, 1901), 222; *The New York Times*, January 9, 1864. Western North Carolina experienced the war very differently to many other areas of the state. For more on this, see for example, David Silkenat, *Driven from Home: North Carolina's Civil War Refugee Crisis* (Athens: The University of Georgia Press, 2016); William L. Barney, *The Making of a Confederate: Walter Lenoir's Civil War* (New York: Oxford University Press, 2008).

2. Barton A. Myers, "A More Rigorous Style of Warfare: Wild's Raid, Guerrilla Violence, and Negotiated Neutrality in Northeastern North Carolina," in Escott, *North Carolinians*, 37–68 (quotation p. 39); *The New York Times*, January 9, 1864.

3. Cornelia Phillips Spenser, *The Last Ninety Days of the War in North-Carolina* (New York: Watchman Publishing Company, 1866), 31, Documenting the American South, University of North Carolina, Chapel Hill, accessed November 12, 2015, http://docsouth.unc.edu/true/spencer/spencer.html; John G. Barrett, "Sherman and Total War in the Carolinas," *The North Carolina Historical Review* 37 (1960), 367–81.

4. William Tecumseh Sherman, *Memoirs of General William T. Sherman, Volume II*, 2nd ed. (New York: D. Appleton, 1904), 175; Barrett, "Sherman and Total War in the Carolinas," 370; Jane Constance Miller Hinton, "The Reminiscences of the Key Basket of a Southern Matron," 1890, 1895, and undated, Laurens Hinton Papers, 1825–1896, Southern Historical Collection, The Wilson Library, University of North Carolina at Chapel Hill, hereafter cited as Laurens Hinton Papers.

5. Letter to Matilda Abernethy, February 25, 1865, William G. Dickson Papers, 1767–1920, Southern Historical Collection, Wilson Library, University of North Carolina at Chapel Hill, hereafter cited as William G. Dickson Papers.

6. According to David Brown, desertion and the ambivalence of many North Carolinians toward the Civil War was not necessarily a reflection of diminishing support for the Confederacy. Instead, Brown argues that this apparent disloyalty to the Confederate cause was a result of strenuous wartime conditions, particularly the way in which these conditions impacted upon the soldiers' families at home, as well as unfair conscription laws and tax policies. See David Brown, "North Carolinian Ambivalence: Rethinking Loyalty and Disaffection in the Civil War Piedmont," in Escott, *North Carolinians*, 7–36. According to Steven E. Nash, about 24,000 North Carolinians deserted the Confederate army. Nonetheless, the state contributed more than 120,000 soldiers to the Confederate war effort "which exceeded the number of soldiers from any other southern state." Steven E. Nash, "North Carolina," in *Encyclopedia of the Reconstruction Era: M–Z and Primary Documents, Volume 2*, ed. Richard Zuczek (Westport, CT: Greenwood Press, 2006), 446. See also William T. Auman, *Civil War in the North Carolina Quaker Belt: The Confederate Campaign Against Peace Agitators, Deserters, and Draft Dodgers* (Jefferson, NC: McFarland & Company, Inc., 2014), 69.

7. Walter H. Conser and Robert J. Cain, *Presbyterians in North Carolina: Race, Politics and Religious Identity in Historical Perspective* (Knoxville: University of Tennessee Press, 2010), 131; Barrett, "Sherman and Total War in the Carolinas," 379.

8. Raphael O'Hara Boyd, "Service in the Midst of the Storm: James Edward O'Hara and Reconstruction in North Carolina," *The Journal of Negro History* 86 (Summer 2001): 319–35 (quotation p. 320); Mary Barbour, in *Federal Writers' Project: Slave Narrative Project, Vol. 11, North Carolina, Part 1, Adams-Hunter*, 1936, Manuscript/Mixed Material, accessed December 12, 2023, https://www.loc.gov/item/mesn111/; H. S. Beals, *American Missionary* (January 1867), 4; Elizabeth James, *American Missionary* (June 1864), 140–41.

9. Elizabeth James, *American Missionary* (February 1864), 39–40; J. W. Burghduff, *The National Freedman* (February 1868), 365; Sarah P. Freeman, *The Freedmen's Advocate* (August 1864), 25–26.

10. John Hope Franklin, *The Free Negro in North Carolina, 1790–1860*, reprint (New York: W. W. Norton, 1971), 9; Delphina Mendenhall to John Ham, February 1, 1869,

Paul W. Bean Civil War Papers, University of Maine, accessed August 22, 2024, https://digitalcommons.library.umaine.edu/paul_bean_papers/54.

11. Samuel S. Ashley to Samuel Hunt, December 20, 1865, American Missionary Association archives, Amistad Research Center at Tulane University, New Orleans, Louisiana, accessed at The New York Public Library, hereafter cited as AMAA; Testimony of James Sinclair in United States Congress, *Report of the Joint Committee on Reconstruction, at the First Session Thirty-Ninth Congress* (Washington, D.C.: Government Printing Office, 1866), 174; Joel Ashworth to Nathan Hill, April 15, 1867, Nathan Hill Papers, David M. Rubenstein Rare Book & Manuscript Library, Duke University, Durham, North Carolina, hereafter cited as Nathan Hill Papers; Diary of Robert G. Fitzgerald, September 28, 1869, Fitzgerald Family Papers, 1864–1954, Southern Historical Collection, The Wilson Library, University of North Carolina at Chapel Hill, hereafter cited as Diary of Robert Fitzgerald.

12. Testimony of Colonel E. Whittlesey, in United States Congress, *Report of the Joint Committee on Reconstruction*, 182. In April 1866, a federal investigation was conducted into the Freedmen's Bureau in North Carolina and Virginia. Headed by Joseph S. Fullerton and James B. Steedman, the subsequent Steedman–Fullerton report that was delivered to Congress in May 1866 cost Whittlesey his job. In this report, Whittlesey was charged with exploiting his position for personal gain. For more information, see Daniel Brown, "The Freedmen's Bureau in Reconstruction North Carolina," PhD Diss. (Queen's University Belfast, 2012), 105–6. See also Brian Kelly, "Black Laborers, the Republican Party, and the Crisis of Reconstruction in Lowcountry South Carolina," *International Institute of Social History* 51 (2006): 375–414.

13. Eric Foner, "The Civil War and the Story of American Freedom," *Art Institute of Chicago Museum Studies* 27 (2001): 8–26 (quotation p. 19), 100–101.

14. See for example, C. Vann Woodward, *The Strange Career of Jim Crow* (New York: Oxford University Press, 1955).

15. Testimony of Lieutenant George O. Sanderson, in United States Congress, *Report of the Joint Committee on Reconstruction*, 175.

16. Report of Horace James, included in testimony of Colonel E. Whittlesey, in United States Congress, *Report of the Joint Committee on Reconstruction*, 187–88.

17. Report of Horace James, 187.

18. "Two North Carolina Freedwomen Testify Against Their Former Owner," After Slavery: Race, Labor and Politics in the Post-Emancipation Carolinas, Lowcountry Digital History Initiative, accessed November 16, 2015, http://ldhi.library.cofc.edu/exhibits/show/after_slavery_educator/unit_one_documents/document_six.

19. Anthony L. Brown, "Counter-Memory and Race: An Examination of African American Scholars' Challenges to Early Twentieth Century K-12 Historical Discourses," *The Journal of Negro Education* 79 (2010): 54–65.

20. *The North Carolinian*, March 7, 1868.

21. "Poor Whites of North Carolina," *Boston Daily Advertiser* reprinted in *The Freedmen's Record* (November 1865), 186–87.

22. Tennessee was excluded from this act because it had already ratified the Fourteenth Amendment to the United States Constitution and was readmitted to the Union. "Act of March 2, 1867," reprinted in *Reconstruction: A Historical Encyclopedia of the American Mosaic*, ed. Richard Zuczec (Santa Barbara, CA: ABC-CLIO, 2016), 390–91

(quotation p. 391); Chandler Davidson, "The Voting Rights Act: A Brief History," in *Controversies in Minority Voting: The Voting Rights Act in Perspective*, eds. Bernard N. Grofman and Chandler Davidson (Washington, D.C.: Brookings Institution, 1992), 7.

23. Gordon B. McKinney, *Zeb Vance: North Carolina's Civil War Governor and Gilded Age Political Leader* (Chapel Hill: University of North Carolina Press, 2004), 273; Pauli Murray, *Proud Shoes: The Story of an American Family* (New York: Harper & Row, 1956), 195; Hilary Nicole Green, "Educational Reconstruction: African American Education in the Urban South," PhD diss. (University of North Carolina at Chapel Hill, 2010), 100–101. One hundred and seven of the elected delegates were Republican. This number included eighteen northern white "carpetbaggers," fifteen Black men, and seventy-four southern white "scalawags." William S. Powell, *North Carolina Through Four Centuries* (Chapel Hill: University of North Carolina Press, 1989), 392.

24. Stephen Middleton, *Black Congressmen During Reconstruction: A Documentary Sourcebook* (Westport, CT: Greenwood Press, 2002), 277; Ronald E. Butchart et al., "The Freedmen's Teacher Project: Teachers Among the Freed People in the U.S. South, 1861–1877," Harvard Dataverse, V3 (2022), https://doi.org/10.7910/DVN/0HBDZD, hereafter cited as The FTP. For a comprehensive overview of the life and work of James Walker Hood, see Sandy Dwayne Martin, *For God and Race: The Religious and Political Leadership of AMEZ Bishop James Walker Hood* (Columbia: University of South Carolina Press, 1999). The conventions held by southern Black men before, during, and after the Civil War have been termed "colored conventions" by P. Gabrielle Foreman et al. For the purpose of this book, the conventions held in North Carolina after the Civil War will be referred to as "Freedmen's Conventions" because these were the terms used in the archival documents, namely the conventions' minutes. See Freedmen's Convention of North Carolina, *Minutes of The Freedmen's Convention Held in the City of Raleigh on the 2nd, 3rd, 4th and 5th of October, 1866* (Raleigh, NC: Standard Book and Job Office, 1866). On the "colored conventions movement" see P. Gabrielle Foreman, Jim Casey, and Sarah Lynn Patterson, eds., *The Colored Conventions Movement: Black Organizing in the Nineteenth Century* (Chapel Hill: University of North Carolina Press, 2021).

25. Diary of Robert G. Fitzgerald, April 22, 1868, Fitzgerald Family Papers, 1864–1954, Southern Historical Collection, Wilson Library, University of North Carolina at Chapel Hill, hereafter cited as Diary of Robert Fitzgerald; John Haley, *Charles N. Hunter and Race Relations in North Carolina* (Chapel Hill: University of North Carolina Press, 1987), 19.

26. Diary of Robert Fitzgerald, November 3, 1868. The seven eligible states were Alabama, Florida, Georgia, Louisiana, Tennessee, North Carolina, and South Carolina. The remaining four Confederate states had not yet been admitted to the Union so neither whites nor Blacks could vote.

27. Allyson Hobbs, *A Chosen Exile: A History of Racial Passing in American Life* (Cambridge, MA: Harvard University Press, 2014), 80–81; Horace James, *Annual Report of the Superintendent of Negro Affairs in North Carolina, 1864* (Boston: W. F. Brown & Co. Printers, 1865), 45. For an analysis of the freedpeople's perspective on the franchise and freedom, see for example, Heather Andrea Williams, "'Clothing Themselves in Intelligence': The Freedpeople, Schooling, and Northern Teachers, 1861–1871," *The Journal of African American History* 87 (2002): 372–89; James D. Anderson, *The Education of Blacks in the South, 1860–1935* (Chapel Hill: University of North Carolina Press, 1988), 18.

28. New England Freedmen's Aid Society, *Extracts from Letters of Teachers and Superintendents of the New England Freedmen's Aid Society, Fifth Series* (Boston: John Wilson & Co., 1864), 13 (first quotation); John W. Alvord, *First Semi-Annual Report on Schools and Finances of Freedmen, January 1, 1866* (Washington, D.C., 1868; reprint, New York: AMS Press, Inc., 1980), 15; "North Carolina Freedmen's Address (1865)," reprinted in Scot J. Hammond, Kevin R. Hardwick, and Howard L. Lubert, eds., *Classics of American Political and Constitutional Thought, Volume 2: Reconstruction to the Present* (Indianapolis, IN: Hackett Publishing Company, 2007), 38. On complex labor contracts, see also, Charles Hill to Horace James, September 6, 1865, Records of the Field Offices for the State of North Carolina, Bureau of Freedmen, Refugees, and Abandoned Lands, 1865–1872, M1909:35; Christopher M. Span, *From Cotton Field to Schoolhouse: African American Education in Mississippi, 1861–1875* (Chapel Hill: University of North Carolina Press, 2009), 47; Leon F. Litwack, *Been in the Storm So Long: The Aftermath of Slavery* (New York: Alfred A. Knopf, 1980), 473. For more on the sharecropping system that emerged after the Civil War, see Donald Spivey, *Schooling for the New Slavery: Black Industrial Education, 1868–1915* (Westport, CT: Greenwood Press, 1978).

2. To "Enjoy the Benefits of a School": Black North Carolinians and the Quest for Education

1. Michael P. Jerkins to Edward P. Smith, January 29, 1869, American Missionary Association archives, Amistad Research Center, Tulane University, New Orleans, Louisiana, accessed at The New York Public Library, hereafter cited as AMAA; H. S. Beals in *American Missionary* (January 1867), 4. See also, *American Missionary* (March 1867), 49; Vincent Colyer, *Report of the Services Rendered by the Freed People to the United States Army: In North Carolina in the Spring of 1862, After the Battle of Newbern* (New York: Vincent Colyer, 1864), 43; Northern soldier cited in Judkin Browning, "'Bringing Light to Our Land. . .When She Was Dark as Night': Northerners, Freedpeople, and Education During Military Occupation in North Carolina, 1862–1865," *Nineteenth Century American History* 9, no. 1 (2008): 1–17 (quotation p. 4).

2. John W. Alvord, *First Semi-Annual Report on Schools and Finances of Freedmen, January 1, 1866* (Washington, D.C., 1868; reprint, New York: AMS Press, 1980), 10.

3. Harriet Beecher Stowe, "The Education of Freedmen," *The North American Review* 128 (1879): 605–15, emphasis in original; Ronald E. Butchart, *Northern Schools, Southern Blacks, and Reconstruction: Freedmen's Education, 1862–1875* (Westport, CT: Greenwood Press, 1980), 13; Jessica Enoch, *Refiguring Rhetorical Education: Women Teaching African American, Native American, and Chicano/a Students, 1865–1911* (Carbondale: Southern Illinois University Press, 2008), 41; Anthony L. Brown, "Counter-Memory and Race: An Examination of African American Scholars Challenges to Early Twentieth Century K-12 Historical Discourses," *The Journal of Negro Education* 79, no. 1 (2010): 54–65. Rufus Saxton, a Union army brigadier general and Freedmen's Bureau official, wrote a description of the freedpeople as childlike and submissive which epitomizes the way in which many white northerners viewed the freedpeople. See *The Freedmen's Record* (August 1865), 121.

4. Freedpeople cited in Roberta S. Alexander, *North Carolina Faces the Freedmen: Race Relations During Presidential Reconstruction, 1865–1867* (Durham, NC: Duke

University Press, 1865), 152; William Birnie to H. C. Vogell, November 10, 1868, Records of the Superintendent of Education, M844:10; Samuel J. Whiton to E. P. Smith, January 1, 1867, AMAA; *Raleigh Register,* October 25, 1867.

    5. John Haley, *Charles N. Hunter and Race Relations in North Carolina* (Chapel Hill: University of North Carolina Press, 1987), 9; Alexander, *North Carolina,* 17; John Richard Dennett, *The South as It Is: 1865–1866* (New York: Viking Press, 1965), 95 (quotation), 149, 154; *The New York Times,* October 1, 1865. On white hostility toward the freedpeople's political endeavors, see for example, John K. Chapman, "Black Freedom and the University of North Carolina, 1793–1960," PhD diss. (University of North Carolina at Chapel Hill, 2006), 92; Dennett, *The South as It Is,* 149.

    6. Ronald E. Butchart et al., "The Freedmen's Teacher Project: Teachers Among the Freed People in the U.S. South, 1861–1877," Harvard Dataverse, V3 (2022), https://doi.org/10.7910/DVN/0HBDZD, hereafter cited as The FTP. Appointment to the New England Freedmen's Aid Society, August 31, 1865, James Henry Harris (ca. 1830–1891) papers, North Carolina State Archives, Raleigh; Haley, *Charles N. Hunter,* 10.

    7. The Freedmen's Convention of North Carolina, *Minutes of the Freedmen's Convention Held in the City of Raleigh on the 2nd, 3rd, 4th and 5th of October, 1866* (Raleigh, NC: Standard Book and Job Office, 1866), 12, accessed October 8, 2015, http://docsouth.unc.edu/nc/freedmen/freedmen.html; State Superintendent's Monthly School Reports, December 1866, Records of the Superintendent of Education for the State of North Carolina, Bureau of Refugees, Freedmen, and Abandoned Lands, M844:13, hereafter cited as Records of the Superintendent of Education.

    8. Charles W. Chesnutt, *The Journals of Charles W. Chesnutt,* ed. Richard Brodhead (Durham, NC: Duke University Press, 1993); Mark Andrew Huddle, "To Educate a Race: The Making of the First State Colored Normal School, Fayetteville, North Carolina, 1865–1877," *The North Carolina Historical Review* 74, no. 2 (1997): 154–57.

    9. F. A. Fiske to General N. A. Miles, January 1, 1868, Records of the Superintendent of Education, M844:2; Alvord, *First Semi-Annual Report on Schools,* 9.

    10. Ira C. Colby, "The Freedmen's Bureau: From Social Welfare to Segregation," *Phylon* 46 (1985): 219–30 (quotation p. 219). For a firsthand account of the establishment of the Bureau, see Oliver O. Howard, *Autobiography of Oliver Otis Howard, Major General, United States Army: Volume 2* (New York: Baker &Taylor, 1908).

    11. E. Allan Richardson, "Architects of a Benevolent Empire: The Relationship Between the American Missionary Association and the Freedmen's Bureau in Virginia, 1865–1872," in *The Freedmen's Bureau and Reconstruction: Reconsiderations,* ed. Paul A. Cimbala and Randall M. Miller (New York: Fordham University Press, 1999), 119–39. See also, Colby, "The Freedmen's Bureau," 222; Bruce E. Baker, *What Reconstruction Meant: Historical Memory in the American South* (Charlottesville: University of Virginia Press, 2007), 13.

    12. Gregory P. Downs, "Anarchy at the Circumference: Statelessness and the Reconstruction of Authority in Emancipation North Carolina," in *After Slavery: Race, Labor, and Citizenship in the Reconstruction South,* ed. Bruce E. Baker and Brian Kelly (Gainesville: University Press of Florida, 2013), 98–121 (quotation p. 105). On the Bureau's attempts to regulate labor, see for example, Daniel Brown, "The Freedmen's Bureau in Reconstruction North Carolina," PhD diss. (Queen's University Belfast, 2012), 4; Jacque-

line Jones, *Soldiers of Light and Love: Northern Teachers and Georgia Blacks, 1865–1873* (Chapel Hill: University of North Carolina Press, 1980), 27.

13. Cimbala and Miller, introduction to *The Freedmen's Bureau and Reconstruction,* xxix. See also Eric Foner, *Reconstruction: America's Unfinished Revolution, 1863–1877* (New York: Harper & Row, 1988), 143; Adriane Ruggiero, *American Voices from Reconstruction* (New York: Marshall Cavendish Benchmark, 2007), 24; Howard, *Autobiography of Oliver Otis Howard,* 263–65 (first quotation p. 263); Colby, "The Freedmen's Bureau," 226 (second quotation). In 1866, federal appropriations to finance the Bureau were amended to include $21,000 for school superintendents' salaries and $500,000 for repairs to and the rental of schoolhouses and asylums. Later, in 1867, Congress awarded an additional $500,000 for Bureau schools and asylums. William Preston Vaughn, *Schools for All: Blacks and Public Education in the South* (Lexington: The University Press of Kentucky, 1974), 11.

14. Walter H. Conser and Robert J. Cain, *Presbyterians in North Carolina: Race, Politics, and Religious Identity in Historical Perspective* (Knoxville: University of Tennessee Press, 2010), 137; Michael Goldhaber, "Mission Unfulfilled: Freedpeople's Education in North Carolina, 1865–1870," *The Journal of Negro History* 77, no. 4 (1992): 199–210; Roberta Sue Alexander, "Hostility and Hope: Black Education in North Carolina During Presidential Reconstruction, 1865–1867," *The North Carolina Historical Review* 53, no. 2 (1976): 113–32, see p. 131 specifically; Joe M. Richardson, *Christian Reconstruction: The American Missionary Association and Southern Blacks, 1861–1890* (Tuscaloosa: University of Alabama Press, 1986), 178–79; New England Freedmen's Aid Society, *Second Annual Report of the New England Freedmen's Aid Society* (Boston: Office of the Society, 1864), 3. For a detailed examination of the federal government's role in freedpeople's education, both before and after the creation of the Freedmen's Bureau, see Vaughn, *Schools for All,* 7–11. In 1869, L. E. Rice was appointed superintendent of education for the new third congressional district of North Carolina which comprised twelve counties.

15. Butchart et al., *The FTP*; Report of James W. Hood in Samuel S. Ashley, *Report of the Superintendent of Public Instruction of North Carolina for the Year 1869* (Raleigh, NC: M. S. Littlefield, 1869), 16, 24 (quotations), accessed November 8, 2015, http://docsouth.unc.edu/nc/report1869/report1869.html.

16. Conser and Cain, *Presbyterians in North Carolina,* 137; F. A. Fiske to O. O. Howard, January 30, 1867, Records of the Superintendent of Education, M844:1.

17. Alexander, "Hostility and Hope," 131; Sidney Busbee, "Snowhill, Greene CO, N.C.," *The Freedmen's Record* (November 1866), 198.

18. *The American Freedman* (April 1868), 388 (first quotation), 380–81 (second and third quotations); Charles N. Hunter, *Review of Negro Life in North Carolina, With My Recollections* (Raleigh: N.p, n.d), 17, Internet Archive, accessed January 18, 2024, https://archive.org/details/reviewofnegrolifoohunt/mode/2up?view=theater; O'Hara cited in New England Freedmen's Aid Society, *Extracts from Letters of Teachers and Superintendents of the New England Freedmen's Aid Society, Fifth Series* (Boston: John Wilson & Co., 1864), 16.

19. On the requirement to labor, see for example, Fannie Graves and Annie P. Merriam, *The Freedman's Record* (July 1865), 117; New England Freedmen's Aid Society,

Second Annual Report, 33; Diary of Robert Fitzgerald, September 12, 1869, September 5, 1870; Robert Harris to Samuel Hunt, March 1, 1866, AMAA. The impact of white terror on school attendance is addressed in more detail in Chapter 6. Goldhaber, "Mission Unfulfilled," 199.

20. Butchart et al., The FTP; Howard, *Autobiography of Oliver Otis Howard*, 221; See Damon D. Hickey, "Pioneers of the New South: The Baltimore Association and North Carolina Friends in Reconstruction," *Quaker History* 74, no. 1 (1985): 1–17.

21. Butchart et al., The FTP. On the various activities performed by the aid associations, see for example, New England Freedmen's Aid Society, *Extracts from Letters*, 6. For a complete list of the aid and missionary organizations that operated throughout the South during the Civil War and Reconstruction period, see Howard, *Autobiography of Oliver Otis Howard*, 196.

22. See for example, Presbyterian Committee on Missions for Freedmen, *Second Annual Report*, 4; Protestant Episcopal Freedman's Commission, *Occasional Paper, January 1866* (Boston: Geo. C. Rand & Avery, 1866), Internet Archive, accessed August 30, 2024, https://archive.org/details/protestantepiscoooepis; Protestant Episcopal Church, *Journal of the General Convention of the Protestant Episcopal Church* (New York, 1868), 340; Methodist Episcopal Church, *Minutes of the Cincinnati Conference of the Methodist Episcopal Church* (Cincinnati, OH: R. P. Thompson, 1866), 40l; Gardiner H. Shattuck Jr., *Episcopalians and Race: Civil War to Civil Rights* (Lexington: University Press of Kentucky, 2010), 10; Conser and Cain, *Presbyterians in North Carolina*, 136.

23. Presbyterian Committee on Missions for Freedmen, *Annual Report of the Presbyterian Committee on Missions for Freedmen* (Pittsburgh, PA: J. M'Millin, Steam Job and Book Printers, 1871), 6, emphasis in original; Butchart et al., The FTP.

24. Report of James W. Hood in Ashley, *Report of the Superintendent*, 21.

25. Butchart et al., The FTP.

26. Butchart et al., The FTP; Hickey, "Pioneers of the New South," 3, 6; Brewer (first quotation) cited in John K. Chapman, "Black Freedom and the University of North Carolina, 1793–1960," PhD diss. (University of North Carolina at Chapel Hill, 2006), 124; Brewer (second quotation) cited in Alexander, *North Carolina*, 157; Maxine D. Jones, "The American Missionary Association and the Beaufort, North Carolina School Controversy, 1866–67," *Phylon (1960-)* 48, no. 2 (1987): 103–11. For more information on the white schools established in North Carolina, see New England Freedmen's Aid Society, *Second Annual Report*, 34.

27. Hosmer cited in Judkin Browning, *Shifting Loyalties: The Union Occupation of Eastern North Carolina* (Chapel Hill: University of North Carolina Press, 2011), 109–10; F. A. Fiske to Willis L. Miller, February 13, 1868, Records of the Superintendent of Education, M844:2; Browning, "Bringing Light to Our Land," 1–17 (quotation p. 6); *Unity* (November 1879), 275.

28. The AMA sponsored 220 of the teachers in the FTP database at one point in their southern missionary careers. Butchart et al., The FTP; Richardson, *Christian Reconstruction*, 146; Jones, *Soldiers of Light and Love*, 16, 18; "Qualifications of American Missionary Association Teachers," Roanoke Island Freedmen's Colony, accessed August 30, 2024, https://www.roanokefreedmenscolony.com/missqual.pdf.

29. National Freedman's Relief Association, *First Annual Report of the National Freedman's Relief Association of the District of Columbia* (Washington, D.C.: M'Gill & Witherow, printers, 1863), accessed September 26, 2022, https://digital.history.pcusa.org/islandora/object/islandora:112859#page/1/mode/1up; *The American Freedman* (October 1866), 1, 108.

30. Report of James W. Hood in Ashley, *Report of the Superintendent*, 17; Revered O. B. Frothingham cited in *The American Freedman* (October 1866), 108; American Baptist Home Mission Society, *Thirty-First Report of the American Baptist Home Mission Society* (New York: American Baptist Home Mission Rooms, 1863), 33; Burnap cited in Patricia C. Click, *A Time Full of Trial: The Roanoke Island Freedmen's Colony, 1862–1867* (Chapel Hill: University of North Carolina Press, 2001), 90, emphasis in original.

31. Protestant Episcopal Freedman's Commission, *Occasional Paper*, 8; James cited in Browning, "Bringing Light to Our Land," 2. Some teachers shared these views. See "An Appeal from Trent Camp," *The American Freedman* (April 1868), 389.

32. *American Missionary* (December 1868), 275.

33. *American Missionary* (December 1868), 275; Butchart, *Northern Schools*, 39. James McPherson reiterated Butchart's argument and found that Catholic schools were "sustained primarily by local parishes or dioceses" and not established on a large scale. James M. McPherson, *The Abolitionist Legacy: From Reconstruction to the NAACP* (Princeton, NJ: Princeton University Press, 1975), 155. For more on fears surrounding the Roman Catholic Church's participation in education, see for example, Ward McAfee, *Religion, Race, and Reconstruction: The Public School in the Politics of the 1870s* (Albany: State University of New York Press, 1998).

34. *The American Freedman* (March 1868), 378.

35. J. P. Patterson, "The Cultural Reform Project of Northern Teachers of the Freed People, 1862–1870," PhD Diss. (University of Iowa, 2012), 101–15. Eric Foner describes some northern teachers' role in freedpeople's education as "cultural imperialism." See Foner, "Reconstruction Revisited," *Reviews in American History* 10, no. 1 (1982): 82–100. For other interpretations of cultural colonialism, see for example, Angela Onwuachi-Willig, "The Return of the Ring: Welfare Reform's Marriage Cure as the Revival of Post-Bellum Control," *California Law Review* 93, no. 6 (2005): 1647–96; Herbert Schiller, *Communication and Cultural Domination* (New York: International Arts and Sciences Press, 1976); Anne McClintock, *Imperial Leather: Race, Gender and Sexuality in the Colonial Contest* (New York: Routledge, 1995).

36. Janice E. Hale, *Black Children: Their Roots, Culture, and Learning Styles* (Baltimore, MD: John Hopkins University Press, 1982), 154. For more on systems of education within colonized societies, see for example, Patrick Walsh, "Education and the 'Universalist' Idiom of Empire: Irish National School Books in Ireland and Ontario," *History of Education* 37, no. 5 (2008): 645–60. A more detailed examination of the curriculum used in freedpeople's schools is provided in Chapter 5.

37. Butchart, *Northern Schools*, 31; Horace James, *Annual Report of The Superintendent of Negro Affairs in North Carolina, 1864* (Boston: W. F. Brown & Co., 1865), 45.

38. Alexander, "Hostility and Hope ," 113–32, specifically p. 121; Phillips cited in Alexander, "Hostility and Hope," 158; Eric Thomas Duncan, "'Make the Letters Big and Plain':

A History of Black Education in North Carolina," MA Diss. (North Carolina State University, 2011), 43; *Raleigh Sentinel,* March 12, 1866; Alexander, "Hostility and Hope," 122.

39. *Journal of the Constitutional Convention of the State of North Carolina, at Its Session 1868* (Raleigh, NC: Joseph W. Holden, Convention Printer, 1868), 338, 339–41, Documenting the American South, University of North Carolina, Chapel Hill, accessed January 10, 2024, http://docsouth.unc.edu/nc/conv1868/conv1868.html.

40. *Journal of the Constitutional Convention, 1868,* 342–43; Vaughn, *Schools for All,* 62; *Journal of the Constitutional Convention, 1868,* 342–43; *The Daily North Carolinian,* March 7, 1868.

41. *Raleigh Sentinel,* March 7, 1868, emphasis in original.

42. *The Daily Standard,* March 7, 1868 (first, second, and third quotations); Sarah Caroline Thuesen, *Greater Than Equal: African American Struggles for Schools and Citizenship in North Carolina, 1919–1965* (Chapel Hill: University of North Carolina Press, 2013), 6; Adam Fairclough, *A Class of Their Own: Black Teachers in the Segregated South* (Cambridge, MA: Harvard University Press, 2007), 61–62; *Journal of the Constitutional Convention, 1868,* 342 (fourth quotation).

43. Daniel J. Whitener, "The Republican Party and Public Education in North Carolina, 1867–1900," *The North Carolina Historical Review* 37 (July 1960): 382–96. In 1875, an amendment to North Carolina's constitution was made which declared, "And the children of the white race and the children of the colored race shall be taught in separate public schools; but there shall be no discrimination made in favor of, or to the prejudice of, either race." See Thuesen, *Greater Than Equal,* 5–6.

44. *School Laws of North Carolina, As Ratified April 12th, A. D. 1869* (Raleigh, NC: M. S. Littlefield, State Printer and Binder, 1869), 57, Internet Archive, accessed November 18, 2015, https://archive.org/stream/schoollawsofnortnort#page/n5/mode/2up/search/four. For a comprehensive overview of the specific actions undertaken by Ashley and Hood in fulfilling their duties as superintendent and assistant superintendent see for example, Ashley, *Report of the Superintendent,* 2–4.

45. Ashley, *Report of the Superintendent,* 2; *School Laws of North Carolina,* 27, 18.

46. Report of James W. Hood in Ashley, *Report of the Superintendent,* 25; Howard N. Rabinowitz, "Half a Loaf: The Shift from White to Black Teachers in Negro Schools of the Urban South, 1865–1890," in *Race, Ethnicity, and Urbanization: Selected Essays,* ed. Howard Rabinowitz (Columbia: University of Missouri Press, 1994), 90–116; John W. Alvord, *Ninth Semi-Annual Report on Schools for Freedmen, January 1, 1870* (Washington, D.C.: Government Printing Office, 1870), 17, and *Tenth Semi-Annual Report on Schools for Freedmen, January 1, 1870* (Washington, D.C.: Government Printing Office, 1870), 6. Northern aid and missionary societies began withdrawing their support from North Carolinian schools at various times. The Howard School in Fayetteville, for instance, stopped receiving AMA support in 1872. However, in many cases, both secular and denominational schools continued supporting schools in North Carolina until 1875 at least. See Huddle, "To Educate a Race," 120; Butchart et al., The FTP.

47. John L. Bell, "Samuel S. Ashley: Carpetbagger and Educator," *The North Carolina Historical Review* 71, no. 4 (1995): 480–81; Rabinowitz, "Half a Loaf," 111.

48. Rabinowitz, "Half a Loaf," 100, 106; Ronald E. Butchart, *Schooling the Freed People: Teaching, Learning, and the Struggle for Black Freedom* (Chapel Hill: University Of North Carolina Press, 2010), 154; Frenise A. Logan, *The Negro in North Carolina, 1876–1894* (Chapel Hill: University of North Carolina Press, 1964),105–16. For more on the creation of a professional class of Black teachers, see Hilary Green, *Educational Reconstruction: African American Education in the Urban South, 1865–1890* (New York: Fordham University Press, 2016).

49. Bell, "Samuel S. Ashley," 481; Rabinowitz, "Half a Loaf," 111; Whitener, "The Republican Party and Public Education," 389; McIver cited in M. C. S. Nobel, *A History of the Public Schools of North Carolina* (Chapel Hill: University of North Carolina Press, 1930), 355.

50. Diary of Robert Fitzgerald, January 25, 1870 (first and second quotations); Pauli Murray, *Proud Shoes: The Story of an American Family* (New York: Harper & Row, 1956), 224; Diary of Robert Fitzgerald, September 17, 1870.

51. Ashley, *Report of the Superintendent*, 33; Hunter, *Review of Negro Life*, 17; Alvord, *Ninth Semi-Annual Report, January 1, 1870*, 21. L. E. Rice was appointed superintendent of education for the new third congressional district of North Carolina in 1869 which comprised twelve counties. Vogell remained superintendent of education for all other areas of the state.

52. Ashley, *Report of the Superintendent*, 33; Report of James W. Hood in Ashley, *Report of the Superintendent*, 26; *American Missionary* (March 1867), 59; Goldhaber, "Mission Unfulfilled," 205–6.

53. Biddle Memorial Institute, *Fifth Annual Catalogue and Circular of the Biddle Memorial Institute, Charlotte, N.C. 1873–1874* (Pittsburgh, PA: J. M'Millin, Steam Job and Book Printers, 1874), 5, 14; Butchart et al., The FTP; M. W. Williams and George W. Watkins, *Who's Whom Among North Carolina Negro Baptists, With a Brief History of Negro Baptist Organizations* (1940), 353, October 15, 2015, Internet Archive, https://archive.org/stream/whoswhoamongnortoowill#page/n3/mode/2up; Rabinowitz, "Half a Loaf," 569.

54. Diary of Robert Fitzgerald, March 24, 1868; Huddle, "To Educate a Race," 158; Cardozo cited in *American Missionary* (March 1867), 58.

3. A Diverse Group of Educators: Freedpeople's Teachers in North Carolina

1. Ronald E. Butchart et al., "The Freedmen's Teacher Project: Teachers among the Freed People in the U.S. South, 1861-1877," Harvard Dataverse, V3 (2022), https://doi.org/10.7910/DVN/0HBDZD, hereafter cited as The FTP. As outlined in the Introduction, Butchart's database provides biographical data on the men and women who engaged in freedpeople's education from the beginning of the Civil War in 1861 to 1875. Limited data is provided for some teachers during the 1875–1876 school year. Of the 1,419 teachers identified in the database, 705 were Black, 523 were white, and the race of 191 is unknown. 613 of the Black teachers were from the South. Only twenty-nine Black teachers have been identified as former slaves. Although Butchart speculated that most of the southern Black teachers were probably former slaves rather than freeborn, he admitted

that there was no way of confirming this. "It is often not possible to establish the slave or free status of African Americans," he explained. "If they appear in the decennial census, they were most likely free. However, many free blacks avoided census takers, and census takers may have not bothered to enumerate free blacks." Butchart, *Schooling the Freed People: Teaching, Learning, and the Struggle for Black Freedom* (Chapel Hill: University of North Carolina Press, 2010), 201. 371 of the 534 northern teachers were white. Eighty-five were Black, and the race for the remainder is unknown. 210 of the 371 northern white teachers were from New England. A total of seventeen teachers came from countries outside of the US, including the Bahamas, Canada, England, Ireland, and the West Indies. 143 teachers have been positively identified as white southerners. Although this may initially seem like an insignificant number, it is likely that due to the paucity of records which support their work, the actual number of southern white teachers was greater than can definitely be accounted for.

2. Between 1861 and 1876, 720 men taught the freedpeople compared to 666 women. The gender for thirty-three teachers is unknown. Butchart et al., The FTP.

3. Horace James cited in New England Freedmen's Aid Society, *Second Annual Report of the New England Freedmen's Aid Society* (Boston: Office of the Society, 1864), 44, 71; Patricia Click, *A Time Full of Trial: The Roanoke Island Freedmen's Colony, 1862–1867* (Chapel Hill: University of North Carolina Press, 2001), 85, 107, 236. Although Massachusetts native Betsey L. Canedy is usually credited with establishing North Carolina's first missionary-sponsored school in New Bern during the summer of 1863, it is likely that Culling's was the first independently supported school. Depending upon the source, Betsey is sometimes identified as Bessie, or her surname is misspelled as Canady. Her name, as it appears in this book, is how it is identified in the FTP and in Horace James's 1864 report. See Horace James, *Annual Report of the Superintendent of Negro Affairs in North Carolina, 1864* (Boston: W. F. Brown & Co. Printers, 1865), 41.

4. For a comprehensive analysis of education in slavery, see Heather Andrea Williams, *Self-Taught: African American Education in Slavery and Freedom* (Chapel Hill: University of North Carolina Press, 2005); Janet Duitsman Cornelius, *"When I Can Read My Title Clear": Literacy, Slavery, and Religion in the Antebellum South* (Columbia: University of South Carolina Press, 1991). Exact figures relating to the deaths of whites and Blacks during the Stono Rebellion remain unclear, but it is generally thought that it resulted in the deaths of over twenty whites and approximately thirty-five Blacks. See Mark Smith, ed., *Stono: Documenting and Interpreting a Southern Slave Revolt* (Columbia: University of South Carolina Press, 2005), xiii.

5. North Carolina anti-literacy law reprinted in Williams, *Self-Taught*, 206.

6. Eugene D. Genovese, *Roll, Jordan, Roll: The World the Slaves Made* (New York: Vintage Books, 1972), 563; Henry Clapp cited in Judkin Browning, "'Bringing Light to Our Land...When She Was Dark as Night': Northerners, Freedpeople, and Education During Military Occupation in North Carolina, 1862–1865," *American Nineteenth Century History* 1 (2008): 1–17.

7. Union officer cited in Browning "Bringing Light to Our Land," 3; John Sella Martin, "My Slave Life," *Good Words* (May 1867), 317. See also, *American Missionary* (September 1867), 194–95.

8. Hannah Crafts, *A Bondswoman's Narrative*, ed. Henry Louis Gates Jr. (New York: Warner Books, 2002), 4; Adora Rienshaw, in *Federal Writers' Project: Slave Narrative Project, Vol. 11, North Carolina, Part 2, Jackson-Yellerday*, 1936, Manuscript/Mixed Material, accessed January 01, 2024, https://www.loc.gov/resource/mesn.112/?sp=217&st=image; Mary Anngady, in *Federal Writers' Project: Slave Narrative Project, Vol. 11, North Carolina, Part 1, Adams-Hunter*, 1936, Manuscript/Mixed Material, accessed December 12, 2023, https://www.loc.gov/resource/mesn.111/?sp=37&st=image&r=-0.508,0.116,2.015,0.847,0; James Curry, *Narrative of James Curry: A Fugitive Slave*, Documenting the American South, University of North Carolina, Chapel Hill, accessed October 11, 2015, http://docsouth.unc.edu/neh/curry/curry.html.

9. Maxine D. Jones, "They Are My People: Black American Missionary Association Teachers in North Carolina During the Civil War and Reconstruction," *The Negro Educational Review* 36, no. 2 (1985): 79, 82. See also, Robert Harris to George Whipple, August 26, 1864, American Missionary Association archives, Amistad Research Center at Tulane University, New Orleans, Louisiana, accessed at The New York Public Library, hereafter cited as AMAA; North Carolina anti-literacy law reprinted in Williams, *Self-Taught*, 206.

10. Williams, *Self-Taught*, 8 (first quotation); Rienshaw, in *Slave Narrative Project*, accessed January 01, 2024, https://www.loc.gov/resource/mesn.112/?sp=217&st=image; Heather Andrea Williams, "'Clothing Themselves in Intelligence': The Freedpeople, Schooling, and Northern Teachers, 1861–1871," *The Journal of African American History* 87 (2002): 372 (second quotation); American Tract Society, *Fifty-Second Annual Report of the American Tract Society* (Boston: American Tract Society, 1866), 51 (third quotation).

11. John W. Alvord, *First Semi-Annual Report on Schools and Finances of Freedmen, January 1, 1866* (Washington, D.C., 1868; reprint, New York: AMS Press, Inc., 1980), 9.

12. Chaney Hews, in *Federal Writers' Project: Slave Narrative Project, Vol. 11, North Carolina, Part 1, Adams-Hunter*, 1936, Manuscript/Mixed Material, accessed December 12, 2023, https://www.loc.gov/resource/mesn.111/?sp=410&st=image; Sam T. Stewart, in *Federal Writers' Project: Slave Narrative Project, Vol. 11, North Carolina, Part 2, Jackson-Yellerday*, 1936, Manuscript/Mixed Material, accessed January 01, 2024, https://www.loc.gov/resource/mesn.112/?sp=320&st=image.

13. John Haley, preface to *Charles N. Hunter and Race Relations in North Carolina* (Chapel Hill, University of North Carolina Press, 1987); Butchart et al., The FTP; Charles N. Hunter, *Review of Negro Life in North Carolina, With My Recollections* (Raleigh: N.p, n.d), 17, accessed January 18, 2024, Internet Archive, https://archive.org/details/reviewofnegrolifoohunt/mode/2up?view=theater; Hampton Normal and Agricultural Institute, *Twenty-Two Years' Work of the Hampton Normal and Agricultural Institute at Hampton Virginia* (Hampton, VA: Normal School Press, 1893), 76.

14. Some southern states prohibited the education of free Blacks. In 1800, South Carolina revised its anti-literacy law of 1740 to prohibit the education of both slaves and free Blacks. This was because, as Heather A. Williams found, the original statute had proved insufficient at preventing enterprising Blacks from attending or conducting clandestine schools. Williams, *Self-Taught*, 13; Interview with Mrs. Colman Freeman in Benjamin Drew, *A North-Side View of Slavery. The Refugee: Or the Narratives of Fugitive*

Slaves in Canada (Boston: John P. Jewett, 1856), 333, Documenting the American South, University of North Carolina, Chapel Hill, accessed August 20, 2024, https://docsouth.unc.edu/neh/drew/drew.html.

15. *Raleigh Register*, August 25, 1808; John Hope Franklin, *The Free Negro in North Carolina, 1790–1860* (reprint, New York: W. W. Norton, 1971), 18; Karin L. Zipf, *Labor of Innocents: Forced Apprenticeship in North Carolina, 1715–1919* (Baton Rouge: Louisiana State University Press, 2005), 8.

16. United States House of Representatives, *Black Americans in Congress* (Washington, D.C.: US Government Printing Office, 2008), 54; Butchart et al., The FTP.

17. Butchart et al., The FTP.; Richard R. Wright, *Centennial Encyclopedia of the African Methodist Episcopal Church Containing Principally the Biographies of the Men and Women, Both Ministers And Laymen, Whose Labors During a Hundred Years, Helped Make The A.M.E. Church What it is* (Philadelphia: Book Concern of the AME Church, 1916), accessed October 15, 2015, Documenting the American South, University of North Carolina, Chapel Hill, http://docsouth.unc.edu/church/wright/wright.html.

18. Although Mary Jane is usually credited with being the first Black woman to earn a bachelor's degree, Dorothy Sterling found that Grace A. Mapps, a Black woman from Philadelphia, graduated from New York Central College at McGrawville in the 1850s. Dorothy Sterling, ed. *We Are Your Sisters: Black Women in The Nineteenth Century* (New York: W. W. Norton, 1984), 202.

19. Jerry Aldridge and Lois McFadyen Christensen, *Stealing from the Mother: The Marginalization of Women in Education and Psychology from 1900–2010* (New York: Rowman & Littlefield Publishers, 2013), 79; Oberlin College, *Seventy-Fifth Anniversary General Catalogue of Oberlin College, 1833–1908, Including an Account of The Principal Events in The History of The College, With Illustrations of the College Building* (Oberlin, 1909), 745; Butchart et al., The FTP.

20. Butchart et al., The FTP. Lucy Brown to F. A. Fiske, March 21, 1868, Records of the Superintendent of Education, M844:7. Although the FTP identifies the names of teachers who taught beyond 1875, data relating to the school's location and sponsoring organization/affiliation is not provided.

21. A total of seventy-two Black teachers have been identified in the FTP as having served seven or more years. Butchart et al., The FTP. McLean is identified as a native of Greensboro, North Carolina, in the FTP and of Greensboro, South Carolina, in the Hampton Institute publication. Hampton Normal Institute, *Twenty-Two Years' Work*, 40–41; Registers and Reports of Registrars Recommended for the Election of Delegates to the Constitutional Convention, Unbound Reports, Records of the Assistant Commissioner for the State of North Carolina, Bureau of Refugees, Freedmen, and Abandoned Lands, 1865–1870, M843:32; A. W. Pegues, *Our Baptist Ministers and Schools* (Springfield, MA: Willey & Co., 1892), 316–19.

22. A total of forty-three southern Black teachers were not from North Carolina, thirty-six of whom were men. The education level is known for twenty-three of these teachers and the alma mater for a further nineteen. Only two of the eight institutions identified in the FTP for this group of educators were based in the North. Butchart et al., The FTP; Hampton Normal Institute, *Twenty-Two Years' Work*, 27.

23. Of the 613 southern Black teachers, 396 were men, 203 were women, and the gender of fourteen is unknown. Butchart et al., The FTP; National Freedman's Relief Association, *Third Annual Report of the National Freedman's Relief Association* (Washington, D.C.: M'Gill & Witherow, 1865), 7; Esther A. Williams, February 17, 1865, Roanoke Island Freedmen's Colony, accessed September 16, 2015, http://www.roanokefreedmenscolony.com/let11.pdf; Lucy Brown to F. A. Fiske, March 21, 1868, Records of the Superintendent of Education, M844:7; Thavolia Glymph, *Out of the House of Bondage: The Transformation of the Plantation Household* (Cambridge: Cambridge University Press, 2008), 158.

24. Butchart et al., The FTP; Samuel S. Ashley and Horace James cited in Jones, "They Are My People," 82, 87; Ellen Garrison Jackson to S. S. Jocelyn, June 13, 1863, reprinted in Sterling, *We Are Your Sisters*, 264.

25. Jones, "They Are My People," 81; Butchart et al., The FTP; Report of James W. Hood in Samuel S. Ashley, *Report of the Superintendent of Public Instruction of North Carolina for the Year 1869* (Raleigh, NC: MS Littlefield, 1869), 22, Documenting the American South, University of North Carolina, Chapel Hill, accessed November 8, 2015, http://docsouth.unc.edu/nc/report1869/report1869.html.

26. New England Freedmen's Aid Society, *Extracts from Letters of Teachers and Superintendents of the New England Freedmen's Aid Society, Fifth Series* (Boston: John Wilson & Co., 1864), 16; Christopher M. Span, *From Cotton Field to Schoolhouse: African American Education in Mississippi, 1861–1875* (Chapel Hill: University of North Carolina Press, 2009), 41; Diary of Robert Fitzgerald, March 6, 1868; Butchart et al., The FTP.

27. Click, *A Time full of Trial*, 86–86; Butchart et al., The FTP; 1880 United States Census Bureau, Salisbury, Rowan County Country, North Carolina, January 10, 2023, www.ancestry.com. For more on the work of Black soldiers who also served as educators, see Williams, "Clothing Themselves in Intelligence," 372–90.

28. Robert Harris to George Whipple, August 26, 1864, AMAA; Harris to Whipple, June 28, 1865, AMAA; Butchart, *Schooling*, 23; Butchart et al., The FTP. For more information on the Harris brothers, see for example, Earle H. West, "The Harris Brothers: Northern Teachers in the Reconstruction South," *The Journal of Negro Education* 48, no. 2 (1979): 126–38; Mark Andrew Huddle, "To Educate a Race: The Making of the First State Colored Normal School, Fayetteville, North Carolina, 1865–1877," *The North Carolina Historical Review* 74, no. 2 (1997): 135–60.

29. *New Era*, March 17, 1870; Butchart et al., The FTP. A more comprehensive discussion on the location of schools is discussed in Chapter 2.

30. Of the forty northern Black teachers whose educational attainment is known, twelve attended a high school, normal school, academy, or commercial college, twelve attended college, and eleven graduated from college. Jonathan Clarkson Gibbs, a Presbyterian missionary who later became the first Black secretary of state in Florida, engaged in postgraduate work at Princeton University although he did not achieve a degree. Butchart et al., The FTP.

31. Fifteen northern Black teachers attended Lincoln University. Eight attended Philadelphia's Institute for Colored Youth while five attended Oberlin College. Butchart et al., The FTP; Alphonso W. Knight Sr., *Historically Black Colleges and Universities: What You Should Know* (Bloomington, IN: Xlibris, 2014), 65; Pauli Murray, *Proud Shoes:*

The Story of an American Family (New York: Harper & Row, 1956), 177; J. Brent Morris, *Oberlin, Hotbed of Abolitionism: College Community, and the Fight for Freedom and Equality in Antebellum America* (Chapel Hill: University of North Carolina Press, 2014), 4, (quotation, emphasis in original); Report of James W. Hood in Ashley, *Report of the Superintendent*, 22; Butchart, *Schooling*, 18. For more on Oberlin College, see Ronald E. Butchart, "Mission Matters: Mount Holyoke, Oberlin, and the Schooling of Southern Blacks, 1871–1917," *History of Education Quarterly* 42, no. 1 (2002): 1–17.

32. For more on how the antebellum common school system served Black children, see for example, Hilary Moss, *Schooling Citizens: The Struggle for African American Education in Antebellum America* (Chicago: University of Chicago Press, 2009), 13; Butchart, *Schooling*, 20. For more on the educational opportunities available to Black women in the antebellum North, see Kabria Baumgartner, *In Pursuit of Knowledge: Black Women and Educational Activism in Antebellum America* (New York: New York University Press, 2019).

33. Newspaper clippings of Ashmun Institute and Lincoln University, 1853–1874, HBCU Library Alliance, accessed February 26, 2016, http://contentdm.auctr.edu/cdm/compoundobject/collection/lupa/id/2044.

34. A total of nine northern Black men and women worked as teachers before securing a position in the southern missionary field. Between 1865 and 1872, the Cardozos taught the freedpeople in Charleston, South Carolina; Baltimore, Maryland; Elizabeth City, North Carolina; and Vicksburg, Mississippi in that order. In 1866, after the school in Baltimore lost its funding, the Cardozos moved to New York and succeeded in raising funds for the National Freedman's Relief Association to open the school in Elizabeth City. Thomas's brother Francis also worked in schools for the freedpeople but not in North Carolina. Butchart et al., The FTP. Neil Kinghan, "A Brief Moment in the Sun: Francis Cardozo and Reconstruction in South Carolina," PhD diss. (Institute of the Americas, University College London, 2019); Euline W. Brock, "Thomas W. Cardozo: Fallible Black Reconstruction Leader," *The Journal of Southern History* 47 (1981): 183–206 (quotation p. 204).

35. Although O'Hara was elected during the period of "Redemption" which is characterized by restrictive laws that attempted to restore the antebellum southern social order, his political accomplishments were ultimately facilitated by Democratic gerrymandering which created the Black-majority Second Congressional District. Raphael O'Hara Boyd, "Service in the Midst of the Storm: James Edward O'Hara and Reconstruction in North Carolina," *The Journal of Negro History* 86 (Summer 2001): 319–35; Stephen Middleton, *Black Congressmen During Reconstruction: A Documentary Sourcebook* (Westport, CT: Greenwood Press, 2002), 277; Butchart et al., The FTP; W.E.B. Du Bois, *Black Reconstruction in America 1860–1880* (New York: Harcourt Brace, and Co., 1935), 30.

36. Butchart et al., The FTP.

37. Butchart et al., The FTP; *The Freedmen's Record* (January 1865), 3–4. The New England Freedmen's Aid Society's monthly organ, *The Freedmen's Record*, shows that the Beverly branch did not sponsor any teacher for the school year 1865–1866. *The Freedmen's Record* (November 1865), 185.

38. Butchart et al., The FTP; Barbara E. Mattick, *Ministries in Black and White: The Catholic Sisters of St. Augustine, Florida, 1859-1920*, Doctoral diss. (Florida State University, 2008) 76.

39. Letter from Jennie S. Bell, August 22, 1867, register of letters received, August 29, 1867, Records of the Superintendent of Education, M844:8; Butchart et al., The FTP; F. A. Fiske to William Alexander Graham, September 29, 1867, Records of the Superintendent of Education, M844:2. For more on the Peabody Educational Fund, see Huddle, "To Educate a Race," 135–60. According to the FTP, Jennie S. Bell taught the freedpeople in Harker's Island, North Carolina; Fredericksburg, Virginia; Ashland, Virginia; and Beaufort, North Carolina, sometime between 1863 and 1869 or 1870. Depending upon the source, Bell's name is occasionally misspelled. In the *Second Annual Report of the New England Freedmen's Aid Society* (initially known as the Educational Commission for Freedmen), Bell is identified as Jeannie L. Bell. According to this report, Jeannie L. Bell was teaching white students in a school in Harker's Island near Beaufort between 1863 and 1864. This information corroborates what is supplied for Jennie S. Bell in both the FTP database and her letter to F. A. Fiske. In Horace James's 1864 report, Bell is identified as Jennie B. Bell, a self-supporting teacher. However, as self-supporting northern white female teachers were rare, it is likely that he was referring to Jennie S. Bell. Admittedly, the FTP identifies another northern white female teacher named Jennie Bell who worked in what was most likely an independently supported school in Charlotte, North Carolina, sometime between 1869/1870 and 1871. New York is identified as her home state. It is possible there are two entries for Jennie S. Bell in the FTP and that she relocated to Charlotte from her previous post in Beaufort. As Jennie S. Bell was not sponsored by a northern aid or missionary association, her movements are more difficult to track. In the 1890s, Jennie S. Bell was principal of a graded school in Oneida, New York, which may account for some of the misinterpretations. See New England Freedmen's Aid Society, *Second Annual Report of the New England Freedmen's Aid Society* (Boston: Office of the Society, 1864), 71; James, *Annual Report*, 42; Butchart et al., The FTP; State of New York Department of Public Instruction, *Forty-First Annual Report of the State Superintendent for the School Year Ending July 31st, 1894* (Albany, NY: James B. Lyon, State Printer, 1895), 636.

40. James, *Annual Report*, 13; Butchart et al., The FTP; Malcolm McG. Dana, *The Annals of Norwich, New London County, Connecticut in the Great Rebellion of 1861–1865* (Norwich, CT: J. H. Jewett and Company, 1873), 180; Rosalind Gillette Shawe, *Notes for Visiting Nurses and All Those Interested in the Working and Organization of District, Visiting, Or Parochial Nurse Societies* (Philadelphia: P. Blakiston, Son & Co., 1983), 138.

41. The school year 1865–1866 was the northern white teachers' peak year of participation whereby a total of 117 men and women were working in schools throughout the state. As educational opportunities increased in North Carolina, northern white teachers gradually became outnumbered by Black North Carolinians and by 1875, only forty-four white northerners remained in North Carolina's schools for the freedpeople. Most returned home although a minority began working within the new public school system. For the purpose of this study, "young" is considered anyone under the age of thirty. Although the marital status has been established for just 102 women, fifty-four, or over half, remained single until at least 1880. Butchart et al., The FTP.

42. Although teaching was traditionally a male-dominated profession, female teachers significantly outnumbered male teachers on the eve of the Civil War, constituting between 65 and 85 percent of the teachers in the northern states of America. Mary Kelley, *Learning to Stand and Speak: Women, Education, and Public Life in America's Republic* (Chapel Hill: University of North Carolina Press, 2006), 10; Carl Kaestle, *Pillars of the Republic: Common Schools and American Society, 1780–1860* (New York: Hill and Wang, 1983), 62–63, 76. The cult of domesticity also facilitated the participation of women in social reform and missionary work which is possible why there were so many female teachers. For more on the ideology of domesticity, or cult of true womanhood as it is often referred to, see Barbara Welter, "The Cult of True Womanhood: 1820–1860," *American Quarterly* 18 (1966): 151–74. The impact of sentimental literature on anti-slavery movements is discussed more thoroughly in Chapter 4.

43. Kaestle, *Pillars of the Republic*, ix; Alison Prentice and Marjorie R. Theobald, "The Historiography of Women Teachers: A Retrospect," in *Women Who Taught: Perspectives on the History of Women and Teaching*, ed. Prentice and Theobald (Toronto: University of Toronto Press, 1991), 5. See also Kaestle, *Pillars of the Republic*, 122–23; The General Assembly's Committee on Freedmen of the Presbyterian Church, *Second Annual Report of the Committee on Freedmen, from May 1, 1866, to May 1, 1867* (Pittsburgh, PA: 1867), 10; Ashley, *Report of the Superintendent*, 6. See also a similar statement from the Presbyterian Committee on Missions for Freedmen in The General Assembly's Committee on Freedmen of the Presbyterian Church, *Second Annual Report of the Committee on Freedmen*, 10.

44. Mary Kelley, "Reading Women/Women Reading: The Making of Learned Women in Antebellum America," *The Journal of American History* 83, no. 2 (1996): 407.

45. During the early stages of freedpeople's education, teaching credentials were not always necessary although some classroom experience was advantageous. To be considered for a teaching position with the AMA, for instance, one had to possess a missionary spirit, good health, energy, culture and common sense, good personal habits, and "experience in teaching ... especially as *disciplinarians*," in that order. The education is known for sixty-two northern white teachers. Butchart et al., The FTP; Morris, *Oberlin, Hotbed of Abolitionism*, 3.

46. Butchart et al., The FTP; Butchart, "Mission Matters," 1–17. The educational institution is known for sixty-three teachers, sixteen of whom attended Mount Holyoke.

47. *American Missionary* (October 1873), 231.

48. *American Missionary* (October 1873), 232. The work of female missionaries with native communities was often justified on similar grounds. See Barbara Welter, "She Hath Done What She Could: Protestant Women's Missionary Careers in Nineteenth-Century America," *American Quarterly* 30, no. 5 (1978): 630.

49. Butchart et al., The FTP.

50. Butchart et al., The FTP. Although the marital status has been established for just fifty-four of the ninety-five male teachers, thirty-four were married before being appointed to a Black school.

51. Of the eighty-three women who were aged thirty or older when they first entered a Black school, only nineteen taught for one year. Butchart et al., The FTP.

52. Butchart et al., The FTP.

53. At least seventeen of the ninety-five northern white male teachers identified in the North Carolina section of the FTP fought in the Union army. Butchart et al., The FTP. These figures are quite similar to Butchart's findings in 2012 which concluded that almost 30 percent of the northern white male teachers were Union veterans. However, he equally acknowledged that this figure could be larger. "Many [Union veterans] can never be positively identified because of the large number of men with the same names," he concluded. See Butchart, *Schooling,* 85, 223 (n. 19). For more on the life and work of Henry Martin Tupper, see H. L. Morehouse, *H.M. Tupper, D.D.: A Narrative of Twenty-Five Years' Work in the South, 1865–1890* (New York: The American Baptist Home Mission Society, 1890). For more on the life and work of Albion Tourgée, which will be examined in more detail in Chapter 4, see Mark Elliott, *Color-Blind Justice: Albion Tourgée and the Quest for Racial Equality, From the Civil War to Plessy V. Ferguson* (New York: Oxford University Press, 2006), 3, 115.

54. Kelley, *Learning to Stand and Speak*, 4. Thirty-one teachers were ministers before entering the classroom while thirteen others were the sons or daughters of ministers. The occupation is known for the parents of ninety-nine teachers. Farmers accounted for forty-five of the professions while twenty professions were listed as "business professionals." Butchart et al., The FTP.

55. During the 1867–1868 school year, a total of sixty-three southern white teachers were teaching the freedpeople in North Carolina. For comparison, during that same period, a total of 106 white northerners, 130 Black southerners, and thirty-five Black northerners were laboring in North Carolina's schools for the freedpeople. Although the home state has been identified for almost every teacher in the FTP database, the race for 112 is as yet unknown. Butchart et al., The FTP; Howard N. Rabinowitz, "Half A Loaf: The Shift from White to Black Teachers in Negro Schools of The Urban South, 1865–1890," in *Race, Ethnicity, And Urbanization: Selected Essays*, ed. Howard Rabinowitz (Columbia: University of Missouri Press, 1994), 106.

56. Butchart et al., The FTP; Vincent Colyer, *Report of the Services Rendered by the Freed People to the United States Army: In North Carolina in the Spring of 1862, After the Battle of Newbern* (New York: Vincent Colyer, 1864); *Harper's Weekly*, June 21, 1862. Stanley was also criticized for returning an escaped slave to his former owner. See William C. Harris, *With Charity for All: Lincoln and the Restoration of the Union* (Lexington: University Press of Kentucky, 1997), 66; Steven E. Nash, "North Carolina," in *Encyclopedia of the Reconstruction Era: M–Z and Primary Documents, Volume 2*, ed. Richard Zuczek (Westport, CT: Greenwood Press, 2006), 447.

57. Francis King cited in Damon D. Hickey, "Pioneers of the New South: The Baltimore Association and North Carolina Friends in Reconstruction," *Quaker History* 74 (1985): 1–17; Ronald E. Butchart, "Troops to Teachers, 19th Century Style: Civil War Veterans as Teachers of the Freed People," American Educational Research Association (San Francisco, 2013): 1–23. The teachers' motivations will be explored more fully in Chapter 4.

58. Most of the southern white teachers examined in this study were natives of North Carolina. Only four teachers came from outside the state, namely Florida, South

Carolina, and Virginia. Butchart et al., The FTP. It seems as though Sarah Elvira Pearson went by her middle name, Elvira, as documented in numerous Freedmen's Bureau records. Hannibal D. Norton to Jacob F. Chur, November 8, 1867, Records of the Field Offices for the State of North Carolina, Bureau of Freedmen, Refugees, and Abandoned Lands, 1865–1872, M1909:31; Martha C. Avery to Mrs. R. L. Patterson, February 21, 1866, Jones and Patterson Family Papers, 1777–1993, Southern Historical Collection, Wilson Library, University of North Carolina, Chapel Hill; Hannibal D. Norton to Rev. J. B. Smith, December 18, 1876, Records of the Field Offices for the State of North Carolina, Bureau of Freedmen, Refugees, and Abandoned Lands, 1865–1872, M1909:31; See also, Steven E. Nash, *Reconstruction's Ragged Edge: The Politics of Postwar Life in the Southern Mountains* (Chapel Hill: University of North Carolina Press, 2016), 101.

59. Seventy-nine, or over half, of the southern white teachers examined in this study spent one year in the classroom. Welborn taught beyond 1875, most likely within the new public school system, although corresponding data is not available for those years. Mendenhall received five dollars in monthly rental from the Freedmen's Bureau while Welborn received ten dollars. These payments were used to supplement their salary. Butchart et al., The FTP; Records of the Assistant Commissioner for the State of North Carolina, Bureau of Refugees, Freedmen, and Abandoned Lands, 1865–1870, M843:30; Judith Mendenhall to F. A. Fiske, June 19, 1867, Records of the Superintendent of Education, M844:7; Schedule of Schools and Rental Accounts, North Carolina, March 31, 1870, Records of the Education Division of the Bureau of Refugees, Freedmen, and Abandoned Lands, 1865–1871, M803:34.

60. The sponsoring organization has not been identified for eighty-nine, just over 60 percent, of the southern white teaching force. Butchart et al., The FTP; Hickey, "Pioneers of the New South," 7; Presbyterian Church in the United States of America, *Minutes of the General Assembly of the Presbyterian Church in the United States of America* (Philadelphia: Presbyterian Board of Publication, 1866), 443.

61. The religion is known for fifty-seven southern white teachers. Forty-one of these men and women were Quakers. The remaining sixteen southern white teachers whose religion is known were of the Presbyterian or Protestant Episcopal faith. Butchart et al., The FTP; Butchart, *Schooling*, 64; Judith Mendenhall to F. A. Fiske, June 19, 1867, Records of the Superintendent of Education, M844:7; William T. Auman, *Civil War in the North Carolina Quaker Belt: The Confederate Campaign Against Peace Agitators, Deserters, and Draft Dodgers* (Jefferson, NC: McFarland & Company, Inc., 2014), 22; US, Quaker Meeting Records, 1681–1935, (www.ancestry.com) (March 3, 2015); A. H. Jones to H. C. Vogell, December 5, 1868, Records of the Superintendent of Education, M844:10. Although they are not listed in the FTP, A. H. Jones taught in Company Shops (present day Burlington) under the sponsorship of the Friends' Freedmen's Association. Their race has not been identified. See "Names of Teachers Employed in the South by Benevolent Associations, 1865–1872," Records of the Superintendent of Education and of the Division of Education, Family Search, accessed January 19, 2023, https://familysearch.org/ark:/61903/3:1:3Q9M-C9TH-GS6W-M?cc=2427894&wc=3139-16F.

62. Levi Coffin, *Reminiscences of Levi Coffin, the Reputed President of the Underground Railroad*, 2nd ed. (Cincinnati: Robert Clarke & Co., 1880), 630, 646 (quotation).

63. Butchart et al., The FTP; Coffin, *Reminiscences*, 689, 704 (quotation); William P. Vaughn, *Schools for All: The Blacks and Public Education in the South, 1865–1877* (Lexington: University of Kentucky Press, 1974), 4. Irish and British Quakers also funded many of the efforts undertaken by the Baltimore Association and North Carolina Friends to provide educational opportunities for white children in the South, and North Carolina in particular. See Hickey, "Pioneers of the New South," 3–6.

64. Butchart et al., The FTP; Freedmen's Bureau Monthly Rent Receipt, Nathan Hill Papers, David M. Rubenstein Rare Book & Manuscript Library, Duke University, Durham, North Carolina, hereafter cited as Nathan Hill Papers; Asenath H. Reese to Nathan Hill, June 23, 1867, Nathan Hill Papers.

65. Between 1861 and 1875, 105 southern white men taught the freedpeople compared to thirty-eight southern white women. Butchart et al., The FTP; Drew G. Faust, *Mothers of Invention in the American Civil War* (Chapel Hill: University of North Carolina Press, 1996), 82. Butchart, *Schooling*, 56 (quotation). For more on the working habits of southern white women, particularly in the field of education, see Kim Tolley, *Heading South to Teach: The World of Susan Nye Hutchinson, 1815–1845* (Chapel Hill: University of North Carolina Press, 2015), 5.

66. Twenty-three teachers have been positively identified as Confederate veterans. Butchart et al., The FTP; Butchart, *Schooling*, 81, 213 (n. 27); Butchart, "Troops to Teachers."

67. Seventeen teachers have been positively identified as slaveowners or from a slaveholding family. Butchart et al., The FTP; Butchart, *Schooling*, 61; 1860 US Federal Census, Slave Schedules, Davidson County, North Carolina, November 17, 2015, www.ancestry.com; Samuel Alexander cited in Inez M. Parker, *The Biddle-Johnson C. Smith University Story* (Charlotte, NC: Johnson C. Smith University Press, 1975), 5.

4. Answering the Call to Teach: Interrogating Teacher Motivations

1. Jon Butler, *Awash in a Sea of Faith: Christianizing the American People*, (Cambridge, MA: Harvard University Press, 1990), 129; Mary Ann Burnap, January 7, 1865, emphasis in original, Roanoke Island Freedmen's Colony, accessed March 26, 2015, https://www.roanokefreedmenscolony.com/let8.pdf; Robert Harris to Samuel Hunt, March 1, 1866, American Missionary Association Archives, Amistad Research Center at Tulane University, New Orleans, Louisiana, accessed at The New York Public Library, hereafter cited as AMAA; Diary of Robert G. Fitzgerald, March 8, 1868, Fitzgerald Family Papers, 1864–1954, Southern Historical Collection, The Wilson Library, University of North Carolina at Chapel Hill, hereafter cited as Diary of Robert Fitzgerald. For other examples of northern Black and white teachers' efforts to spread religion, see Elizabeth James, December 29, 1864, Roanoke Island Freedmen's Colony, accessed March 26, 2015, http://www.roanokefreedmenscolony.com/let7.pdf; Sallie Daffin to George Whipple, March 30, 1864, cited in James Paul Patterson, "The Cultural Reform Project of Northern Teachers of the Freed People, 1862–1870," PhD diss. (University of Iowa, 2012), 223; Sara Stanley in the *American Missionary* (March 1867), 55–56.

2. Jonathan W. White and Lydia J. Davis, eds., *My Work Among the Freedmen: The Civil War and Reconstruction Letters of Harriet M. Buss* (Charlottesville: University of

Virginia Press, 2021), 148; *The Presbyterian*, August 27, 1902. For more on the proselytizing mission of northern teachers, see for example, Judkin Browning, "Visions of Freedom and Civilization Opening Before Them: African Americans Search for Autonomy During Military Occupation in North Carolina," in *North Carolinians in the Era of The Civil War and Reconstruction,* ed. Paul D. Escott (Chapel Hill: University of North Carolina Press, 2008), 69–100. For more on the Great Awakening, see Joseph Conforti, "The Invention of the Great Awakening, 1795–1842," *Early American Literature* 26, no. 2 (1991): 99–118; John G. West Jr., "Nineteenth-Century America," in *Building a Healthy Culture: Strategies for an American Renaissance,* ed. Don Eberly (Grand Rapids, MI: Eerdmans Publishing, 2001), 181–99.

3. Ella Roper cited in Patricia C. Click, *A Time Full of Trial: The Roanoke Island Freedmen's Colony, 1862–1867* (Chapel Hill: University of North Carolina Press, 2001), 119; J. W. Burghduff in *The American Freedman* (April 1868), 389; Samuel J. Whiton to E. P. Smith, January 1, 1867, AMAA; Robert Harris to Samuel Hunt, March 1, 1866, AMAA.

4. Butler, *Awash in a Sea of Faith;* American Baptist Home Mission Society, preface to *Thirty-Fifth Annual Report of the American Baptist Home Mission Society* (New York: American Baptist Home Mission Rooms, 1867); Presbyterian Committee on Missions for Freedmen, *Annual Report of the Presbyterian Committee of Missions for Freedmen* (Pittsburgh, PA: J. M'Millin, Steam Job and Book Printers, 1871), 8, emphasis in original; Presbyterian Church in the United States of America, *Minutes of the General Assembly of the Presbyterian Church in the United States of America* (Philadelphia: Presbyterian Board of Publication, 1866), 443.

5. State Superintendent's Monthly School Reports, December 1865, Records of the Superintendent of Education, M844:13; *The North Carolina Presbyterian*, August 29, 1866.

6. *The Presbyterian,* August 27, 1902; Ronald E. Butchart, *Schooling the Freed People: Teaching, Learning, and the Struggle for Black Freedom* (Chapel Hill: University of North Carolina Press, 2010), 212; Ronald E. Butchart et al., "The Freedmen's Teacher Project: Teachers Among the Freed People in the U.S. South, 1861–1877," Harvard Dataverse, V3 (2022), https://doi.org/10.7910/DVN/0HBDZD, hereafter cited as The FTP.

7. Henry L. McCrorey, *A Brief History of Johnson C. Smith University* (Charlotte, NC: Johnson C. Smith University, 1935), 2; Walter H. Conser and Robert J. Cain, *Presbyterians in North Carolina: Race, Politics and Religious Identity in Historical Perspective* (Knoxville: University of Tennessee Press, 2010), 136; Testimony of James Sinclair, in United States Congress, *Report of the Joint Committee on Reconstruction, at the First Session Thirty-Ninth Congress* (Washington. D.C.: Government Printing Office, 1866), 174; Biddle Memorial Institute, *First Annual Catalogue and Circular of the Biddle Memorial Institute, Charlotte, N.C. 1867–68* (Pittsburgh, PA: J. M'Millin, 1868), 6; *The Presbyterian* August 27, 1902. The practice of teaching during the summer months continued well beyond the Reconstruction Era. While studying at Fisk University, W. E. B. Du Bois and others like him taught in rural Black schools during the summer vacation. See James D. Anderson, *The Education of Blacks in the South, 1860–1935* (Chapel Hill: University of North Carolina Press, 1988), 282. When the Civil War broke out, the Presbyterian and Episcopalian churches broke into southern and northern factions. See Conser and Cain, *Presbyterians in North Carolina,* 113; Gardiner H. Shattuck, *Episcopalians and Race: Civil War to Civil Rights* (Lexington: University Press of Kentucky, 2000), 9.

8. Willis L. Miller to F. A. Fiske, March 23, 1868, and April 18, 1868, Records of the Superintendent of Education, M844:7; Shattuck, *Episcopalians and Race*, 10; Presbyterian Church in the United States of America, *Minutes of the General Assembly of the Presbyterian Church*, 443; *The Presbyterian* August 27, 1902.

9. Biddle Institute, *First Annual Catalogue*, 5; W. L. Miller to F. A. Fiske, June 9, 1868, Records of the Superintendent of Education, M844:7, emphasis in original. Shaw University had a similar enrolment policy. See White and Davis, *My Work Among the Freedmen*, 122.

10. Charles Phillips to F. A. Fiske, August 20, 1867, Records of the Superintendent of Education, M844:7.

11. Letter from Charles Phillips, May 4, 1868, Charles Phillips Papers, 1807–1868, Southern Historical Collection, Wilson Library, University of North Carolina at Chapel Hill; John V. Orth and Paul Martin Newby, *The North Carolina State Constitution* (Oxford: Oxford University Press, 2013), 24; "The Amendments of 1873 to North Carolina's Constitution of 1868," North Carolina Legislative Library, accessed November 9, 2015, http://www.ncleg.net/library/Documents/Amdts_1873.pdf. Similar situations existed throughout the Reconstruction South. In 1868, the University of South Carolina began admitting Black students who made up the majority by 1873 until the university was resegregated in 1877. See Tyler D. Parry, "The Radical Experiment of South Carolina: The History and Legacy of a Reconstructed University," *Journal of African American History* 105, no. 4 (Fall 2020): 539–66; Robert Greene II and Tyler D. Parry, eds., *Invisible No More: The African American Experience at the University of South Carolina* (Columbia: University of South Carolina Press, 2021).

12. Butchart, *Schooling*, 107; Finney cited in Butchart, *Schooling*, 107; White and Davis, *My Work Among the Freedmen*, 160; Elizabeth and Horace James cited in Click, *A Time Full of Trial*, 82; Butchart et al., The FTP. For more on Elizabeth James's work in the South, see some of her letters which have been reprinted online. Patricia C. Click, "Letters from Roanoke Island Missionary Teachers," The Roanoke Island Freedmen's Colony, 2001, accessed August 22, 2024, https://www.roanokefreedmenscolony.com/docs.html.

13. Joanna P. R. Hanly, *Memoirs of the Late Joseph J. Hanly, M.D.*, 2nd ed. (Philadelphia: Sherman & Co., 1869); Joanna P. R. Hanly to O. O. Howard, March 23, 1869, Letters Received, Entered in Register 4, A – W, Records of the Assistant Commissioner for the State of North Carolina, Bureau of Refugees, Freedmen, and Abandoned Lands, 1865–1870, M843:15, National Museum of African American History and Culture, Smithsonian Institution; Joanna P. R. Hanly to H. C. Vogell, September 2, 1868, Records of the Superintendent of Education, M844:8; Butchart et al., The FTP; Ronald E. Butchart, "Mission Matters: Mount Holyoke, Oberlin, and the Schooling of Southern Blacks, 1871–1917," *History of Education Quarterly* 42, no. 1 (2002): 1–17 (quotation 12).

14. James O. Whittemore to H. C. Vogel, April 10, 1869, Letters Received, Entered in Register 4, A – W, Records of the Assistant Commissioner for the State of North Carolina, Bureau of Refugees, Freedmen, and Abandoned Lands, 1865–1870, M843:15, National Museum of African American History and Culture, Smithsonian Institution; Butchart et al., The FTP; New England Freedmen's Aid Society, *Second Annual Report of the New England Freedmen's Aid Society* (Boston: Office of the Society, 1864), 71.

15. Butchart, "Mission Matters," 10, 12; Letter from Ella Roper, February 12, 1865, Roanoke Island Freedmen's Colony, accessed May 7, 2015, http://roanokefreedmenscolony.com/let10.pdf; Roper cited in Click, *A Time Full of Trial*, 83; Butchart et al., The FTP.

16. Joe M. Richardson, *Christian Reconstruction: The American Missionary Association and Southern Blacks, 1861–1890* (Tuscaloosa: University of Alabama Press, 1986), 4–5; White and Davis, *My Work Among the Freedmen*, 133, 139, 149.

17. Sarah P. Freeman, "Roanoke Island," *The National Freedman* (January 1866), 13–14 (first quotation); Sarah P. Freeman, "Industrial School, Roanoke Island," *The National Freedman* (August 1866), 215–16 (second quotation). Harriet M. Buss offered a similar argument. See White and Davis, *My Work Among the Freedmen*, xxvi.

18. *The Presbyterian*, August 27, 1902.

19. Anderson, *The Education of Blacks in the South*, 6; Teacher in Elizabeth City, *The National Freedman* (May 1866), 142.

20. Robert Harris to H. C. Vogell, November 12, 1868, Records of the Superintendent of Education, M844:10; See also, Diary of Robert Fitzgerald, July 27, 1867; Mary Ann Burnap, January 1865, Roanoke Island Freedmen's Colony, accessed October 4, 2015, http://www.roanokefreedmenscolony.com/let8.pdf; H. S. Beals in the *American Missionary* (January 1868), 6; John Haley, *Charles N. Hunter and Race Relations in North Carolina* (Chapel Hill, University of North Carolina Press, 1987), 28. In 1867, a teacher in Beaufort banned tobacco from their morning school but conceded that "the old people are so addicted to its use it will be long before they give it up." See "Extracts from Teachers' Letters," *American Missionary* (May 1867), 100.

21. *The Freedmen's Record* (June 1865), 94; General Saxton in *The Freedmen's Record* (August 1865), 121; George Newcomb in *The National Freedman* (May 1866), 142. Frances Graves, a Mount Holyoke graduate from Hatfield, Massachusetts, taught the freedpeople for a total of nine years while Annie Merriam from Worcester, Massachusetts, taught for a total of six. Butchart et al., The FTP.

22. Frances E. Bonnell in *The Freedmen's Record* (June 1865), 96; Martha L. Kellogg in *American Missionary* (March 1863), 64–65. Kellogg spent a total of seven years in the South, one of which was in Wilmington, North Carolina. Butchart et al., The FTP. See also a remark by General Armstrong, a Freedmen's Bureau officer, regarding the ability of Black students in North Carolina in *American Missionary* (September 1867), 194.

23. Butchart, *Schooling*, 116; White and Davis, *My Work Among the Freedmen*, 144.

24. Sarah P. Freeman, July 26, 1866, Roanoke Island Freedmen's Colony, accessed October 4, 2015, http://www.roanokefreedmenscolony.com/let21.pdf; *Harper's Weekly*, February 10, 1866; Click, *A Time Full of Trial*, 120; Letter from Horace James in New England Freedmen's Aid Society, *Second Annual Report*, 73. Instilling the freedpeople with the "habits of punctuality," a hallmark of nineteenth century industrialization, was also considered an important aspect of southern Black schooling and Freedmen's Bureau Superintendent of Education in North Carolina F. A. Fiske, regularly encouraged teachers to keep "*stated* hours, both for the commencement and close of" daily school. F. A. Fiske to A. M. (?) Hall, July 29, 1868, Records of the Superintendent of Education, M844:2, emphasis in original.

25. New England Freedmen's Aid Society, *Second Annual Report*, 3; *The Freedmen's Record* (June 1867), 98; Protestant Episcopal Freedman's Commission, *Occasional Paper*,

January 1866 (Boston: Geo. C. Rand & Avery, 1866), 6, Internet Archive, accessed August 30, 2024. https://archive.org/details/protestantepiscoooepis; National Freedman's Relief Association, *National Freedman's Relief Association*, 1863, Houghton Library, Harvard University, Cambridge, MA., accessed August 27, 2024, https://nrs.lib.harvard.edu/urn-3:fhcl.hough:100511357?n=3.

26. *The Freedmen's Record* (July 1865), 108; *The Freedmen's Record* (June 1867), 98–99.

27. Sarah P. Freeman, January 3, 1866, Roanoke Island Freedmen's Colony, accessed August 23, 2022, https://www.roanokefreedmenscolony.com/let19.pdf.

28. Testimony of Lieutenant George O. Sanderson, in United States Congress, *Report of the Joint Committee on Reconstruction*, 180–81.

29. *The Freedman* (December 1865), emphasis in original. In the end, formerly enslaved men and women refused to continue laboring under a system that resembled slavery, thus giving rise to the sharecropping system. See for example, Bart Landry, *Black Working Wives: Pioneers of the American Family Revolution* (Berkeley: University of California Press, 2000), 43–44.

30. Letter from O. O. Howard reprinted in *The Freedman's Record* (August 1865), 130; Oliver O. Howard, *Autobiography of Oliver Otis Howard, Major General, United States Army: Volume 2* (New York: Baker & Taylor, 1908), 222–23, 227, 247. Other practical reasons compelled freedpeople to return to the plantation and in 1866 an AFUC teacher in Elizabeth City admitted that due to the prevalence of smallpox, efforts were being made to remove the freedpeople to the plantations where the disease had yet to surface. *The National Freedman* (May 1866), 142.

31. Samuel S. Ashley to N. A. McLean, February 7, 1866, American Missionary Association archives, Amistad Research Center, Tulane University, New Orleans, Louisiana, accessed at The New York Public Library, hereafter cited as AMAA.

32. Butchart et al., The FTP; *Journal of the Constitutional Convention of the State of North Carolina at Its Session 1868* (Raleigh, NC, 1868), 338–41, Documenting the American South, University of North Carolina, Chapel Hill, accessed November 9, 2014, http://docsouth.unc.edu/nc/conv1868/conv1868.html; *School Laws of North Carolina, as Ratified April 12th, A. D. 1869* (Raleigh, NC: M. S. Littlefield, State Printer and Binder, 1869), 5, Internet Archive, accessed November 18, 2015, https://archive.org/stream/schoollawsofnortnort#page/n5/mode/2up/search/four; John L. Bell, "Samuel S. Ashley, Carpetbagger and Educator," *The North Carolina Historical Review* 71, no. 4 (1995): 456–83; J. G. de Roulhac Hamilton, *History of North Carolina: North Carolina Since 1860* (Chicago: Lewis Publishing Co., 1919), 352.

33. Daniel J. Whitener, "The Republican Party and Public Education in North Carolina, 1867–1900," *The North Carolina Historical Review* 37, no. 3 (1960): 382–96; Samuel S. Ashley to George Whipple, November 23, 1870, AMAA; Bell, "Samuel S. Ashley," 481–84.

34. F. A. Fiske to Ms. Stevenson, September 15, 1866, Records of the Superintendent of Education, M844:1 (first quotation); Samuel S. Ashley to F. A. Fiske, May 5, 1866, Records of the Superintendent of Education, M844:10; John W. Alvord, *First Semi-Annual Report on Schools for Freedmen, January 1, 1866* (Washington, Government Printing Office, 1868), 13; *The Fayetteville News*, September 11, 1866. For more on the response of whites in Fayetteville to freedpeople's education, see Mark Andrew Huddle, "To Educate

a Race: The Making of the First State Colored Normal School, Fayetteville, North Carolina, 1865–1877," *The North Carolina Historical Review* 74, no. 2 (1997): 135–60.

35. Letter from W. A. Graham, Freedmen's Convention of North Carolina, *Minutes of the Freedmen's Convention Held in the City of Raleigh on the 2nd, 3rd, 4th and 5th of October, 1866* (Raleigh, NC: Standard Book and Job Office, 1866), 10, Documenting the American South, University of North Carolina, Chapel Hill, accessed November 11, 2022, http://docsouth.unc.edu/nc/freedmen/freedmen.html. For more on changing attitudes toward freedpeople's education in the southern white community, see Roberta Sue Alexander, *North Carolina Faces the Freedmen: Race Relations During Presidential Reconstruction* (Durham, NC: Duke University Press, 1985), 153.

36. F. A. Fiske to A. Thurston, November 2, 1866, Records of the Superintendent of Education, M844:1; F. A. Fiske to W. H. Worden, October 12, 1866, Records of the Superintendent of Education, M844:1.

37. Fiske to Worden, November 2, 1866, Records of the Superintendent of Education, M844:1; Fiske to Worden, November 28, 1866 and November 14, 1866, Records of the Superintendent of Education, M844:1; Endorsements Sent, Vol. 1 (15), Records of the Assistant Commissioner for the State of North Carolina, Bureau of Refugees, Freedmen and Abandoned Lands, 1865–1870, M843:3; Butchart et al., The FTP.

38. Martha C. Avery to Mrs. R. L. Patterson, February 21, 1866, Jones and Patterson Family Papers, 1777–1993, Southern Historical Collection, Wilson Library, University of North Carolina, Chapel Hill; F. A. Fiske to Jacob F. Chur, October 22, 1866, Records of the Superintendent of Education, M844:1.

39. Sallie Daffin to Samuel Hunt cited in Maxine D. Jones, "They Are My People: Black American Missionary Association Teachers in North Carolina During the Civil War and Reconstruction," *The Negro Educational Review* 36, no. 2 (1985): 9.

40. Butchart et al., The FTP; Sallie Daffin to George Whipple cited in Christina Lenore Davis, "The Collective Identities of Women Teachers in Black Schools in the Post-Bellum South," PhD diss. (The University of Georgia, 2016), 100. Daffin attended the Institute for Colored Youth in Philadelphia.

41. Sara G. Stanley to George Whipple, March 4, 1864, AMAA; Judith Weisenfeld, "'Who is Sufficient for These Things': Sara G. Stanley and the American Missionary Association, 1864–1868," *Church History* 60, no. 4 (1991): 493–507; Butchart et al., The FTP.

42. John Richard Dennett, *The South as It Is: 1865–1866* (New York: Viking Press, 1965), 152–53; Harris cited in Howard N. Rabinowitz, "Half A Loaf: The Shift from White to Black Teachers in Negro Schools of the Urban South, 1865–1890," in *Race, Ethnicity, And Urbanization: Selected Essays*, ed. Howard Rabinowitz (Columbia: University of Missouri Press, 1994), 579.

43. Robert Harris to George Whipple, August 24, 1864, AMAA; Mary A. Best to W. W. Holden, February 2, 1869, Records of the Superintendent of Education, M844:11; Robert P. Martin to F. A. Fiske, September 30, 1867, Records of the Superintendent of Education, M844:7.

44. Butchart et al., The FTP; Mark Elliott, *Color-Blind Justice: Albion Tourgée and the Quest for Racial Equality, From the Civil War to Plessy V. Ferguson* (New York: Oxford University Press, 2006), 3, 115.

45. Albion W. Tourgée to Nathan H. Hill, July 17, 1867, Nathan Hill Papers, David M. Rubenstein Rare Book & Manuscript Library, Duke University, Durham, North Carolina, hereafter cited as Nathan Hill Papers; Elliott, *Color-Blind Justice*, 145, 4.

46. Albion Tourgée to A. H. Cole, October 11, 1884, Albion W. Tourgée (1838–1905) Papers, North Carolina State Archives, Raleigh, North Carolina.

47. Albion Tourgée to A. H. Cole, October 11, 1884, Albion W. Tourgée (1838–1905) Papers, North Carolina State Archives, Raleigh, North Carolina. See also, Gregory P. Downs, "Anarchy at the Circumference: Statelessness and the Reconstruction of Authority in Emancipation North Carolina," in *After Slavery: Race, Labor, and Citizenship in the Reconstruction South*, ed. Bruce E. Baker and Brian Kelly (Gainesville: University Press of Florida, 2013), 116. Albion W. Tourgée, *A Fool's Errand: By One of the Fools* (New York: Fords, Howard & Hulbert, 1879), Documenting the American South, University of North Carolina, Chapel Hill, accessed April 12, 2015, http://docsouth.unc.edu/church/tourgee/tourgee.html.

48. The Freedmen's Teacher Project (FTP) identifies seventeen northern white teachers who were prewar abolitionists while there is evidence to suggest that a further eight were also active in the movement. Such teachers include Elizabeth James, Horace James, Martha Kellogg, and Samuel Ashley, all of whom are mentioned at various points throughout this book. Butchart et al., The FTP; *The Friend* (August 1866), 390; *The Friend* (April 1868), 253.

49. Martha Kellogg in *American Missionary* (June 1868), 136; Butchart et al., The FTP.

50. Horace James, *Annual Report of the Superintendent of Negro Affairs in North Carolina, 1864* (Boston: W. F. Brown & Co. Printers, 1865), 45.

51. Karen Sanchez-Eppler, "Bodily Bonds: The Intersecting Rhetorics of Feminism and Abolition," in *The Culture of Sentiment: Race, Gender, and Sentimentality in Nineteenth-Century America*, ed. Shirley S. Samuels (New York: Oxford University Press, 1992), 92–114; Harryette Mullen, "Runaway Tongue: Resistant Orality in *Uncle Tom's Cabin, Our Nig, Incidents in the Life of a Slave Girl*, and *Beloved*," in Samuels, *The Culture of Sentiment*, 244–64.

52. Sanchez-Eppler, "Bodily Bonds," 98; Carolyn L. Karcher, "Rape, Murder, and Revenge in 'Slavery's Pleasant Homes': Lydia Marie Child's Antislavery Fiction and the Limits of the Genre," in Samuels, *The Culture of Sentiment*, 58–72. Bruce Dorsey argued that female abolitionists helped to develop a gendered discourse of race and slavery that was rooted in the "sentimentalized portrayal of slaves as feminized." Bruce Dorsey, *Reforming Men and Women: Gender in the Antebellum City* (Ithaca. NY: Cornell University Press, 2002), 140; Christopher M. Span, *From Cotton Field to Schoolhouse: African American Education in Mississippi, 1862–1875* (Chapel Hill: University of North Carolina Press, 2009), 40.

53. Span, *From Cotton Field to Schoolhouse*, 103; Butchart et al., The FTP; Edward Payson Hall to F. A. Fiske, August 7, 1867, Records of the Superintendent of Education, M844:7; Butchart, *Schooling*, 64.

54. Mary Bowers to F. A. Fiske, March 21, 1866, Records of the Superintendent of Education, M844:10, emphasis in original.

55. Jordan Swain to F. A. Fiske, November 29, 1866, Records of the Superintendent of Education, M844:10; Bowers to Fiske, April 4, 1866, Records of the Superintendent of Education, M844:10.

56. Jordan Swain to F. A. Fiske, November 29, 1866, Records of the Superintendent of Education, M844:10.

57. Testimony of James Sinclair, in United States Congress, *Report of the Joint Committee on Reconstruction*, 174. In his testimony to the Joint Committee on Reconstruction, a congressional committee set up in 1865 to inquire into the condition of the former Confederate states, Sinclair claimed that he did not engage in the war willingly. Married to a slaveholding woman of prominent social standing, Sinclair inadvertently blackened his wife's name and reputation on the eve of the Civil War by advising his congregants to ignore the talk of secession that was currently underway in neighboring South Carolina. "That sermon made a great noise in the church," confessed Sinclair, "and I lost my church in consequence of what was called my abolition sermon." Thus, Sinclair entered the war to protect his wife's reputation as well as his life. After the Civil War, Sinclair severed his ties with the Confederacy and served as an agent for the Freedmen's Bureau.

58. Butchart et al., The FTP. Clumfort's Creek, as described in James's *Annual Report*, was a small stream in Carteret County. The surrounding area was home to a large population of Black men and women who had been free before the war. Because of this, it was deemed "a good position for a school." James, *Annual Report of the Superintendent*, 20.

59. Admittedly, this was not Ferebee's first experience of school. During the Civil War, twelve-year-old Ferebee attended a private school in New Bern that was taught by a Black minister and ex-slave. London R. Ferebee, *A Brief History of the Slave Life of Rev. L. R. Ferebee, and the Battles of Life, and Four Years of His Ministerial Life* (Raleigh, NC: Edwards, Broughton & Co., 1882), Documenting the American South, University of North Carolina, Chapel Hill, accessed October 22, 2015, http://docsouth.unc.edu/fpn/ferebee/ferebee.html; Butchart et al., The FTP.

60. Charles N. Hunter, *Review of Negro Life in North Carolina, With My Recollections* (Raleigh, NC: N.p, n.d), 17, Internet Archive, accessed January 18, 2024, https://archive.org/details/reviewofnegrolifoohunt/mode/2up?view=theater; Haley, *Charles N. Hunter*, 15, 34; United States House of Representatives, *Black Americans in Congress* (Washington, D.C.: Government Printing Office, 2008), 54. James Henry Harris was more tolerable to the southern white community in Fayetteville because he was southern. See Huddle, "To Educate a Race." For a more comprehensive analysis of Black accomodationism, see C. Vann Woodward, *The Strange Career of Jim Crow*, reprint (New York: Oxford University Press, 2002), 28. Although Revels was born free in North Carolina, he represented Mississippi in the Senate in 1870 and 1871.

61. Hunter to the editor, newspaper clipping, March 17, 1877, scrapbook, various dates, Hunter Papers.

62. Fiske cited in *The Raleigh Register*, October 25, 1867; Diary of Robert Fitzgerald, July 10, 1867.

63. William Birnie to H. C. Vogell, November 30, 1868, Records of the Superintendent of Education, M844:10; Butchart et al., The FTP; Ronald E. Butchart, "Wealth Database" (2013), used by permission.

64. Butchart et al., The FTP; Butchart, *Schooling*, 62.

65. Butchart et al., The FTP; Butchart, "Wealth Database"; US Civil War Soldier Records and Profiles, 1861–1865, October 17, 2015; Noah Hancock Pension Application, June 3, 1885, North Carolina Digital Collections, accessed August 25, 2022, https://digital.ncdcr.gov/documents/mirador/321702.

66. M. A. Chambers to E. C. [H. C.] Vogell, July 26, 1869, Records of the Superintendent of Education, M844:11; Mary A. Chambers to H. C. Vogell, August 27, 1869, Records of the Superintendent of Education, M844:11; Butchart et al., The FTP; William Preston Vaughn, *Schools for All: Blacks and Public Education in the South* (Lexington: The University Press of Kentucky, 1974), 25.

67. William R. Ashworth to Nathan Hill, August 13, 1867, Nathan Hill Papers, David M. Rubenstein Rare Book & Manuscript Library, Duke University, Durham, North Carolina, hereafter cited as Nathan Hill Papers; Registers of Letters Received, Vol. 2 (3), Records of the Assistant Commissioner for the State of North Carolina, Bureau of Refugees, Freedmen and Abandoned Lands, 1865–1870, M843:5; Endorsements Sent, Vol. 2 (18), Records of the Assistant Commissioner for the State of North Carolina, Bureau of Refugees, Freedmen and Abandoned Lands, 1865–1870, M843:4; North Carolina Death Certificates, 1909–1976, www.ancestry.com; Butchart et al., The FTP; *Randolph County Business Directory* (Raleigh, NC: Levi Branson, 1894), 89; 1880 United States Census Bureau, Cedar Grove Township, Randolph Country, North Carolina, November 10, 2015, www.ancestry.com.

68. Elliott, *Color-Blind Justice*, 116; Joel Ashworth to Nathan Hill, April 15, 1867, Nathan Hill Papers; H. C. Talley to Nathan Hill, August 1867, Nathan Hill Papers.

5. The Textbooks Used in North Carolina's Schools for the Freedpeople

1. Christopher M. Span, *From Cotton Field to Schoolhouse: African American Education in Mississippi, 1862–1875* (Chapel Hill: University of North Carolina Press, 2009), 65; Mark Andrew Huddle, "To Educate a Race: The Making of the First State Colored Normal School, Fayetteville, North Carolina, 1865–1877," *The North Carolina Historical Review* 74, no. 2 (1997): 135–60; Heather Andrea Williams, *Self-Taught: African American Education in Slavery and Freedom* (Chapel Hill: University of North Carolina Press, 2005), 130; Christine E. Sleeter and Carl A. Grant, "Race, Class, Gender, and Disability in Current Textbooks," in *The Textbook as Discourse: Sociocultural Dimensions of American Schoolbooks*, ed. Annis N. Shaver, Eugene F. Provenzo Jr., and Manuel Bello (New York: Routledge, 2011), 203.

2. A more comprehensive overview of the aims of the common school movement is provided in Chapter 3. For analyses of nineteenth-century common school textbooks, see for example, David E. Tanner, "The Textbook as a Political Instrument," *The High School Journal* 72 (1989): 182–87; AnneMarie Brosnan, "Representations of Race and Racism in the Textbooks Used in Southern Black Schools During the American Civil War

and Reconstruction Era, 1861–1876," *Paedagogica Historica* 52 (2016): 718–33; Ruth M. Elson, *Guardians of Tradition: American Schoolbooks of the Nineteenth Century* (Lincoln: University of Nebraska Press, 1964), 1; Noah Webster, *The American Spelling Book: Containing the Rudiments of the English Language, for the Use of Schools in the United States* (Brattleboro, VT: Holbrook and Fessenden, 1820), vi.

3. See for example, George Dixon to Nathan Hill, January 1867, Nathan H. Hill papers, David M. Rubenstein Rare Book & Manuscript Library, Duke University, North Carolina; Letter from B. L. Canedy, July 27, 1863, in *Report of the Executive Board of the Friends' Association of Philadelphia and the Vicinity for the Relief of Colored Freedmen*, Friends' Freedmen's Association (Philadelphia: C. Sherman, Son & Co. Printers, 1864), 23; H. C. Vogell's report in John W. Alvord, *Ninth Semi-Annual Report on Schools for Freedmen, January 1, 1870* (Washington: Government Printing Office, 1870), 18. See also H. C. Vogell's report in John W. Alvord, *Tenth Semi-Annual Report on Schools for Freedmen, July 1, 1870* (Washington: Government Printing Office, 1870), 16. Depending upon the source, Betsey is sometimes identified as Bessie or her surname is misspelled as Canady. Her name, as it appears in this book, is how it is identified in the FTP and in Horace James's 1864 report. See Horace James, *Annual Report of the Superintendent of Negro Affairs in North Carolina, 1864* (Boston: W. F. Brown & Co. Printers, 1865), 41.

4. Edgar W. Knight, *Public School Education in North Carolina* (Boston: Houghton Mifflin, c. 1916), 278; Ronald E. Butchart, *Schooling the Freed People: Teaching, Learning, and the Struggle for Black Freedom* (Chapel Hill: University of North Carolina Press, 2010), 126.

5. American Baptist Publication Society, *Forty-First Annual Report of the American Baptist Publication Society, 1865* (Philadelphia: American Baptist Publication Society, 1865), 24. A special thanks is owed to Ashlee Mason-Cleary for sharing her unpublished research with me on the topic of these textbooks, many which she uncovered for the first time and which have not been examined heretofore.

6. Robert C. Morris reprinted a total of ten freedmen's textbooks in a series of six volumes. See Robert C. Morris, ed., *Freedmen's Schools and Textbooks*, vols. 1–6 (New York: AMS Press, 1980); Williams, *Self-Taught*; Ashley M. Swarthout, "Textbooks, Teachers, and Compromise: The Political Work of Freedmen Education," MA diss. (The University of Texas at El Paso, 2013); Brosnan, "Representations of Race and Racism."

7. *The American Freedman* (May 1866), 32, emphasis in original.

8. American Tract Society, *Fifty-Second Annual Report of the American Tract Society* (Boston, 1866), 17; *The Freedman* (March 1867; reprint, New York, 1980), 3; *The Freedman* (August 1868; reprint, New York, 1980), 4. See also, *The Freedman's Second Reader*, 52–55, 57; American Tract Society, *Fifty-Second Annual Report*, 17. For lessons on temperance in northern common school textbooks, see for example, Marcius Willson, *The Third Reader of the School and Family Series* (New York: Harper & Brothers, 1860), 61; Webster, *The American Spelling Book*, 154; Marcius Willson, *The Second Reader of the School and Family Series* (New York: Harper & Brothers, 1860), 91–92, 120–21. Paternalistic lessons were also included in tracts intended for members of the poor white population. See for example, New England Society, *Tracts Published by the New England Society* (Andover, MA: Flagg and Gould, 1814); *American Missionary* (April 1867), 82, emphasis in original.

9. Laura F. Edwards, *Gendered Strife and Confusion: The Political Culture of Reconstruction* (Champaign: University of Illinois Press, 1997), 31; Katherine M. Franke, "Becoming a Citizen: Reconstruction Era Regulation of African American Marriages," *Yale Journal of Law & The Humanities* 1, no. 2 (1999): 251–309.

10. Franke, "Becoming a Citizen," 262; Clinton B. Fisk, *Plain Counsels to Freedmen in Sixteen Brief Lectures* (Boston: American Tract Society, 1866), 31. J. B. Waterbury issued a similar warning in *Friendly Counsels for Freedmen* (New York: American Tract Society, 1864; reprint, New York, 1980), 14–15.

11. Stuart M. Taylor, "Marriage Rules," in United States Congress, *Executive Documents of the House of Representatives During the First Session of the Thirty-Ninth Congress, 1865–1866* (Washington: Government Printing Office, 1866), 109; Franke, "Becoming a Citizen," 278.

12. Angela Onwuachi-Willig, "The Return of the Ring: Welfare Reform's Marriage Cure as the Revival of Post-Bellum Control," *California Law Review* 93 (2005): 1647–96; Edwards, *Gendered Strife and Confusion*, 35, 37; Franke, "Becoming a Citizen," 262, 251, 302; Fisk, *Plain Counsels*, 32; Waterbury, *Friendly Counsels for Freedmen*, 20 (quotation), 26.

13. Fisk, *Plain Counsels*, 26–27. See a similar lesson in Waterbury, *Friendly Counsels for Freedmen*, 14–15. For analyses on the perception of Black women as seducers, see for example, Shirley J. Yee, *Black Women Abolitionists: A Study in Activism, 1828–1860* (Knoxville: University of Tennessee Press, 1992), 42–43; Franke, "Becoming a Citizen," 259; Deborah Gray White, *Ar'n't I a Woman? Female Saves in the Plantation South*, 2nd ed. (New York: W. W. Norton, 1999), 27–61.

14. In its original format, many of the words in this lesson were hyphenated to support beginning readers. *The Freedman* (December 1865; reprint, New York, 1980), 46. For lessons on industry in northern common school textbooks, see for example, Webster, *The American Spelling Book*, 64, 166.

15. Span, *From Cotton Field to Schoolhouse*, 43; Fisk, *Plain Counsels*, 41–42; Waterbury, *Friendly Counsels for Freedmen*, 5. See also Helen E. Brown, *John Freeman and His Family* (Boston: American Tract Society, 1862; reprint, New York, 1980), 7; Fisk, *Plain Counsels*, 12; Donald Spivey, *Schooling for The New Slavery: Black Industrial Education, 1868–1915* (Westport, CT: Greenwood Press, 1978), 6.

16. *The Freedman* (February 1866; reprint, New York, 1980), 2; Willson, *The Third Reader*, 68; Willson, *The Second Reader*, 126; *The Freedman* (March 1867; reprint, New York, 1980), 2; Samuel Mitchell, *A System of Modern Geography, Comprising a Description of the World, and Its Five Great Divisions, American, Europe, Asia, Africa, and Oceania with Their Several Empires, Kingdoms, States, Territories, etc.*, 2nd Edition (Philadelphia: Thomas Cowperthwait & Co., 1848), 48. For examples of religious content in northern textbooks, see for example, Willson, *The Third Reader*, iv, 60; William H. McGuffey, *McGuffey's New First Eclectic Reader for Little Children* (Cincinnati, OH: W. B. Smith & Co., 1857), 29, 56; Webster, *The American Spelling Book*, 62. Textbooks from the revolutionary period were decidedly more religious than the textbooks used in antebellum common schools, namely because many of these textbooks explicitly taught religious catechism. See for example, *The New England Primer* (Boston: Edward Draper, 1777), Internet Archive, accessed August 22, 2024, https://archive.org/details/newenglandprimer00west/page/n9/mode/2up.

17. Brown, *John Freeman and His Family*, 71; Barbara Welter, "The Cult of True Womanhood: 1820–1860," *American Quarterly* 18, no. 1 (1966): 151–74.

18. *The Freedman's Spelling Book* (Boston: The American Tract Society, 1866; Reprint. New York: 1980), 22; Isaac W. Brinkerhoff, *Advice to Freedmen* (New York: American Tract Society, 1864), 7; For studies of Black Union soldiers, see for example, John David Smith, ed., *Black Soldiers in Blue: African American Troops in the Civil War Era* (Chapel Hill: University of North Carolina Press, 2002); Hondon B. Hargrove, *Black Union Soldiers in the Civil War* (Jefferson, NC: McFarland & Company, 1988).

19. Samuel Augustus Mitchell, *An Easy Introduction to the Study of Geography: Designed for the Instruction of Children in Schools and Families* (Philadelphia: Thomas Cowperthwait & Co., 1845), 144; Francis McNally, *An Improved System of Geography: Designed for Schools, Academies and Seminaries* (New York: A. S. Barnes & Co., 1859), 83; Mitchell, *An Easy Introduction to the Study of Geography*, 137. Native Americans were also heavily stereotyped by textbook authors and producers. See for example, James Monteith, *First Lessons in Geography, Or, Introduction to "Youth's Manual of Geography"* (New York: A. S. Barnes & Co., 1856), accessed September 17, 2015, http://www.gutenberg.org/files/11722/11722-h/11722-h.htm.

20. Mitchell, *A System of Modern Geography*, 41, 2.

21. Ken Montgomery, "Banal Race-Thinking: Ties of Blood, Canadian History Textbooks, and Ethnic Nationalism," *Paedagogica Historica: International Journal of the History of Education* 41, no. 3 (2005): 313–36; Mitchell, *An Easy Introduction to the Study of Geography*, 37; Mitchell, *An Easy Introduction to the Study of Geography*, 138–39. A similar lesson on Liberia can be found in *The Freedman's Third Reader*, 227. New Englanders, in particular, achieved very high praise, which is unsurprising considering Mitchell, like many other textbook authors of the era, was from that region of the country. See Mitchell, *An Easy Introduction to the Study of Geography*, 43; Elson, *Guardians of Tradition*, 7.

22. Fisk, *Plain Counsels*, 7–8 (first quotation), 14 (second quotation); Lydia Marie Child, *The Freedmen's Book* (Boston: Ticknor & Fields, 1865), 110, 271 (third quotation), 259–60 (fourth quotation). See a similar lesson in Brown, *John Freeman and His Family*, 18.

23. Child, preface to *The Freedmen's Book*; Jessica Enoch, *Refiguring Rhetorical Education: Women Teaching African American, Native American, and Chicano/a Students, 1865–1911* (Carbondale: Southern Illinois University Press, 2008), 67, 52. For an example of a lesson in Child's book which contradicted the more conservative lessons in the text, see Frederick Douglass's contribution "A Pertinent Question," 94.

24. Provenzo, Shaver, and Bello, introduction to *The Text as Discourse*, 1; Morris, introduction to Robert C. Morris, ed. *Freedmen's Schools and Textbooks. Vols. 1–6* (New York: AMS Press, 1980), Volume 4.; *The Freedman* (August 1864; reprint, New York, 1980), 30.

25. Butchart, *Schooling*, 126; Patricia Young, "Roads to Travel: A Historical Look at The Freedman's Torchlight–An African American Contribution to 19th Century Information Technologies," *Journal of Black Studies* 31, no. 5 (2001): 671–98; *The Freedman's Torchlight* (December 1866), 1.

26. *The Freedman's Torchlight* (December 1866), 1.

27. Brown, *John Freeman and His Family*, 65; Miranda Branson Moore, *The First Dixie Reader: Designed to Follow the Dixie Primer* (Raleigh, NC: Branson, Farrar, & Co.,

1863), 14, Documenting the American South, University of North Carolina, Chapel Hill, accessed September 15, 2015, http://docsouth.unc.edu/imls/moore2/moore.html. Other textbooks penned by Moore include *The Dixie Primer, for the Little Folks, The First Dixie Reader: Designed to Follow the Dixie Primer,* and *The Geographical Reader for Dixie Children.* The image of the "happy slave" in both elementary and high school textbooks persisted until the twentieth century. See James A. Banks, "The Lives and Values of Researchers: Implications for Educating Citizens in a Multicultural Society," *Educational Researcher* 27, no. 7 (1998): 4–17. For references to slavery in northern textbooks, see for example, Monteith, *First Lessons in Geography;* Mitchell, *An Easy Introduction to the Study of Geography,* 48, 148, 135; *The Freedman's Third Reader,* 227.

28. James D. Anderson, "Secondary School History Textbooks and the Treatment of Black History," in *The State of Afro-American History: Past, Present, and Future,* ed. D. C. Hine (Baton Rouge: Louisiana State University Press, 1986), 253; Williams, *Self-Taught,* 137; Jesus Garcia, "The Changing Image of Ethnic Groups in Textbooks," *The Phi Delta Kappa* 75 (1993): 29–35; Janice Radway, "Reading is Not Eating: Mass-Produced Literature and the Theoretical, Methodological, and Political Consequence of a Metaphor," *Book Research Quarterly* 2 (1986): 7–29; Elson, *Guardians of Tradition,* viii; William F. Pinar et al., *Understanding Curriculum: An Introduction to the Study of Historical and Contemporary Curriculum Discourse,* revised edition (New York: Peter Lang, 2008), 777; Kim Tolley, *Heading South to Teach: The World of Susan Nye Hutchison, 1815–1845* (Chapel Hill: University of North Carolina Press, 2015), 79; Lunsford Lane, *A Narrative of Lunsford Lane* (Boston: J. G. Torrey, 1842), 21, Documenting the American South, University of North Carolina, Chapel Hill, accessed January 6, 2024, http://docsouth.unc.edu/neh/lanelunsford/lane.html.

29. Elson, *Guardians of Tradition,* 66; Helen Fox, *When Race Breaks Out: Conversations About Race and Racism in College Classrooms* (New York: Peter Lang, 2001), 12; Sleeter and Grant, "Race, Class, Gender," 203.

6. Life in Reconstruction North Carolina

1. "Roanoke Island," *The National Freedman* (September 15, 1865), 259–60. Although it is not clear whether Freeman was successful in securing a teacher for the freedpeople in Edenton, correspondence between the Freedmen's Bureau and D. Edson Smith, a white New Yorker who taught in Edenton between 1866 and 1867, indicates that local freedpeople had been refused federal aid because the funds were not available. Petitioning the Bureau on their behalf, Edson wrote, "I know of no people more worthy of aid than this. They will do all they can for themselves, and a little help just at this point will do much good." D. Edson Smith to F. A. Fiske, November 20, 1866, Records of the Superintendent of Education, M844:10.

2. Patricia C. Click, *A Time Full of Trial: The Roanoke Island Freedmen's Colony, 1862–1867* (Chapel Hill: University of North Carolina Press, 2001), 128; Emily Gill cited in Judkin Browning, "'Bringing Light to Our Land...When She Was Dark as Night': Northerners, Freedpeople, And Education During Military Occupation in North Carolina, 1862–1865," *American Nineteenth Century History* 1, no. 1 (2008): 6; Ronald E. Butchart et al., "The Freedmen's Teacher Project: Teachers Among the Freed People

in the U.S. South, 1861–1877," Harvard Dataverse, V3 (2022), https://doi.org/10.7910/DVN/0HBDZD, hereafter cited as The FTP. Emily Gill was a white woman from Philadelphia, Pennsylvania.

3. See for example, Esther A. Williams, February 17, 1865, Roanoke Island Freedmen's Colony, accessed September 16, 2015, http://www.roanokefreedmenscolony.com/let11 .pdf; "Roanoke Island: Mrs. Freeman's Letter," *The Freedmen's Advocate* (December 1864), 42.

4. Elizabeth James, *American Missionary* (February 1864), 39–40; Eliza P. Perkins to Hattie, January 10, 1864, Tryon Palace Archives, New Bern, North Carolina; F. A. Fiske to Samuel Hunt, October 13, 1866, Records of the Superintendent of Education, M844.

5. M. N. Thorpe, "A 'Yankee Teacher' in North Carolina," *The North Carolina Historical Review* 30, no. 4 (October 1953): 570; Susan Odell, *The National Freedman* (June 1865), 153–54; Click, *A Time Full of Trial*, 120.

6. Diary of Robert Fitzgerald, June 29, 1867; Robert Harris to Samuel Hunt, January 1, 1866, American Missionary Association archives, Amistad Research Center at Tulane University, New Orleans, Louisiana, accessed at The New York Public Library, hereafter cited as AMAA; Letter from B. L. Canedy, July 27, 1863, in Friends' Freedmen's Association, *Report of the Executive Board of the Friends' Association of Philadelphia and the Vicinity for the Relief of Colored Freedmen*, (Philadelphia: C. Sherman, Son & Co., Printers, 1864), 23; New England Freedmen's Aid Society, *Extracts from Letters of Teachers and Superintendents of the New England Freedmen's Aid Society, Fifth Series* (Boston: John Wilson & Co., 1864), 14.

7. Diary of Robert Fitzgerald, June 16, 1867, June 22, 1867, September 1, 1867.

8. Charles N. Hunter, *Review of Negro Life in North Carolina, With My Recollections*. Raleigh: N.p, n.d., 13–14, Internet Archive, accessed August 22, 2024, https://archive.org/details/reviewofnegrolifoohunt/mode/2up?view=theater; Robert Harris to Samuel Hunt, January 1, 1866, AMAA, emphasis in original.

9. See Ronald E. Butchart, *Schooling the Freed People: Teaching, Learning, and the Struggle for Black Freedom* (Chapel Hill: University of North Carolina Press, 2010), 97; *The Freedmen's Record* (January 1865), 9; Joe M. Richardson, *Christian Reconstruction: The American Missionary Association and Southern Blacks, 1861–1890* (Tuscaloosa: University of Alabama Press, 1986), 178–79; Robert Harris to Edward P. Smith, January 9, 1867, AMAA. The teachers who assisted Harris were Mary Payne and Carolina Bryant. See Mark Andrew Huddle, "To Educate a Race: The Making of the First State Colored Normal School, Fayetteville, North Carolina, 1865–1877," *The North Carolina Historical Review* 74, no. 2 (1997): 157.

10. Edward P. Smith to Michael P. Jerkins, June 23, 1869, AMAA.

11. Jerkins to W. E. Whiting, November 7, 1869, AMAA; Jerkins to Edward P. Smith, December 14, 1869, AMAA, emphasis in original; Jerkins to Smith, December 18, 1869, AMAA; Maxine D. Jones, "They Are My People: Black American Missionary Association Teachers in North Carolina During the Civil War and Reconstruction," *The Negro Educational Review* 36, no. 2 (1985): 86; Samuel C. Alexander to H. C. Vogell, November 7, 1868, Records of the Superintendent of Education, M844:10; William Birnie to H. C. Vogell, November 10, 1868, Records of the Superintendent of Education, M844:10.

12. Testimony of Colonel E. Whittlesey, in United States Congress, *Report of the Joint Committee on Reconstruction, at the First Session Thirty-Ninth Congress* (Washington. D.C.: Government Printing Office, 1866), 183. See also, Roberta Sue Alexander, "Hostility and Hope: Black Education in North Carolina During Presidential Reconstruction, 1865–1867," *The North Carolina Historical Review* 53, no. 2 (1976); Richardson, *Christian Reconstruction*, 178–79; Butchart, *Schooling*, 97.

13. James cited in Click, *A Time Full of Trial*, 88.

14. Jonathan W. White and Lydia J. Davis, eds. *My Work Among the Freedmen: The Civil War and Reconstruction Letters of Harriet M. Buss* (Charlottesville: University of Virginia Press, 2021), 127, 125; Thorpe, "A 'Yankee Teacher' in North Carolina," 581.

15. Jones, "They Are My People," 86.

16. Samuel Ashley cited in Jones, "They Are My People," 87.

17. Butchart et al., The FTP.

18. Hunter, *Review of Negro Life*, 19–20; Diary of Robert Fitzgerald, September 22, 1868. For more on Fitzgerald's ancestry and upbringing, see Pauli Murray, *Proud Shoes: The Story of an American Family* (New York: Harper & Row, 1956).

19. White and Davis, *My Work Among the Freedmen*, 127. See also Elizabeth James, April 7, 1864, Roanoke Island Freedmen's Colony, accessed November 2, 2015, http://www.roanokefreedmenscolony.com/let2.pdf; Freeman, *The Freedmen's Advocate* (August 1864), 25–26.

20. Superintendent Reverend William Briggs cited in Browning, "Bringing Light to our Land," 8; Nellie F. Stearns to Lizzie, November 5, 1865, emphasis in original, Nellie F. Stearns Papers, David M. Rubenstein Rare Book & Manuscript Library, Duke University, Durham, North Carolina, hereafter cited as Nellie F. Stearns Papers. Nellie is listed as Ellen in the Freedmen's Teacher Project database. Butchart et al., The FTP.

21. L. W. Montgomery, *Sketches of Old Warrenton, North Carolina: Traditions and Reminiscences of the Town and People Who Made It* (Raleigh, NC: Edwards and Broughton, 1924), 275–76; Thorpe, "A 'Yankee Teacher' in North Carolina," 570.

22. Thorpe, "A 'Yankee Teacher' in North Carolina," 578, 574.

23. North Carolina teacher cited in Leon Litwack, *Been in the Storm So Long: The Aftermath of Slavery* (New York: Alfred A. Knopf, 1980), 478–79.

24. C. Vann Woodward, *The Strange Career of Jim Crow* (New York: Oxford University Press, 1955), 21.

25. Fisk Parsons Brewer, "South Carolina University–1876," ed. William P. Vaughn, *South Carolina Historical Magazine* 76 (October 1975): 225–31; Kemp Battle cited in John K. Chapman, "Black Freedom and the University of North Carolina, 1793–1960," PhD diss. (University of North Carolina at Chapel Hill, 2006), 127. Battle briefly served as North Carolina's superintendent of Public Instruction in 1873.

26. A. C. Blandin to E. P. Smith, March 29, 1869, AMAA (first quotation); *The Presbyterian*, August 27, 1902; Margaret S. Clark to F. A. Fisk, May 30, 1868, Records of the Superintendent of Education, M844:7 (second quotation).

27. North Carolina has often been described as lenient or racially progressive due to the relatively low number of antebellum slaveholders and the fact that it was the last state to secede from the Union. See for example, United States Congress, *Report of the Joint*

Committee on Reconstruction, at the First Session Thirty-Ninth Congress (Washington. D.C.: Government Printing Office, 1866), 183; Michael Goldhaber, "Mission Unfulfilled: Freedpeople's Education in North Carolina, 1865–1870," *The Journal of Negro History* 77, no. 4 (1992): 99–210.

28. William Elliott to F. A. Fisk, April 14, 1866, Records of the Superintendent of Education, M844:10. By May 1866, Elliott was still attempting to locate a schoolhouse for the local freedpeople or site on which to build one. Although his efforts were initially fruitless, he later found work on the Wilden plantation and Hinton farm. Elliott to Fisk, May 16, 1866, Records of the Superintendent of Education, M844:10; Butchart et al., The FTP.

29. Alexander, "Hostility and Hope," 113–32. Richardson, *Christian Reconstruction*, 178–79; Butchart, *Schooling*, 97; Harris to Hunt, March 1, 1866, AMAA.

30. White and Davis, *My Work Among the Freedmen*, 127, 139, 129; Huddle, "To Educate a Race," 135–60; Oliver O. Howard, *Autobiography of Oliver Otis Howard, Major General, United States Army: Volume 2* (New York: Baker & Taylor, 1908), 276. For more on the postwar military occupation of the South, see Gregory P. Downs, *After Appomattox: Military Occupation and the Ends of War* (Cambridge, MA: Harvard University Press, 2015).

31. State Superintendent's Monthly School Report, February 1866, Records of the Superintendent of Education, M844:13; Butchart et al., The FTP; John W. Alvord, *Ninth Semi-Annual Report on Schools for Freedmen, January 1, 1870* (Washington: Government Printing Office, 1870), 17; Robert Harris to Samuel Hunt, March 1, 1866, AMAA.

32. United States Congress, *Report of the Joint Committee on Reconstruction*, 183; State Superintendent's Monthly School Report, April 1866, Records of the Superintendent of Education, M844:13; F. A. Fisk to Jacob Chur, April 11, 1867, Records of the Superintendent of Education, M844:2. For more examples of incendiarism, see Alexander, "Hostility and Hope," 115.

33. Goldhaber, "Mission Unfulfilled," 200; Horace James to F. A. Fisk, September 29, 1865, Records of the Superintendent of Education, M844:10.

34. State Superintendent's Monthly School Reports for April 1868, March, April and May 1868, and September 1868, Records of the Superintendent of Education, M844:13.

35. For a comprehensive overview of Klan violence in North Carolina, see Bruce E. Stewart, "'When Darkness Reigns Then is the Hour to Strike': Moonshining, Federal Liquor Taxation, and Klan Violence in Western North Carolina, 1868–1872," *The North Carolina Historical Review* 80, no. 4 (October 2003): 453–74; "Albion W. Tourgée Reports on KKK Violence in North Carolina," After Slavery: Race, Labor, and Politics in the Post-Emancipation Carolinas, Lowcountry Digital History Initiatives, accessed October 17, 2015, http://ldhi.library.cofc.edu/exhibits/show/after_slavery_educator/unit_nine_documents/document_8.

36. *The Weekly Pioneer*, November 9, 1871. On gendered Klan violence see Butchart, *Schooling*, 169.

37. *The Daily Standard*, September 28, 1870; For KKK trial documentation relating to North Carolina, see *Testimony Taken by the Joint Select Committee to Inquire into the Condition of Affairs in the Late Insurrectionary States, North Carolina* (Washington, D.C.: Government Printing Office, 1872).

38. Thomas B. Barton to F. A. Fisk, March 24, 1867, Records of the Superintendent of Education, M844:10; Barton's attackers cited in Alexander, "Hostility and Hope," 116; Butchart et al., The FTP.

39. On the experience of the Corliss couple, see Edward J. Blume, *Reforging the White Republic: Race, Religion, and American Nationalism, 1865–1898* (Baton Rouge: Louisiana State University Press, 2005), 79; Mark L. Bradley, *Bluecoats and Tar Heels: Soldiers and Civilians in Reconstruction North Carolina* (Lexington: The University Press of Kentucky, 2009), 212; Richardson, *Christian Reconstruction*, 227; *American Missionary* (January 1892), 57.

40. Diary of Robert Fitzgerald, September 29, 1869, September 1, 1869.

41. Testimony of William G. Bowers, Orange City, N.C., report #7, office #507, Denied Claim, Papers of the Southern Claims Commission, accessed December 6, 2015, www.ancestry.com. For traditional interpretations of freedpeople's education and the role of Klan violence, see for example, Henry L. Swint, *The Northern Teacher in the South, 1862–1870* (Nashville, TN: George Peabody College for Teachers, 1941), 136; Edgar W. Knight, "The 'Messianic' Invasion of the South After 1865," *School and Society* 57, no. 1484 (1943): 645–51; William Preston Vaughn, *Schools for All: Blacks and Public Education in the South* (Lexington: The University Press of Kentucky, 1974), 25.

42. Newspaper clipping, *Greensboro Daily News*, April 6, 1941, in The Caswell County Historical Collection, 1791–2000s, Southern Historical Collection, Wilson Library, University of North Carolina at Chapel Hill, hereafter cited as The Caswell County Historical Collection.

43. Newspaper clipping, *Greensboro Daily News*, undated 1960, The Caswell County Historical Collection.

44. Newspaper clipping, unidentified periodical, October 2, 1935, The Caswell County Historical Collection.

45. Newspaper clipping, *Daily News*, May 1870, The Caswell County Historical Collection (first quotation); Newspaper clipping, unidentified periodical, October 2, 1935, The Caswell County Historical Collection (second and third quotations).

46. For more information on Wyatt Outlaw's murder, see Carole Watterson Troxler, "'To Look More Closely at the Man': Wyatt Outlaw, a Nexus of National, Local and Personal History," *The North Carolina Historical Review* 77, no. 4 (2000): 403–33; Samuel Ashley cited in John L. Bell, "Samuel S. Ashley: Carpetbagger and Educator," *The North Carolina Historical Review* 71, no. 4 (1995): 480. For an overview of the period known as "Redemption," see for example, Woodward, *The Strange Career of Jim Crow*.

47. Butchart et al., The FTP; Nellie F. Stearns to Lizzie, November 5, 1865, Nellie F. Stearns Papers; Sarah Freeman, July 7, 1864, Documenting the American South, University of North Carolina, Chapel Hill, accessed September 16, 2015, http://www.roanokefreedmenscolony.com/let3.pdf; Thorpe, "A 'Yankee Teacher' in North Carolina," 581. In August of 1865, an epidemic raged through the eastern portion of North Carolina which proved fatal for both Blacks and whites and left many unable to work. See J. W. Burghduff, *The National Freedman* (February 1868), 365.

Epilogue: The Struggle for Educational Equality Continues

1. Frenise A. Logan, "The Legal Status of Public School Education for Negroes in North Carolina, 1877–1894," *The North Carolina Historical Review* 32, no. 3 (1955): 346–57; M. C. S. Nobel, *A History of the Public Schools of North Carolina* (Chapel Hill: University of North Carolina Press, 1930), 403. "Redemption" refers to the period in which Southern Democrats, known as "Redeemers," attempted to redeem the South by overturning many of the progressive policies initiated under Republican rule, especially as they related to the extension of Black freedom. Graded schools organized students into different levels or grades in order to ensure their systematic progression from elementary to secondary education.

2. Nobel, *A History of the Public Schools*, 368; Mark Andrew Huddle, "To Educate a Race: The Making of the First State Colored Normal School, Fayetteville, North Carolina, 1865–1877," *The North Carolina Historical Review* 74, no. 2 (1997): 136; Ronald E. Butchart, *Schooling the Freed People: Teaching, Learning, and the Struggle for Black Freedom* (Chapel Hill: University of North Carolina Press, 2010), 177; W. Fitzhugh Brundage, *Lynching in the New South: Georgia and Virginia, 1880–1903* (Champaign: University of Illinois Press, 1993). For more on the Wilmington massacre, see for example, David S. Cecelski and Timothy B. Tyson, eds., *Democracy Betrayed: The Wilmington Race Riot of 1898 and Its Legacy* (Chapel Hill: University of North Carolina Press, 2000); David Zucchino, *Wilmington's Lie: The Murderous Coup of 1898 and the Rise of White Supremacy* (New York: Grove Atlantic, 2020); H. Leon Prather, *We Have Taken A City: The Wilmington Racial Massacre and Coup of 1898* (Rutherford, NJ: Fairleigh Dickinson University Press, 1984). For more on Klan violence beyond 1877, see Bradly David Proctor, "Whip, Pistol, and Hood: Ku Klux Klan Violence in the Carolinas During Reconstruction," PhD Diss. (University of North Carolina, Chapel Hill, 2013), 16–17.

3. Logan, "The Legal Status of Public School Education," 348.

4. Logan, "The Legal Status of Public School Education," 352; Louis R. Harlan, *Separate and Unequal: Public School Campaigns and Racism in the Southern Seaboard States, 1901–1915* (Chapel Hill: University of North Carolina Press, 1958), 14; Booker T. Washington and W. E. B. Du Bois, *The Negro in the South: His Economic Progress in Relation to His Moral and Religious Development* (Philadelphia: George W. Jacobs & Company Publishers, 1907), 103.

5. *Goldsboro Messenger*, February 28, 1887; Willard B. Gatewood, "North Carolina and Federal Aid to Education: Public Reaction to the Blair Bill, 1881–1890," *The North Carolina Historical Review* 40, no. 4 (1963): 465–88; H. N. Green, "Educational Reconstruction: African American Education in the Urban South, 1865–1890," PhD Diss. (University of North Carolina, Chapel Hill, 2010), 186. By 1900, Black men in most southern states had been effectively excluded from the political sphere through disenfranchisement. See J. Morgan Kousser, *The Shaping of Southern Politics: Suffrage Restrictions and the Establishment of the One-Party South* (New Haven, CT: Yale University Press, 1974).

6. Green, "Educational Reconstruction," 186; Washington and Du Bois, *The Negro in the South*, 102; James D. Anderson, *The Education of Blacks in the South, 1860–1935* (Chapel Hill: University of North Carolina Press, 1988), 26. For more on the fusionists'

impact on North Carolina's public school system, see for example, Daniel J. Whitener, "The Republican Party and Public Education in North Carolina, 1867–1900," *The North Carolina Historical Review* 37, no. 3 (July 1960): 393–95; James S. Ferguson, "An Era of Educational Change," *The North Carolina Historical Review* 46, no. 2 (1969): 130–41.

7. Green, "Educational Reconstruction," 193. For more information on Booker T. Washington and his vision of Black education and Black freedom, see Robert J. Norrell, *Up from History: The Life of Booker T. Washington* (Cambridge, MA: Belknap, 2009).

8. A. D. Mayo, *An Address Delivered Before The State Agricultural and Mechanical College for the Colored Race at Greensboro NC, May 26, 1898* (Hampton, VA: Press of Hampton Institute, 1898), 11; Charles W. Chesnutt, *The Journals of Charles W. Chesnutt*, ed. Richard Brodhead (Durham, NC: Duke University Press, 1993), 154–55.

9. Vanessa Siddle Walker, *Their Highest Potential: An African American School Community in the Segregated South* (Chapel Hill: University of North Carolina Press, 1996), 3; Adam Fairclough, *A Class of Their Own: Black Teachers in the Segregated South* (Cambridge, MA: Harvard University Press, 2007), 3; Butchart, *Schooling*, 157.

10. *The New York Times*, June 29, 2023.

Bibliography

Manuscript Collections and Archives
Duke University, David M. Rubenstein Rare Book & Manuscript Library
  Charles N. Hunter Papers
  Nathan H. Hill Papers
  Nellie F. Stearns Papers
Guilford College, Hege Library, Friends Historical Collection
  Delphina E. Mendenhall Papers
Library of Congress, Manuscripts Division, Washington, D.C.
  National Archives and Records Administration
  Bureau of Refugees, Freedmen, and Abandoned Lands. Record Group 105
  Records of the Assistant Commissioner for the State of North Carolina, 1865–1870, Bureau of Refugees, Freedmen, and Abandoned Lands. Microfilm M843
  Records of the Field Offices for the State of North Carolina, 1865–1872, Bureau of Refugees, Freedmen, and Abandoned Lands. Microfilm M1909
North Carolina State Archives
  Albion W. Tourgée Papers, 1838–1905
  James Henry Harris Papers, 1830–1891
Tulane University, Amistad Research Center, New Orleans, Louisiana
  American Missionary Association Archives
Tryon Palace, New Bern, North Carolina
  Letter from Eliza Perkins to "Hattie," Dec. 9, 1863
  Letter from Eliza Perkins to "Hattie," Jan. 10, 1864
University of North Carolina at Chapel Hill, Wilson Library
  A. J. McIntire Diaries, 1864, 1867–1868
  Charles Phillips Papers, 1807–1868
  Fitzgerald Family Papers, 1864–1954
  Hobbs and Mendenhall Family Papers, 1787–1949
  Jones and Patterson Family Papers, 1777–1993
  Laurens Hinton Papers, 1825–1896
  The Caswell County Historical Collection, 1791–2000s
  William G. Dickson Papers, 1767–1920
  Records of the Superintendent of Education for the State of North Carolina, 1865–1870, Bureau of Refugees, Freedmen, and Abandoned Lands. Microfilm M844

Newspapers and Periodicals
The American Freedman
American Missionary

The Daily North Carolinian
The Daily Standard
The Fayetteville News
The Freedman
The Freedman's Torchlight
The Freedmen's Record
The Friend Goldsboro Messenger
Good Words
Harper's Weekly
The Liberator
The National Freedman
New Era
The New York Times
The North Carolinian
The North Carolina Presbyterian
The Presbyterian
The Raleigh Register
Raleigh Sentinel
Unity
The Weekly North Carolina Standard
The Weekly Pioneer

Published Primary Sources

"Albion W. Tourgée Reports on KKK Violence in North Carolina." After Slavery: Race, Labor, and Politics in the Post-Emancipation Carolinas. Lowcountry Digital History Initiatives. Accessed October 17, 2015. http://ldhi.library.cofc.edu/exhibits/show/after_slavery_educator/unit_nine_documents/document_8.

Alvord, John W. *Semi-Annual Report on Schools for Freedmen, Numbers 1–10, January 1866–July 1870*. Washington: Government Printing Office, 1866–1870; Reprint, New York: AMS Press, Inc., 1980.

The Amendments of 1873 to North Carolina's Constitution of 1868. North Carolina Legislative Library. Accessed November 9, 2015. http://www.ncleg.net/library/documents/amdts_1873.pdf 09.

American Anti-Slavery Society. *Constitution of the Anti-Slavery Society*. Boston: Isaac Knapp, 1838.

American Baptist Home Mission Society. *Thirty-First Report of the American Baptist Home Mission Society*. New York: American Baptist Home Mission Rooms, 1863.

———. *Thirty-Second Annual Report of the American Baptist Home Mission Society*. New York: American Baptist Home Mission Rooms, 1864.

———. *Thirty-Fifth Annual Report of the American Baptist Home Mission Society*. New York: American Baptist Home Mission Rooms, 1867.

American Baptist Publication Society. *Forty-First Annual Report of the American Baptist Publication Society, 1865*. Philadelphia: American Baptist Publication Society, 1865.

American Tract Society. *Fifteenth Annual Report of the American Tract Society.* New York: American Tract Society, 1840.
———. *Fifty-Second Annual Report of the American Tract Society.* Boston: American Tract Society, 1866.
———. *The Freedman's Spelling Book.* Boston, 1866; Reprint, New York: American Tract Society, 1980.
———. *The Freedman's Second Reader.* Boston, 1865; Reprint, New York: American Tract Society, 1980.
———. *The Freedman's Third Reader.* Boston, 1866; Reprint, New York: American Tract Society, 1980.
Ancestry.com. *U.S., Civil War Soldier Records and Profiles, 1861–1865.* Provo, UT: Ancestry.com Operations, Inc., 2009.
———. *North Carolina, U.S. Death Certificates, 1909–1976.* Lehi, UT: Ancestry.com Operations, Inc., 2007.
Ashley, Samuel S. *Report of the Superintendent of Public Instruction for North Carolina, for the Year 1869.* Raleigh, NC: M. S. Littlefield, 1869.
Beecher, Catherine. *A Treatise on Domestic Economy. For the Use of Young Ladies at Home and at School*, Revised Edition. New York: Harper & Brothers, 1845.
Biddle Memorial Institute. *First Annual Catalogue and Circular of the Biddle Memorial Institute, Charlotte, N.C. 1867–1868.* Pittsburgh, PA: J. M'Millin, Steam Job and Book Printers, 1868.
———. *Fifth Annual Catalogue and Circular of the Biddle Memorial Institute, Charlotte. N.C. 1873–1874.* Pittsburgh, PA: J. M'Millin, Steam Job and Book Printers, 1874.
Brinkerhoff, Isaac W. *Advice to Freedmen.* New York: American Tract Society, 1864.
Brown, Helen E. *John Freeman and His Family.* Boston: American Tract Society, 1862.
Burnap, George W. *The Sphere and Duties of Woman: A Course of Lectures.* Baltimore, MD: John Murphy, 1848.
Chesnutt, Charles W. *The Journals of Charles W. Chesnutt.* Edited by Richard Brodhead. Durham, NC: Duke University Press, 1993.
Child, Lydia Marie. *The Freedmen's Book.* Boston: Ticknor & Fields, 1865.
Click, Patricia C. "Letters from Roanoke Island Missionary Teachers." Roanoke Island Freedmen's Colony, 2001. Accessed August 22, 2024. www.roanokefreedmenscolony.com.
Coffin, Levi. *Reminiscences of Levi Coffin: The Reputed President of the Underground Railroad*, 2nd Ed. Cincinnati, OH: Robert Clarke & Co., 1880.
Colyer, Vincent. *Report of the Services Rendered by the Freed People to the United States Army: In North Carolina in the Spring of 1862, After the Battle of Newbern.* New York: Vincent Colyer, 1864.
Crafts, Hannah. *A Bondswoman's Narrative.* Edited by Henry Louis Gates, Jr. New York: Warner Books, 2002.
Creecy, Richard Benbury. *Grandfather's Tales of North Carolina History.* Raleigh, NC: Edwards & Broughton, 1901.
Curry, James. *Narrative of James Curry: A Fugitive Slave.* Documenting the American South. University of North Carolina, Chapel Hill. Accessed October 11, 2015. http://docsouth.unc.edu/neh/curry/curry.html.

Dana, Malcolm McG. *The Annals of Norwich, New London County, Connecticut in the Great Rebellion of 1861–1865.* Norwich, CT: J. H. Jewett and Company, 1873.

Drew, Benjamin. *A North-Side View of Slavery. The Refugee: Or, the Narratives of Fugitive Slaves in Canada.* Boston: John P. Jewett, 1856. Documenting the American South. University of North Carolina, Chapel Hill. Accessed August 22, 2024. https://docsouth.unc.edu/neh/drew/drew.html.

Educational Commission. *First Annual Report of the Educational Commission for Freedmen.* Boston: Prentiss & Deland, Book and Job Printers, 1863.

Federal Writers' Project. *Slave Narrative Project. Vol. 11, North Carolina, Part 1, Adams-Hunter,* 1936. Manuscript/Mixed Material. Accessed December 12, 2023. https://www.loc.gov/item/mesn111/.

———. *Slave Narrative Project. Vol. 11, North Carolina, Part 2, Jackson-Yellerday,* 1936. Manuscript/Mixed Material. Accessed January 01, 2024. https://www.loc.gov/item/mesn112/.

Ferebee, London R. *A Brief History of the Slave Life of Rev. L. R. Ferebee, and the Battles of Life, and Four Years of His Ministerial Life.* Raleigh, NC: Edwards & Broughton, 1882.

Fisk, Clinton B. *Plain Counsels to Freedmen in Sixteen Brief Lectures.* Boston: American Tract Society, 1866.

Fleming, Robert. *The Elementary Spelling Book, Revised and Adapted to the Youth of the Southern Confederacy, Interspersed with Bible Readings on Domestic Slavery.* Atlanta: Job Printing Office, 1863. Internet Archive. Accessed August 22, 2024. https://archive.org/details/elementaryspellioflem.

Freedmen's Convention of North Carolina. *Minutes of the Freedmen's Convention Held in the City of Raleigh on the 2nd, 3rd, 4th and 5th of October, 1866.* Raleigh, NC: Standard Book and Job Office, 1866.

Friends' Freedmen's Association. *Report of the Executive Board of the Friends' Association of Philadelphia and the Vicinity for the Relief of Colored Freedmen.* Philadelphia: C. Sherman, Son & Co. Printers, 1864.

The General Assembly's Committee on Freedmen of the Presbyterian Church. *Second Annual Report of the Committee on Freedmen. From May 1. 1866. To May 1. 1867.* Pittsburgh, PA: J. M'Millin, Steam Job and Book Printers, 1867.

Hampton Normal and Agricultural Institute. *Twenty-Two Years' Work of the Hampton Normal and Agricultural Institute at Hampton Virginia.* Hampton, VA: Normal School Press, 1893.

Howard, Oliver O. *Autobiography of Oliver Otis Howard, Major General, United States Army: Volume 2.* New York: Baker & Taylor, 1908.

Hunter, Charles N. *Review of Negro Life in North Carolina, With My Recollections.* Raleigh, NC: N.p, n.d. Internet Archive. Accessed January 18, 2024. https://archive.org/details/reviewofnegrolifoohunt/mode/2up?view=theater.

James, Horace. *Annual Report of the Superintendent of Negro Affairs in North Carolina, 1864.* Boston: W. F. Brown & Co. Printers, 1865.

Journal of the Constitutional Convention of the State of North Carolina, at Its Session 1868. Raleigh, NC: Joseph W. Holden, Convention Printer, 1868. Documenting the American South. University of North Carolina, Chapel Hill. Accessed January 10, 2024. http://docsouth.unc.edu/nc/conv1868/conv1868.html.

Lane, Lunsford. *A Narrative of Lunsford Lane*, 2nd Edition. Boston: J. G. Torrey, 1842. Documenting the American South. University of North Carolina, Chapel Hill. Accessed January 6, 2024. http://docsouth.unc.edu/neh/lanelunsford/lane.html.

Lee, Laura Elizabeth. *Forget-Me-Nots of the Civil War: A Romance, Containing Reminiscences and Original Letters of Two Confederate Soldiers*. St. Louis, MO: Press A. R. Fleming Printing Co., 1909.

Mayo, A. D. *An Address Delivered Before the State Agricultural and Mechanical College for the Colored Race at Greensboro NC, May 26, 1898*. Hampton, VA: Press of Hampton Institute, 1898.

McGuffey, William H. *The Eclectic First Reader for Young Children*. Cincinnati, OH: Truman & Smith, 1836.

———. *The Eclectic Third Reader for Young Children*. Cincinnati, OH: Truman & Smith, 1836.

———. *McGuffey's New First Eclectic Reader for Little Children*. Cincinnati, OH: W. B. Smith & Co., 1857.

———. *McGuffey's New Third Eclectic Reader for Young Learners*. Cincinnati, OH: W. B. Smith, 1857. Internet Archive. Accessed January 18, 2024. https://archive.org/details/mcguffeysnewthir03mcgu.

McNally, Francis. *An Improved System of Geography: Designed for Schools, Academies and Seminaries*. New York: A. S. Barnes & Co., 1859.

Mendenhall, Delphina E. Delphina E. Mendenhall to John L. Ham, February 1, 1869. Paul W. Bean Civil War Papers. University of Maine. Accessed August 22, 2024. https://digitalcommons.library.umaine.edu/paul_bean_papers/54.

Mitchell, Samuel Augustus. *An Easy Introduction to the Study of Geography: Designed for the Instruction of Children in Schools and Families*. Philadelphia: Thomas Cowperthwait & Co., 1845.

———. *A System of Modern Geography, Comprising a Description of the Present State of the World, and its Five Great Divisions, America, Europe, Asia, Africa, and Oceanica, With Their Several Empires, Kingdoms, States, Territories, etc*, 2nd Edition. Philadelphia: Thomas Cowperthwait & Co., 1848.

Methodist Episcopal Church. *Minutes of the Cincinnati Conference of the Methodist Episcopal Church*. Cincinnati, OH: R. P. Thompson, 1866.

Monteith, James. *First Lessons in Geography, Or, Introduction to "Youth's Manual of Geography."* New York: A. S. Barnes & Co., 1856. Project Gutenberg. Accessed January 17, 2024. http://www.gutenberg.org/files/11722/11722-h/11722-h.htm.

———. *Youth's Manual of Geography Combined with History and Astronomy*, 3rd Edition. New York: A. S. Barnes & Co., 1854.

Montgomery, L. W. *Sketches of Old Warrenton, North Carolina: Traditions and Reminiscences of the Town and People Who Made It*. Raleigh, NC: Edwards & Broughton, 1924.

Moore, Miranda Branson. *The First Dixie Reader: Designed to Follow the Dixie Primer*. Raleigh, NC: Branson, Farrar, & Co., 1863. Documenting the American South. University of North Carolina, Chapel Hill. Accessed January 22, 2024. http://docsouth.unc.edu/imls/moore2/moore.html.

Morehouse, H. L. *H. M. Tupper, D.D.: A Narrative of Twenty-Five Years' Work in the South, 1865–1890.* New York: The American Baptist Home Mission Society, 1890.

The New England Primer. Boston: Edward Draper, 1777. Internet Archive. Accessed August 22, 2024. https://archive.org/details/newenglandprimer00west/page/n9/mode/2up.

New England Society, *Tracts Published by the New England Society.* Andover, MA: Flagg and Gould, 1814.

National Freedman's Relief Association. *First Annual Report of the National Freedman's Relief Association of the District of Columbia.* Washington, D.C.: M'Gill & Witherow, 1863. Accessed September 26, 2022. https://digital.history.pcusa.org/islandora/object/islandora:112859#page/1/mode/1up.

———. *National Freedman's Relief Association.* 1863. Houghton Library. Harvard University, Cambridge, MA. Accessed August 27, 2024. https://nrs.lib.harvard.edu/urn-3:fhcl.hough:100511357?n=3.

New England Freedmen's Aid Society. *Extracts from Letters of Teachers and Superintendents of the New England Freedmen's Aid Society, Fifth Series.* Boston: John Wilson & Co., 1864.

———. *Second Annual Report of the New England Freedmen's Aid Society.* Boston: Office of the Society, 1864.

Oberlin College. *Seventy-Fifth Anniversary General Catalogue of Oberlin College, 1833–1908, Including an Account of the Principal Events in the History of the College, With Illustrations of the College Building.* Oberlin, 1909.

Pegues, A. W. *Our Baptist Ministers and Schools.* Springfield, MA: Willey & Co., 1892.

Presbyterian Church in the United States of America. *Minutes of the General Assembly of the Presbyterian Church in the United States of America.* Philadelphia: Presbyterian Board of Publication, 1866.

Presbyterian Committee on Missions for Freedmen. *Annual Report of the Presbyterian Committee of Missions for Freedmen.* Pittsburgh, PA: J. M'Millin, Steam Job and Book Printers, 1871.

Protestant Episcopal Church. *Journal of the General Convention of the Protestant Episcopal Church.* New York, 1868.

Protestant Episcopal Freedman's Commission. *Occasional Paper, January 1866.* Boston: Geo. C. Rand & Avery, 1866. Internet Archive. Accessed August 30, 2024. https://archive.org/details/protestantepisco00epis.

Randolph County Business Directory. Raleigh, NC: Levi Branson, 1894.

Rice, John H. *A System of Modern Geography, Compiled from Various Sources and Adapted to the Present Condition of the World, Expressly for the Use of Schools and Academies in the Confederate States of America.* Atlanta: Franklin Printing House, 1862. Boston Athenaeum Digital Collections. Accessed August 30, 2024. http://cdm.bostonathenaeum.org/cdm/ref/collection/p16057coll14/id/75495.

School Laws of North Carolina, as Ratified April 12th A. D, 1869. Raleigh, NC: M. S. Littlefield, State Printer and Binder, 1869. Internet Archive. Accessed November 18, 2015. https://archive.org/stream/schoollawsofnortnort#page/n5/mode/2up/search/four.

Sherman, William Tecumseh. *Memoirs of General William T. Sherman. Volume I*, 2nd Edition. New York: D. Appleton, 1904.
Spenser, Cornelia Phillips. *The Last Ninety Days of the War in North-Carolina*. New York: Watchman Publishing Company, 1866. Documenting the American South. University of North Carolina at Chapel Hill. Accessed November 12, 2015. http://docsouth.unc.edu/true/spencer/spencer.html.
Sterling, Richard. *Our Own Third Reader for the Use of Schools and Families*. Greensboro, NC, 1862. Documenting the American South. University of North Carolina at Chapel Hill. Accessed August 30, 2024. http://docsouth.unc.edu/imls/sterling/sterling.html.
Tourgée, Albion W. *A Fool's Errand: By One of the Fools*. New York: Fords, Howard & Hulbert, 1879. Documenting the American South. University of North Carolina, Chapel Hill. Accessed April 12, 2015. http://docsouth.unc.edu/church/tourgee/tourgee.html.
"Two North Carolina Freedwomen Testify Against Their Former Owner." After Slavery: Race, Labor and Politics in the Post-Emancipation Carolinas. Lowcountry Digital History Initiative. Accessed November 16, 2015. http://ldhi.library.cofc.edu/exhibits/show/after_slavery_educator/unit_one_documents/document_six.
United States Census Bureau. *Seventh Census of the United States, 1850*. Washington, D.C.: Robert Armstrong, 1853.
United States Congress. *Executive Documents of the House of Representatives During the First Session of the Thirty-Ninth Congress, 1865–1866*. Washington, D.C.: Government Printing Office, 1866.
———. *Report of the Joint Committee on Reconstruction, at the First Session Thirty-Ninth Congress*. Washington. D.C.: Government Printing Office, 1866.
———. *Testimony Taken by the Joint Select Committee to Inquire into the Condition of Affairs in the Late Insurrectionary States, North Carolina*. Washington, D.C.: Government Printing Office, 1872.
United States House of Representatives. *Black Americans in Congress*. Washington, D.C.: Government Printing Office, 2008.
Walker, David. *Walker's Appeal, In Four Articles: Together with A Preamble, to the Coloured Citizens of The World, but in Particular, and Very Expressly, to Those of the United States of America*. Boston: David Walker, 1830.
Washington, Booker T., and W. E. B. Du Bois. *The Negro in the South: His Economic Progress in Relation to His Moral and Religious Development*. Philadelphia: George W. Jacobs & Company Publishers, 1907.
Waterbury, J. B. *Friendly Counsels for Freedmen*. New York: American Tract Society, 1864.
Webster, Noah. *The American Spelling Book: Containing the Rudiments of the English Language, for the Use of Schools in the United States*, 19th Edition. Philadelphia: Johnson & Warner, 1816.
———. *The American Spelling Book: Containing, the Rudiments of the English Language, for the Use of Schools in the United States*. Brattleboro, VT: Holbrook and Fessenden, 1820.
Wiley, C. H. "Address to the People of North Carolina." Speech Given at the Conference of Teachers and Friends of Education. Raleigh, N.C.: n.p., 1861. Documenting the

American South. University of North Carolina, Chapel Hill. Accessed January 26, 2024. https://docsouth.unc.edu/imls/confteach/confteach.html.

Willson, Marcius. *The Third Reader of the School and Family Series*. New York: Harper & Brothers, 1860.

———. *The Second Reader of the School and Family Series*. New York: Harper & Brothers, 1860.

Wright, Richard R. *Centennial Encyclopedia of the African Methodist Episcopal Church Containing Principally the Biographies of the Men and Women, Both Ministers and Laymen, Whose Labors During a Hundred Years, Helped Make The A.M.E. Church What It Is*. Philadelphia: Book Concern of the AME Church, 1916.

Database Records and Digital Collections

Ancestry. www.ancestry.com.
    Civil War Soldier Records and Profiles, 1861–1865
    Decennial U.S. Census. 1850 and 1860
    North Carolina Death Certificates, 1909–1976
    Quaker Meeting Records, 1681–1935
    Slave Schedules, 1860
    Southern Claims Commission Records

Butchart, Ronald E. "Wealth Database." 2013. Used with permission.

Butchart, Ronald E. et al. "The Freedmen's Teacher Project: Teachers Among the Freed People in the U.S. South, 1861–1877." Harvard Dataverse. V3 (2022) www.doi.org/10.7910/DVN/0HBDZD.

Family Search. www.familysearch.org.
    United States. Freedmen's Bureau. Records of the Superintendent of Education and of the Division of Education, 1865–1872.

HBCU Library Alliance. https://hbcudigitallibrary.auctr.edu/.
    Newspaper Clippings of Ashmun Institute and Lincoln University, 1853–1874.

National Museum of African American History and Culture, Smithsonian Institution.
    Records of the Assistant Commissioner for the State of North Carolina. Bureau of Refugees, Freedmen, and Abandoned Lands, 1865–1870.

North Carolina Digital Collections. www.digital.ncdcr.gov.
    1885 Confederate Pension Applications
    Noah Hancock (Randolph County)

Secondary Books

Aldridge, Jerry, and Lois McFadyen Christensen. *Stealing from the Mother: The Marginalization of Women in Education and Psychology from 1900–2010*. New York: Rowman & Littlefield Publishers, Inc., 2013.

Alexander, Roberta Sue. *North Carolina Faces the Freedmen: Race Relations During Presidential Reconstruction*. Durham, NC: Duke University Press, 1985.

Allen, Timothy J. *North Carolina Quakers: Spring Friends Meeting*. Charleston, SC: Arcadia Publishing, 2011.

Bibliography

Anderson, James D. *The Education of Blacks in the South, 1860–1935*. Chapel Hill: University of North Carolina Press, 1988.
Auman, William T. *Civil War in the North Carolina Quaker Belt: The Confederate Campaign Against Peace Agitators, Deserters, and Draft Dodgers*. Jefferson, NC: McFarland & Company, Inc., 2014.
Baker, Bruce E. *What Reconstruction Meant: Historical Memory in the American South*. Charlottesville: University of Virginia Press, 2007.
Barney, William L. *The Making of a Confederate: Walter Lenoir's Civil War*. New York: Oxford University Press, 2008.
Baumgartner, Kabria. *In Pursuit of Knowledge: Black Women and Educational Activism in Antebellum America*. New York: New York University Press, 2019.
Blume, Edward J. *Reforging the White Republic: Race, Religion, and American Nationalism, 1865–1898*. Baton Rouge: Louisiana State University Press, 2005.
Bowers, Claude G. *The Tragic Era: The Revolution After Lincoln*. Boston: Houghton Mifflin, 1929.
Bradley, Mark L. *Bluecoats and Tar Heels: Soldiers and Civilians in Reconstruction North Carolina*. Lexington: The University Press of Kentucky, 2009.
Brooks, F. Erik, and Glenn L. Starks, eds. *Historically Black Colleges and Universities: An Encyclopedia*. Santa Barbara, CA: Greenwood, 2011.
Brown, Hugh Victor. *A History of the Education of Negroes in North Carolina*. Raleigh, NC: Irving Swain Press, 1961.
Browning, Judkin. *Shifting Loyalties: The Union Occupation of Eastern North Carolina*. Chapel Hill: University of North Carolina Press, 2011.
Brundage, W. Fitzhugh. *Lynching in the New South: Georgia and Virginia, 1880–1903*. Champaign: University of Illinois Press, 1993.
Butchart, Ronald E. *Northern Schools, Southern Blacks, and Reconstruction: Freedmen's Education, 1862–1875*. Westport, CT: Greenwood Press, 1980.
———. *Schooling the Freed People: Teaching, Learning, and the Struggle for Black Freedom*. Chapel Hill: University of North Carolina Press, 2010.
Butler, Jon. *Awash in a Sea of Faith: Christianizing the American People*. Cambridge, MA: Harvard University Press, 1990.
Carpenter, Robert C. *Gaston County, North Carolina, in the Civil War*. Jefferson, NC: McFarland & Company, 2016.
Cash, Wilbur J. *The Mind of the South*. New York: Knopf, 1941.
Cecelski, David S., and Timothy B. Tyson, eds. *Democracy Betrayed: The Wilmington Race Riot of 1898 and Its Legacy*. Chapel Hill: University of North Carolina Press, 2000.
Cimbala, Paul A. *The Freedmen's Bureau: Reconstructing the American South After the Civil War*. Malabar, FL: Krieger, 2005.
Cimbala, Paul A., and Randall M. Miller. *The Freedmen's Bureau and Reconstruction: Reconsiderations*. New York: Fordham University Press, 1999.
Click, Patricia C. *A Time Full of Trial: The Roanoke Island Freedmen's Colony, 1862–1867*. Chapel Hill: University of North Carolina Press, 2001.

Conser, Walter H., and Robert J. Cain. *Presbyterians in North Carolina: Race, Politics, and Religious Identity in Historical Perspective*. Knoxville: University of Tennessee Press, 2010.

Coon, Charles L. *A Statistical Record of the Progress of Public Education in North Carolina, 1870–1906*. Raleigh, NC: Edwards & Broughton, 1906.

Cornelius, Janet Duitsman. *"When I Can Read My Title Clear": Literacy, Slavery, and Religion in the Antebellum South*. Columbia: University of South Carolina Press, 1991.

De Boer, Clara Merritt. *His Truth is Marching On: African Americans Who Taught the Freedmen for the American Missionary Association, 1861–1877*. New York: Garland, 1995.

Dennett, John Richard. *The South as It Is: 1865–1866*. New York: Viking Press, 1965.

Dorsey, Bruce. *Reforming Men and Women: Gender in the Antebellum City*. Ithaca, NY: Cornell University Press, 2002.

Downs, Gregory P. *After Appomattox: Military Occupation and the Ends of War*. Cambridge, MA: Harvard University Press, 2015.

Du Bois, W. E. B. *The Souls of Black Folk: Essays and Sketches*. Chicago: A.C. McClurg & Co., 1903. Documenting the American South. University of North Carolina, Chapel Hill. Accessed August 30, 2024. http://docsouth.unc.edu/church/duboissouls/dubois.html.

———. *Black Reconstruction in America: An Essay Toward a History of the Part Which Black Folk Played in the Attempt to Reconstruct Democracy in America, 1860–1880*. New York: Free Press, 1935.

Dunning, William A. *Essays on the Civil War and Reconstruction and Related Topics*. Reprint. New York: Peter Smith, 1931.

Eberly, Don, ed. *Building a Healthy Culture: Strategies for an American Renaissance*. Grand Rapids, MI: Eerdmans, 2001.

Edwards, Laura F. *Gendered Strife and Confusion: The Political Culture of Reconstruction*. Champaign: University of Illinois Press, 1997.

Elliott, Mark. *Color-Blind Justice: Albion Tourgée and the Quest for Racial Equality from the Civil War to Plessy V. Ferguson*. New York: Oxford University Press, 2006.

Elson, Ruth M. *Guardians of Tradition: American Schoolbooks of the Nineteenth Century*. Lincoln: University of Nebraska Press, 1964.

Enoch, Jessica. *Refiguring Rhetorical Education: Women Teaching African American, Native American. and Chicano/a Students, 1865–1911*. Carbondale: Southern Illinois University Press, 2008.

Escott, Paul D. *Slavery Remembered: A Record of Twentieth-Century Slave Narratives*. Chapel Hill: University of North Carolina Press, 1979.

Escott, Paul D., ed. *North Carolinians in the Era of the Civil War and Reconstruction*. Chapel Hill: University of North Carolina Press, 2008.

Fairclough, Adam. *A Class of Their Own: Black Teachers in the Segregated South*. Cambridge, MA: Harvard University Press, 2007.

Fairclough, Norman. *Critical Discourse Analysis: The Critical Study of Language*. New York: Longman, 1995.

BIBLIOGRAPHY

Faust, Drew G. *Mothers of Invention in the American Civil War.* Chapel Hill: University of North Carolina Press, 1996.

Fleming, Walter L. *The Sequel of Appomattox: A Chronicle of the Reunion of the States.* New Haven, CT: Yale University Press, 1919.

Foner, Eric. *Reconstruction: America's Unfinished Revolution, 1863–1877.* New York: Harper & Row, 1988.

Foner, Philip S., ed. *Frederick Douglass: Selected Speeches and Writings.* Reprint. Chicago: Lawrence Hill, 1999.

Foreman, P. Gabrielle, Jim Casey, and Sarah Lynn Patterson, eds. *The Colored Conventions Movement: Black Organizing in the Nineteenth Century.* Chapel Hill: University of North Carolina Press, 2021.

Fox, Helen. *When Race Breaks Out: Conversations About Race and Racism in College Classrooms.* New York: Peter Lang, 2001.

Franklin, John Hope. *The Free Negro in North Carolina, 1790–1860.* Reprint. New York: W. W. Norton, 1971.

Fredrickson, George M. *The Black Image in the White Mind: The Debate on Afro-American Character and Destiny, 1817–1914.* Middletown, CT: Wesleyan University Press, 1987.

Genovese, Eugene D. *Roll, Jordan, Roll: The World the Slaves Made.* New York: Vintage Books, 1972.

Ginzberg, Lori D. *Women and the Work of Benevolence: Morality, Politics, and Class in the 19th-Century United States.* New Haven, CT: Yale University Press, 1990.

Glymph, Thavolia. *Out of the House of Bondage: The Transformation of the Plantation Household.* Cambridge: Cambridge University Press, 2008.

Green, Hilary. *Educational Reconstruction: African American Education in the Urban South, 1865–1890.* New York: Fordham University Press, 2016.

Greene II, Robert, and Tyler D. Parry, eds. *Invisible No More: The African American Experience at the University of South Carolina.* Columbia: University of South Carolina Press, 2021.

Goluboff, Risa. *Vagrant Nation: Police Power, Constitutional Change, and the Making of the 1960s.* New York: Oxford University Press, 2016.

Hahn, Steven. *A Nation Under Our Feet: Black Political Struggles in the Rural South from Slavery to the Great Migration.* Cambridge: Cambridge University Press, 2003.

Hale, Janice E. *Black Children: Their Roots, Culture, and Learning Styles.* Baltimore, MD: John Hopkins University Press, 1982.

Haley, John. *Charles N. Hunter and Race Relations in North Carolina.* Chapel Hill, University of North Carolina Press, 1987.

Hammond, Scot J., Kevin R. Hardwick, and Howard L. Lubert, eds. *Classics of American Political and Constitutional Thought, Volume 2: Reconstruction to the Present.* Indianapolis, IN: Hackett Publishing Company, 2007.

Hargrove, Hondon B. *Black Union Soldiers in the Civil War.* Jefferson, NC: McFarland & Company, 1988

Harlan, Louis R. *Separate and Unequal: Public School Campaigns and Racism in the Southern Seaboard States, 1901–1915.* Chapel Hill: University of North Carolina Press, 1958.

Harris, William C. *With Charity for All: Lincoln and the Restoration of the Union.* Lexington: University Press of Kentucky, 1997.

Hartman, Saidiya. *Scenes of Subjection: Terror, Slavery, and Self-Making in Nineteenth-Century America.* New York: Oxford University Press, 1997.

Hilty, Hiram H. *Toward Freedom for All: North Carolina Quakers and Slavery.* Richmond, IN: Friends' United Press, 1984.

Hobbs, Allyson. *A Chosen Exile: A History of Racial Passing in American Life.* Cambridge, MA: Harvard University Press, 2014.

Ingham, John N., and Lynne B. Feldman. *African American Business Leaders: A Biographical Dictionary.* Westport, CT: Greenwood Press, 1994.

Inscoe, John C. *Mountain Masters: Slavery Sectional Crisis Western North Carolina.* Knoxville: University of Tennessee Press, 1989.

Jones, Jacqueline. *Soldiers of Light and Love: Northern Teachers and Georgia Blacks, 1865–1873.* Chapel Hill: University of North Carolina Press, 1980.

Joyce, Barry. *The First U.S. History Textbooks: Constructing and Disseminating the American Tale in the Nineteenth Century.* Lanham, MD: Lexington Books, 2015.

Kaestle, Carl. *Pillars of the Republic: Common Schools and American Society, 1780–1860.* New York: Hill and Wang, 1983.

Kelley, Mary. *Learning to Stand and Speak: Women, Education, and Public Life in America's Republic.* Chapel Hill: University of North Carolina Press, 2006.

Kenschaft, Lori. *Lydia Marie Child: The Quest for Racial Justice.* New York: Oxford University Press, 2002.

Knight, Edgar W. *Public School Education in North Carolina.* Boston: Houghton Mifflin, ca. 1916.

Knight, Alphonso W., Sr. *Historically Black Colleges and Universities: What You Should Know.* Bloomington, IN: Xlibris, 2014.

Kousser, J. Morgan. *The Shaping of Southern Politics: Suffrage Restrictions and the Establishment of the One-Party South.* New Haven, CT: Yale University Press, 1974.

Landry, Bart. *Black Working Wives: Pioneers of the American Family Revolution.* Berkeley: University of California Press, 2000.

Leloudis, James L. *Schooling the New South: Pedagogy, Self, and Society in North Carolina, 1880–1920.* Chapel Hill: University of North Carolina Press, 1996.

Litwack, Leon. *Been in the Storm So Long: The Aftermath of Slavery.* New York: Alfred A. Knopf, 1980.

Logan, Frenise A. *The Negro in North Carolina, 1876–1894.* Chapel Hill: University of North Carolina Press, 1964.

Marten, James Allen. *The Children's Civil War.* Chapel Hill: University of North Carolina Press, 1998.

Martin, Sandy Dwayne. *For God and Race: The Religious and Political Leadership of AMEZ Bishop James Walker Hood.* Columbia: University of South Carolina Press, 1999.

McAfee, Ward. *Religion, Race, and Reconstruction: The Public School in the Politics of the 1870s*. Albany: State University of New York Press, 1998.

McClintock, Anne. *Imperial Leather: Race, Gender and Sexuality in the Colonial Contest*. New York: Routledge, 1995.

McCrorey, Henry L. *A Brief History of Johnson C. Smith University*. Charlotte, NC: Johnson C. Smith University, 1935.

McKinney, Gordon B. *Zeb Vance: North Carolina's Civil War Governor and Gilded Age Political Leader*. Chapel Hill: University of North Carolina Press, 2004.

McPherson, James M. *The Abolitionist Legacy: From Reconstruction to the NAACP*. Princeton, NJ: Princeton University Press, 1975.

Meekins, Alex Christopher. *Elizabeth City, North Carolina and the Civil War: A History of Battle and Occupation*. Charleston, SC: History Press, 2007.

Middleton, Stephen. *Black Congressmen During Reconstruction: A Documentary Sourcebook*. Westport, CT: Greenwood Press, 2002.

Milteer, Warren Eugene, Jr. *North Carolina's Free People of Color, 1715–1885*. Baton Rouge: Louisiana State University Press, 2020.

Milteer, Warren Eugene, Jr. *Beyond Slavery's Shadow: Free People of Color in the South*. Chapel Hill: University of North Carolina Press, 2021.

Morris, J. Brent. *Oberlin, Hotbed of Abolitionism: College, Community, and the Fight for Freedom and Equality in Antebellum America*. Chapel Hill: University of North Carolina Press, 2014.

Morris, Robert C. *Reading, 'Riting, and Reconstruction: The Education of Freedmen in the South, 1861–1870*. Chicago: University of Chicago Press, 1981.

Morris, Robert C., ed. *Freedmen's Schools and Textbooks*. Vols. 1–6. New York: AMS Press, 1980.

Moss, Hilary. *Schooling Citizens: The Struggle for African American Education in Antebellum America*. Chicago: University of Chicago Press, 2009.

Murray, Pauli. *Proud Shoes: The Story of an American Family*. New York: Harper & Row, 1956.

Myers, Barton A. *Rebels Against the Confederacy: North Carolina Unionists*. New York: Cambridge University Press, 2014.

Nash, Steven E. *Reconstruction's Ragged Edge: The Politics of Postwar Life in the Southern Mountains*. Chapel Hill: University of North Carolina Press. 2016.

Nobel, M. C. S. *A History of the Public Schools of North Carolina*. Chapel Hill: University of North Carolina Press, 1930.

Norrell, Robert J. *Up from History: The Life of Booker T. Washington*. Cambridge, MA: Harvard University Press, 2009.

Orth, John V., and Paul Newby Martin. *The North Carolina State Constitution*. Oxford: Oxford University Press, 2013.

Prather, H. Leon. *We Have Taken A City: The Wilmington Racial Massacre and Coup of 1898*. Rutherford, NJ: Fairleigh Dickinson University Press, 1984.

Pinar, William F., William M. Reynolds, Patrick Slattery, and Peter M. Taubman, eds. *Understanding Curriculum: An Introduction to the Study of Historical and Contemporary Curriculum Discourse*, revised edition. New York: Peter Lang, 2008.

Parker, Inez M. *The Biddle-Johnson C. Smith University Story*. Charlotte, NC: Johnson C. Smith University Press, 1975.
Powell, William S. *North Carolina Through Four Centuries*. Chapel Hill: University of North Carolina Press, 1989.
Ready, Milton. *The Tar Heel State: A History of North Carolina*. Columbia: University of South Carolina Press, 2005.
Reid, Kevin. *Greensboro*. Charleston, SC: Arcadia Publishing, 2014.
Reid, Richard M. *Freedom for Themselves: North Carolina's Black Soldiers in the Civil War Era*. Chapel Hill: University of North Carolina Press, 2008.
Richardson, Joe M. *Christian Reconstruction: The American Missionary Association and Southern Blacks, 1861–1890*. Tuscaloosa: University of Alabama Press, 1986.
Rose, Willie Lee. *Rehearsal for Reconstruction: The Port Royal Experiment*. New York: Bobbs-Merrill, 1964.
Ruggiero, Adriane. *American Voices from Reconstruction*. New York: Marshall Cavendish Benchmark, 2007.
Schiller, Herbert. *Communication and Cultural Domination*. New York: International Arts and Sciences Press, 1976.
Selleck, Linda B. *Gentle Invaders: Quaker Women Educators and Racial Issues During the Civil War and Reconstruction*. Bloomington: Indiana University Press, 1995.
Shattuck, Gardiner H., Jr. *Episcopalians and Race: Civil War to Civil Rights*. Lexington: University Press of Kentucky, 2010.
Silkenat, David. *Driven from Home: North Carolina's Civil War Refugee Crisis*. Athens: The University of Georgia Press, 2016.
Skrabec, Quentin R., Jr. *William McGuffey: Mentor to American Industry*. New York: Algora Publishing, 2009.
Smith, John David, ed. *Black Soldiers in Blue: African American Troops in the Civil War Era*. Chapel Hill: University of North Carolina Press, 2002.
Smith, Mark, ed. *Stono: Documenting and Interpreting a Southern Slave Revolt*. Columbia: University of South Carolina Press, 2005.
Span, Christopher M. *From Cotton Field to Schoolhouse: African American Education in Mississippi, 1861–1875*. Chapel Hill: University of North Carolina Press, 2009.
Spivey, Donald. *Schooling for the New Slavery: Black Industrial Education, 1868–1915*. Westport, CT: Greenwood Press, 1978.
Sterling, Dorothy, ed. *We Are Your Sisters: Black Women in the Nineteenth Century*. New York: W. W. Norton, 1984.
Swint, Henry L. *The Northern Teacher in the South, 1862–1870*. Nashville, TN: George Peabody College for Teachers, 1941.
Thuesen, Sarah Caroline. *Greater Than Equal: African American Struggles for Schools and Citizenship in North Carolina, 1919–1965*. Chapel Hill: University of North Carolina Press, 2013.
Tolley, Kim. *Heading South to Teach: The World of Susan Nye Hutchinson, 1815–1845*. Chapel Hill: University of North Carolina Press, 2015.
Vaughn, William Preston. *Schools for All: Blacks and Public Education in the South*. Lexington: The University Press of Kentucky, 1974.

Walker, Vanessa Siddle. *Their Highest Potential: An African American School Community in the Segregated South*. Chapel Hill: University of North Carolina Press, 1996.
Wexler, Laura. *Tender Violence: Domestic Visions in an Age of U.S. Imperialism*. Chapel Hill: University of North Carolina Press, 2000.
White, Deborah Gray. *Ar'n't I A Woman? Female Slaves in the Plantation South*, 2nd edition. New York: W.W. Norton, 1999.
White, Jonathan W., and Lydia J. Davis, eds. *My Work Among the Freedmen: The Civil War and Reconstruction Letters of Harriet M. Buss*. Charlottesville: University of Virginia Press, 2021.
Williams, Heather Andrea. *Self-Taught: African American Education in Slavery and Freedom*. Chapel Hill: University of North Carolina Press, 2005.
Woodson, Carter G. *The Mis-Education of The Negro*. Washington, D.C.: Associated Publishers, 1933.
Woodward, C. Vann. *The Strange Career of Jim Crow*. New York: Oxford University Press, 1955.
Yee, Shirley J. *Black Women Abolitionists: A Study in Activism, 1828–1860*. Knoxville: University of Tennessee Press, 1992.
Zipf, Karin L. *Labor of Innocents: Forced Apprenticeship in North Carolina, 1715–1919*. Baton Rouge: Louisiana State University Press, 2005.
Zucchino, David. *Wilmington's Lie: The Murderous Coup of 1898 and the Rise of White Supremacy*. New York: Grove Atlantic, 2020.
Zuczek, Richard, ed. *Encyclopedia of the Reconstruction Era: M–Z and Primary Documents, Volume 2*. Westport, CT: Greenwood Press, 2006.
———. *Reconstruction: A Historical Encyclopedia of the American Mosaic*. Santa Barbara, CA: ABC-CLIO, 2016.

Articles in Periodicals

Alexander, Roberta Sue. "Hostility and Hope: Black Education in North Carolina During Presidential Reconstruction. 1865–1867." *The North Carolina Historical Review* 53, no. 2 (1976): 113–32.
Banks, James A. "A Content Analysis of the Black American in Textbooks." *Social Education* 33, no. 8 (1969): 954–57.
———. "The Lives and Values of Researchers: Implications for Educating Citizens in A Multicultural Society." *Educational Researcher* 27, no. 7 (1998): 4–17.
Barrett, John G. "Sherman and Total War in the Carolinas." *The North Carolina Historical Review* 37, no. 3 (1960): 367–81.
Beck, Scot. "Friends, Freedmen, Common Schools and Reconstruction." *The Southern Friend: Journal of Quaker History* 17, no. 1 (1995): 5–31.
Bell, John L. "Samuel S. Ashley: Carpetbagger and Educator." *The North Carolina Historical Review* 71, no. 4 (1995): 456–83.
Boardman, Kay. "The Ideology of Domesticity: The Regulation of The Household Economy in Victorian Women's Magazines." *Victorian Periodicals Review* 33, no. 2 (2000): 150–64.

Brewer, Fisk Parson, and William P. Vaughn. "'South Carolina University-1876' of Fisk Parsons Brewer." *The South Carolina Historical Magazine* 76 (1975): 225–31.
Brock, Euline W. "Thomas W. Cardozo: Fallible Black Reconstruction Leader." *The Journal of Southern History* 47 (1981): 183–206.
Brosnan, AnneMarie. "Representations of Race and Racism in the Textbooks Used in Southern Black Schools During the American Civil War and Reconstruction Era, 1861–1876." *Paedagogica Historica: International Journal of the History of Education* 52 (2016): 718–33.
———. "'To Educate Themselves': Southern Black Teachers in North Carolina's Schools for the Freedpeople During the Civil War and Reconstruction Period, 1862–1875." *American Nineteenth Century History* 20, no. 3 (2019): 231–48.
Brown, Anthony L. "Counter-Memory and Race: An Examination of African American Scholars' Challenges to Early Twentieth Century K-12 Historical Discourses." *The Journal of Negro Education* 79 (2010): 54–65.
Browning, Judkin. "'Bringing Light to Our Land...When She Was Dark as Night': Northerners, Freedpeople, And Education During Military Occupation in North Carolina, 1862–1865." *American Nineteenth Century History* 1, no. 1 (2008): 1–17.
———. "Removing the Mask of Nationality: Unionism, Racism, and Federal Military Occupation in North Carolina, 1862–1865." *The Journal of Southern History* Lixxi, no. 3 (2005): 589–620.
Butchart, Ronald E. "Black Hope, White Power: Emancipation, Reconstruction, and the Legacy of Unequal Schooling in the US South, 1861–1880." *Paedagogica Historica: International Journal of the History of Education* 46, nos. 1–2 (2010): 33–50.
———. "Mission Matters: Mount Holyoke, Oberlin, and the Schooling of Southern Blacks, 1871–1917." *History of Education Quarterly* 42, no. 1 (2002): 1–17.
Clendenen, Clarence C. "President Hayes' 'Withdrawal' of the Troops: An Enduring Myth." *The South Carolina Historical Magazine* 70, no. 4 (1969): 240–50.
Colby, Ira C. "The Freedmen's Bureau: From Social Welfare to Segregation." *Phylon* 46, no. 3 (1985): 219–30.
Conforti, Joseph. "The Invention of the Great Awakening, 1795–1842." *Early American Literature* 26, no. 2 (1991): 99–118.
Cott, Nancy F. "Young Women in the Second Great Awakening in New England." *Feminist Studies* 3, no. 1/2 (1975): 15–29.
Dal Lago, Enrico. "'States of Rebellion': Civil War, Rural Unrest, and the Agrarian Question in the American South and the Italian Mezzogiorno, 1861–1865." *Comparative Studies in Society and History* 47, no. 2 (2005): 403–32.
Escott, Paul D., and Jeffery J. Crow. "The Social Order and Violent Disorder: An Analysis of North Carolina in the Revolution and Civil War." *The Journal of Southern History* 52, no. 3 (1986): 373–402.
Ferguson, James S. "An Era of Educational Change." *The North Carolina Historical Review* 46, no. 2 (1969): 130–41.
Foner, Eric. "The Civil War and the Story of American Freedom." *Art Institute of Chicago Museum Studies* 27, no. 1 (2001): 8–26, 100–101.
———. "Reconstruction Revisited." *Reviews in American History* 10, no. 4 (1982): 82–100.

Franke, Katherine M. "Becoming a Citizen: Reconstruction Era Regulation of African American Marriages." *Yale Journal of Law & The Humanities* 1, no. 2 (1999): 251–309.

Gatewood, Willard B. "North Carolina and Federal Aid to Education: Public Reaction to the Blair Bill, 1881–1890." *The North Carolina Historical Review* 40, no. 4 (1963): 465–88.

Garcia, Jesus. "The Changing Image of Ethnic Groups in Textbooks." *The Phi Delta Kappan* 75, no. 1 (1993): 29–35.

Goldhaber, Michael. "A Mission Unfulfilled: Freedmen's Education in North Carolina, 1865–1870." *The Journal of Negro History* 77, no. 4 (1992): 199–210.

Hickey, Damon D. "Pioneers of the New South: The Baltimore Association and North Carolina Friends in Reconstruction." *Quaker History* 74, no. 1 (1985): 1–17.

Huddle, Mark Andrew. "To Educate a Race: The Making of the First State Colored Normal School, Fayetteville, North Carolina, 1865–1877." *The North Carolina Historical Review* 74, no. 2 (1997): 135–60.

Jones, Maxine D. "'They Are My People: Black American Missionary Association Teachers in North Carolina During the Civil War and Reconstruction." *The Negro Educational Review* 36, no. 2 (1985): 78–89.

———. "The American Missionary Association and the Beaufort, North Carolina, School Controversy, 1866–67." *Phylon (1960-)* 48, no. 2 (1987): 103–11.

Kelley, Mary. "Reading Women/Women Reading: The Making of Learned Women in Antebellum America." *The Journal of American History* 83, no. 2 (1996): 401–24.

Kelly, Brian. "Black Laborers, the Republican Party, and the Crisis of Reconstruction in Lowcountry South Carolina." *International Review of Social History* 51, no. 3 (2006): 375–414.

———. "Labor and Place: The Contours of Freedpeoples' Mobilization in Reconstruction South Carolina." *The Journal of Peasant Studies* 35, no. 4 (2008): 653–87.

———. "No Way Through: Race, Leadership, and Black Workers at the Nadir." *Labor: Studies in the Working-Class History of the Americas* 7, no. 3 (2010): 79–93.

King, Lagarrett J., Christopher Davis, and Anthony L. Brown. "African American History, Race, and Textbooks: An Examination of the Works of Harold O. Rugg and Carter G. Woodson." *The Journal of Social Studies Research* 36, no. 1 (2012): 57–74.

Knight, Edgar W. "The 'Messianic' Invasion of the South After 1865." *School and Society* 57, no. 1484 (1943): 645–51.

Logan, Frenise A. "The Legal Status of Public School Education for Negroes in North Carolina, 1877–1894." *The North Carolina Historical Review* 32, no. 3 (1955): 346–57.

McPherson, James M. "White Liberals and Black Power in Negro Education." *The American Historical Review* 75, no. 5 (1970): 1357–86.

Milteer, Warren E. "Life in a Great Dismal Swamp Community: Free People of Color in Pre-Civil War Gates County, North Carolina." *The North Carolina Historical Review* 91, no. 2 (2014): 144–70.

Montgomery, Ken. "Banal Race-Thinking: Ties of Blood, Canadian History Textbooks, and Ethnic Nationalism." *Paedagogica Historica: International Journal of the History of Education* 41, no. 3 (2005): 313–36.

O'Hara Boyd, Raphael. "Service in the Midst of the Storm: James Edward O'Hara and Reconstruction in North Carolina." *The Journal of Negro History* 83, no. 3 (2001): 319–35.

Onwuachi-Willig, Angela. "The Return of the Ring: Welfare Reform's Marriage Cure as the Revival of Post-Bellum Control." *California Law Review* 93, no. 6 (2005): 1647–96.

Parry, Tyler D. "The Radical Experiment of South Carolina: The History and Legacy of a Reconstructed University." *Journal of African American History* 105, no. 4 (Fall 2020): 539–66

Radway, Janice. "Reading is Not Eating: Mass-Produced Literature and the Theoretical, Methodological, and Political Consequence of a Metaphor." *Book Research Quarterly* 2 (1986): 7–29.

Sleeter, Christine E. "Decolonizing Curriculum: An Essay Review of the Sacred Hoop: Recovering the Feminine in American Indian Traditions." *Curriculum Inquiry* 40, no. 2 (2010).

Small, Sandra E. "The Yankee Schoolmarm in Freedmen's Schools: An Analysis of Attitudes." *The Journal of Southern History* 45, no. 3 (1979): 381–402.

Stewart, Bruce E. "<HS'When Darkness Reigns Then is the Hour to Strike': Moonshining, Federal Liquor Taxation, and Klan Violence in Western North Carolina, 1868–1872." *The North Carolina Historical Review* 80, no. 4 (October 2003): 453–74.

Stowe, Harriet Beecher. "The Education of Freedmen." *The North American Review* 128 (1879): 605–15.

Tanner, David E. "The Textbook as a Political Instrument." *The High School Journal* 72, no. 4 (1989): 182–87.

Thorpe, M. N. "A 'Yankee Teacher' in North Carolina." *The North Carolina Historical Review* 30, no. 4 (October 1953): 564–82.

Troxler, Carole Watterson. "'To Look More Closely at the Man': Wyatt Outlaw, A Nexus of National, Local, and Personal History." *The North Carolina Historical Review* 77, no. 4 (2000): 403–33.

Walsh, Patrick. "Education and the 'Universalist' Idiom of Empire: Irish National School Books in Ireland and Ontario." *History of Education* 37, no. 5 (2008): 645–60.

Watson, Harry. "The Man with the Dirty Black Beard: Race, Class, and Schools in the Antebellum South." *Journal of the Early Republic* 32, no. 1 (2012): 2–26.

Weisenfeld, Judith. "'Who is Sufficient for These Things': Sara G. Stanley and the American Missionary Association. 1864–1868." *Church History* 60, no. 4 (1991): 493–507.

Welter, Barbara. "She Hath Done What She Could: Protestant Women's Missionary Careers in Nineteenth-Century America." *American Quarterly* 30, no. 5 (1978): 624–38.

———. "The Cult of True Womanhood: 1820–1860." *American Quarterly* 18, no. 2 (1966): 151–74.

Williams, Heather Andrea. "'Clothing Themselves in Intelligence': The Freedpeople, Schooling, and Northern Teachers, 1861–1871." *The Journal of African American History* 87 (2002): 372–89.

Whitescarver, Keith. "School Books, Publishers, and Southern Nationalists: Refashioning the Curriculum in North Carolina's Schools, 1850–1861." *The North Carolina Historical Review* 79, no. 1 (2002): 28–49.

Whitener, Daniel J. "The Republican Party and Public Education in North Carolina, 1867–1900." *The North Carolina Historical Review* 37, no. 3 (July 1960): 382–96.

Zimmerman, Jonathan. "*Brown*-ing the American Textbook: History, Psychology, and the Origins of Modern Multiculturalism." *History of Education Quarterly* 44, no. 1 (2004): 46–69.

Young, Patricia. "Roads to Travel: A Historical Look at *The Freedman's Torchlight*- An African American Contribution to 19th-Century Information Technologies." *Journal of Black Studies* 31, no. 5 (2001): 671–98.

Chapters in Collected Works

Anderson, James D. "Secondary School History Textbooks and the Treatment of Black History." In *The State of Afro-American History: Past, Present, and Future*, edited by D. C. Hine, 253–76. Baton Rouge: Louisiana State University Press, 1986.

Brown, David. "North Carolinian Ambivalence: Rethinking Loyalty and Disaffection in the Civil War Piedmont." In *North Carolinians in the Era of the Civil War and Reconstruction*, edited by Paul D. Escott, 7–36. Chapel Hill: University of North Carolina Press, 2008.

Browning, Judkin. "Visions of Freedom and Civilization Opening Before Them: African Americans Search for Autonomy During Military Occupation in North Carolina." In *North Carolinians in The Era of the Civil War and Reconstruction,* edited by Paul D. Escott, 69–100. Chapel Hill: University of North Carolina Press, 2008.

Davidson, Chandler. "The Voting Rights Act: A Brief History." In *Controversies in Minority Voting: The Voting Rights Act in Perspective*, edited by Bernard N. Grofman and Chandler Davidson, 1–22. Washington, D.C.: Brookings Institution, 1992.

Downs, Gregory P. "Anarchy at the Circumference: Statelessness and the Reconstruction of Authority in Emancipation North Carolina." In *After Slavery: Race, Labor, and Citizenship in the Reconstruction South*, edited by Bruce E. Baker and Brian Kelly, 98–121. Gainesville: University Press of Florida, 2013.

Foner, Eric. "Afterword." In *After Slavery: Race, Labor, and Citizenship in the Reconstruction South,* edited by Bruce E. Baker and Brian Kelly, 221–30. Gainesville: University Press of Florida, 2013.

Huckin, Thomas. "Critical Discourse Analysis and the Discourse of Condescension." In *Discourse Studies in Composition*, edited by Ellen Barton and Gail Stygall, 71–88. New York: Hampton Press, 2002.

Kandaswamy, Priya. "Gendering Racial Formation." In *Racial Formation in the Twenty-First Century*, edited by Daniel Martinez Hosang, Oneka LaBennett, and Laura Pulido, 29–50. Berkeley: University of California Press, 2012.

Karcher, Carolyn L. "Rape, Murder, and Revenge in 'Slavery's Pleasant Homes': Lydia Marie Child's Antislavery Fiction and the Limits of the Genre." In *The Culture of Sentiment: Race, Gender, and Sentimentality in Nineteenth-Century America*, edited by Shirley S. Samuels, 58–72. New York: Oxford University Press, 1992.

Lehuu, Isabelle. "Sentimental Figures: Reading *Godey's Lady's Book* in Antebellum America." In *The Culture of Sentiment: Race, Gender, and Sentimentality in Nineteenth-Century America*, edited by Shirley S. Samuels, 73–91. New York: Oxford University Press, 1992.

Martin, Katherine F. "Phillips, Charles." In *Dictionary of North Carolina Biography*, edited by William S. Powell, vol. 5, P–S. Chapel Hill: University of North Carolina Press, 1994.

Mullen, Harryette. "Runaway Tongue: Resistant Orality in *Uncle Tom's Cabin, Our Nig, Incidents in the Life of a Slave Girl*, and *Beloved*." In *The Culture of Sentiment: Race, Gender, and Sentimentality in Nineteenth-Century America*, edited by Shirley S. Samuels, 244–64. New York: Oxford University Press, 1992.

Myers, Barton A. "A More Rigorous Style of Warfare: Wild's Raid, Guerrilla Violence, and Negotiated Neutrality in Northeastern North Carolina." In *North Carolinians in the Era of the Civil War and Reconstruction*, edited by Paul D. Escott, 37–68. Chapel Hill: University of North Carolina Press, 2008.

Nash, Steven E. "North Carolina." In *Encyclopedia of the Reconstruction Era: M–Z and Primary Documents, Vol 2*, edited by Richard Zuczek. Westport, CT: Greenwood Press, 2006.

O'Donovan, Susan Eva. "Mapping Freedom's Terrain: The Political and Productive Landscapes of Wilmington, North Carolina." In *After Slavery: Race, Labor, and Citizenship in the Reconstruction South*, edited by Bruce E. Baker and Brian Kelly, 201–19. Gainesville: University Press of Florida, 2013.

Prentice, Alison, and Marjorie R. Theobald. "The Historiography of Women Teachers: A Retrospect." In *Women Who Taught: Perspectives on the History of Women and Teaching*, edited by Prentice and Theobald, 3–37. Toronto: University of Toronto Press, 1991.

Eugene F. Pinar, Annis N. Shaver, and Manuel Bello. "Introduction." In *The Textbook as Discourse: Sociocultural Dimensions of American Schoolbooks*, edited by Eugene F. Provenzo, Annis N. Shaver, and Manuel Bello, 1–8. New York: Routledge, 2011.

Rabinowitz, Howard N. "Half A Loaf: The Shift from White to Black Teachers in Negro Schools of the Urban South. 1865–1890." In *Race, Ethnicity, And Urbanization: Selected Essays*, edited by Howard Rabinowitz, 90–116. Columbia: University of Missouri Press, 1994.

Ravitch, Diane. "American Traditions of Education." In *A Primer on America's Schools*, edited by Terry M. Moe, 1–15. Stanford, CA: Hoover Institution Press, 2001.

Richardson, E. Allan. "Architects of a Benevolent Empire: The Relationship Between the American Missionary Association and the Freedmen's Bureau in Virginia, 1865–1872." In *The Freedmen's Bureau and Reconstruction: Reconsiderations*, edited by Paul A. Cimbala and Randall M. Miller, 119–39. New York: Fordham University Press, 1999.

Sanchez-Eppler, Karen. "Bodily Bonds: The Intersecting Rhetorics of Feminism and Abolition." In *The Culture of Sentiment: Race, Gender, and Sentimentality in Nineteenth-Century America*, edited by Shirley S. Samuels, 92–114. New York: Oxford University Press, 1992.

Sleeter, Christine E., and Carl A. Grant. "Race, Class, Gender, and Disability in Current Textbook." In *The Textbook as Discourse: Sociocultural Dimensions of American Schoolbooks*, edited by Eugene F. Provenzo, Annis N. Shaver, and Manuel Bello, 183–216. New York: Routledge, 2011.

Swerdlow, Amy. "Abolition's Conservative Sisters: The Ladies' New York City Anti-Slavery Societies, 1834–1840." In *The Abolitionist Sisterhood: Women's Political Culture in Antebellum America*, edited by Jean Fagan Yellin and John C. Van Horne, 31–44. Ithaca, NY: Cornell University Press, 1994.

West, John. G., Jr. "Nineteenth-Century America." In *Building A Healthy Culture: Strategies for an American Renaissance,* edited by Don Eberly, 181–99. Grand Rapids, MI: Eerdmans, 2001.

Dissertations

Brown, Daniel. "The Freedmen's Bureau in Reconstruction North Carolina." PhD Diss. Queen's University Belfast, 2012.
Chapman, J. K. "Black Freedom and the University Of North Carolina. 1793–1960." PhD Diss. University of North Carolina, Chapel Hill, 2006.
Davis, C. L. "The Collective Identities of Women Teachers in Black Schools in the Post-Bellum South." PhD Diss. The University of Georgia, 2016.
Duncan, Eric Thomas. "'Make the Letters Big and Plain': A History of Black Education in North Carolina." MA Diss. North Carolina State University, 2011.
Green, H. N. "Educational Reconstruction: African American Education in the Urban South. 1865–1890." PhD Diss. University of North Carolina, Chapel Hill, 2010.
Kinghan, N. "A Brief Moment in the Sun: Francis Cardozo and Reconstruction in South Carolina." PhD Diss. Institute of the Americas, University College London, 2019.
Kopp, L. E. "Teaching the Confederacy: Textbooks in the Civil War South." MA Diss. University of Maryland, 2009.
Mattick, Barbara E. "Ministries in Black and White: The Catholic Sisters of St. Augustine. Florida, 1859–1920." PhD Diss. Florida State University, 2008.
Kowalewski, J. "'To Be True to Ourselves': Freedpeople, Schoolbuilding, and Community Politics in Appalachian Tennessee, 1865–1870." MA Diss. University of Tennessee, Knoxville, 2009.
Nash, Stephen E. "The Extremest Condition of Humanity: Emancipation, Conflict, and Progress in Western North Carolina, 1865–1880." PhD Diss. University of Georgia, 2004.
Patterson, J. P. "The Cultural Reform Project of Northern Teachers of the Freed People, 1862–1870." PhD Diss. University of Iowa, 2012.
Proctor, Bradly David. "Whip, Pistol, and Hood: Ku Klux Klan Violence in the Carolinas During Reconstruction." PhD Diss. University of North Carolina, Chapel Hill, 2013.
Swarthout, A. M. "Textbooks, Teachers, and Compromise: The Political Work of Freedmen Education." MA Diss. The University of Texas, El Paso, 2013.

Conference Papers

Butchart, Ronald E. "Troops to Teachers, 19th Century Style: Civil War Veterans as Teachers of the Freed People." At the *American Educational Research Association.* San Francisco, 2013.

Index

ABHMS. *See* American Baptist Home Mission Society
ACS. *See* African Civilization Society
Advice to Freedmen (Brinckerhoff), 97, 103, 106
African Civilization Society (ACS), 98, 106
African Methodist Episcopal Zion Church (AMEZ), 17, 53–54, 85
African spiritual holocaust, 68
AFUC. *See* American Freedmen's Union Commission
aid societies: northern, 35, 37, 83–84; operating in North Carolina, 27–30
Alexander, Samuel C., 63, 70
Allen, Harriett, 50
Allen, J. Timothy, 3
Alvord, John W., 18–19, 21, 36, 44, 83
AMA. *See* American Missionary Association
American Baptist Home Mission Society (ABHMS), 26, 30
American Freedmen's Union Commission (AFUC), 27, 98; and Catholic schools, 32; and naming textbooks, 98; object of, 30
American Missionary Association (AMA), 14, 16, 20; assisting Black teachers, 113–14; and life in Reconstruction North Carolina, 111–14, 118–21; and motivations of teachers, 73–75, 77, 82, 85–86; as premier aid society in North Carolina, 29–30; and quest for education, 20, 26, 28–31, 33; and Roman Catholic Church, 31–32; sponsoring teachers, 141n28; and teachers, 49, 51, 53, 55, 57–59; and textbooks, 99, 105
American Tract Society (ATS), 97
AMEZ. *See* African Methodist Episcopal Zion Church

Angady, Mary, 43
anti-literacy laws, 42–43, 146n14
anti-slavery, 3–5, 42, 57, 74, 88–89
anti-slavery novel, 88–89
Appeal in Favor of That Class of Americans Called Africans, An (Child), 105
Appeal to the Colored Citizens of the World (Walker), 42, 45
Armstrong, Samuel C., 128
Article IX, North Carolina state constitution, 82
Ashley, Samuel S., 14, 16, 33, 38, 49, 57, 81, 82, 114, 121
Ashworth, Joel, 94
Ashworth, William R., 94
ATS. *See* American Tract Society
Auman, William T., 3
Avery, Martha C., 62

Bachelor, Daniel T., 59
Bahel, Eliza A., 28
Baltimore Association for the Moral and Educational Improvement of the Colored People, 28–29, 62
Baptist Institute, 69
Battle of Fort Wagner, 50
Battle, Kemp, 117
Beals, H. S., 20, 77
Beech Grove Quaker Seminary, 45
Bell, Jennie S., 29, 55, 150n39
Bell, John, 37, 82
Bennett College, 60
Best, Mary A., 86
Biddle Institute, 38–39, 70–72
Black communities, determination of, 125–30

Black schooling, 2–3, 8–10; attacks on, 126–27; contributing to growth and development of, 82; engaging in, 46, 61–62, 74; extending reach of, 117–18; and habits of punctuality, 157n24; incendiarism as reaction to, 119; increased opposition to, 120; initial stages of, 111–12; new phase of, 129; northern involvement in, 32–33; Redeemers opposing, 123; Roman Catholic Church threatening, 31–32; slow and haphazard nature of, 38; sustaining, 25
Blair education bill, defeat of, 127–28
Blair, Henry W., 127
Blue-Backed Speller (Webster), 96–97
Bonnell, Frances, 78
Bowers, Mary, 89–90
Brackin, W.C., 120
Brewer, Fisk Parsons, 28–29, 117
Brinckerhoff, Isaac W., 97
Brown v. Board of Education, 129
Brown, Helen E., 107
Brown, Lucy Evelyn Sparhawk, 47, 97
Brunap, Roper and Mary Ann, 113
Bureau of Refugees, Freedmen, and Abandoned Lands. *See* Freedmen's Bureau
Burke Country, North Carolina, 21, 62
Burnap, Mary Ann, 30–31, 42, 54, 68, 76
Burnside, Ambrose E., 11
Burton, W. C., 123
Busbee, Sidney A., 26, 47–48
Buss, Harriet M., 69, 75, 78, 116
Butchart, Ronald E., 2, 31–32, 41, 66, 75, 144n1
Butler, Jon, 68

Canedy, Betsey L., 97, 111
Cardozo, Isaac Nunez, 53, 149n34
Cardozo, Thomas W., 53, 149n34
Catawba Presbytery, 72
Chambers, Mary A., 93–94
Chapel Hill, freedpeople of, 90
Chavis, John, 45
Chesnutt, Charles W., 128–29

Child, Lydia Maria, 97, 98, 104
Chur, Jacob F., 84
Cimbala, Paul A., 24
Civil Rights Act of 1866, 14–15
Civil War, 1, 29, 48, 50–51, 54, 59, 64, 91, 93, 135n6; aid societies established after, 26; apprenticeship laws following, 45; Black labor following, 14–16; Black North Carolinians mobilizing after, 21–22; Black political leadership following, 54; Carolinas Campaign, 12–13; collapse of North Carolina after, 33; and colored conventions, 137n24; eavesdropping during, 43; engagement in education prior to end of, 42; enslaved people in North Carolina during, 13; first year of, 42; foraging during, 12; highly charged religious atmosphere before, 73–74; ignoring talks of secession during, 161n57; increased poverty in aftermath of, 61–62; and life in Reconstruction North Carolina, 109–10, 117–18, 126–30; NEFAS not long after end of, 79; North Carolina after, 11–19; North Carolina constitution following, 17–19; northern Black teachers following, 52–53; northern churches during, 70–71; and northern white teachers, 56, 62; number of white North Carolinian teachers after, 62; poverty during, 13–14; propelling women into paid workforce, 65–67; reluctance to perceive freedpeople following, 15–16; scorched earth policy, 11–12; secret teaching during, 43–44; and Soldiers' Aid Society, 55–56; Special Field Order No. 120, 12; textbooks produced during, 97, 100, 106–8; total war campaign affecting Confederate army, 12–13; white North Carolinians during, 61. *See also* Reconstruction
civilizations, lessons on. *See* white supremacy, promoting
Clapp, Henry, 42–43
Clark, Margaret S., 117

INDEX

Clary, Martha Hale, 58
classes, size of, 110–11
Clumfort's Creek, 161n58
Cock, Jane M., 60
Coffin, Levi, 64–65
Colby, Ira C., 24
colored conventions, 137n24
Colyer, Vincent, 20, 61
common school movement, 57
Company Shops, 121
Confederacy, 3, 12, 24, 45, 66, 72, 93, 107, 135n6, 161n57
Corliss, Alonzo B., 121
Crafts, Hannah, 43
Crawford, James, 84
Croome, Carrie E., 91
Culling, Martha, 41–42
cultural colonialism, 32–33
Curry, James, 43

Daffin, Sallie, 50, 85, 114
Daily Standard, 121
Day, Mary, 43
Democrats, 10, 33, 36, 39, 82, 120, 123, 125–26, 171n1
Dorland, Luke, 60
Dorland, William Gardner, 60
Dorsey, Bruce, 160n52
Douglass, Frederick, 105
Downs, Gregory P., 24
Draper, Edward, 11
Du Bois, W. E. B., 42, 54
DuBois, W. E. B., 128
Durham, Plato, 34

Easy Introduction to the Study of Geography, An (Mitchell), 103
education, quest for: activism in Fayetteville, 23; aid societies, 27–30; attempts to subvert Black education, 37–38; emergence of Freedmen's Bureau, 20–21; establishing system of free public schooling, 33–38; establishing teaching force, 37–39; federal perspective, 23–24;

grassroots level, 21–22; *Lane v. Stanley*, 37; organizing on political level, 22–23; Roman Catholic church as threat, 31–32; rural nature of North Carolina hindering efforts, 25–27; secular organizations, 30–31; thirst for knowledge, 20–21; training institutes for, 38–40; viewing through lens of cultural colonialism, 32–33. *See also* freedpeople's education; North Carolina, freedpeople's education in

Elizabeth City, North Carolina, deterioration of, 11
Elliott, Mark, 86
Elliott, William, 118
Elson, Ruth, 107–8
Emma, Frankie, 53
equality (education), struggle for, 125–30
Etheridge, Antoinette L., 54

Fayetteville State University, 23
Fayetteville, The, 83
Ferebee, London R., 91
Fernald, Anne Shaw, 58
FFA. *See* Friends' Freedmen's Association
Field, Josephine C., 58
Finney, Charles G., 73
First Dixie Reader, 107
First Reconstruction Act, 16
Fisk, Clinton B., 99
Fiske, F. A., 22–23, 25, 47, 55, 70, 84, 89, 110, 118–19
Fitzgerald, Robert G., 17, 37, 39, 50, 52, 92, 110–11, 121–22
Flake, Francis, 93
Foner, Eric, 14, 142n35
Forten, Charlotte, 105
Foster, John G., 20
Franke, Katherine M., 99
Franklin, Benjamin, 48
Freedman, The, 80, 101–2, 106
Freedman's First Reader, The, 97–98
Freedman's Spelling Book, The, 97, 103
Freedman's Torchlight, The, 97–98, 106

Freedmen's Book, The (Child), 98, 104–5
Freedmen's Bureau, 1, 6, 8, 14–15, 18; emergence of, 20–21; and fair and equitable employment, 80–81; from federal perspective, 23–24; and first public school system, 33–38; and freedpeople's teachers in North Carolina, 41, 44, 47, 49, 57, 62–63, 65, 72; funding, 24–25; hindering efforts of, 25–27; interrogating teacher motivations, 72, 74–75, 77, 80, 83–90, 93–95; life in Reconstruction North Carolina, 110, 113, 117–20; partnerships with, 39–40; and textbooks, 100, 102, 106; working for, 53–55; writing to, 47
Freedmen's Association (FFA), 28
Freedmen's Convention of North Carolina, 17, 83
Freedmen's Educational Association of North Carolina, 22–23
Freedmen's Record, The, 79
Freedmen's Teacher Project (FTP), 6–8, 41, 71, 147nn21–22, 160n48; on AMA, 49–50; analysis of, 50; on Black teachers serving in Union army, 50; data on teacher tenure, 47; interrogating teacher motivations, 71, 84, 94–95; North Carolina section of, 49; on Perkins, 56; reporting on Vogelsang, 50
freedpeople, 1; continuing struggle for educational equality, 125–30; documenting education of, 1–3; during Civil War and Reconstruction period, 11–19; instilling with "habits of punctuality," 157n24; life in Reconstruction North Carolina, 109–24; preparing for responsible citizenship, 81–82; quest for education, 20–40; teachers of, 41–47; textbooks used for, 96–108
freedpeople's education: continuing struggle for educational equality, 125–30; during Civil War and early Reconstruction period, 11–19; interrogating teacher motivations in, 68–95;

life in Reconstruction North Carolina, 109–24; quest for education in North Carolina, 20–40; teachers of, 41–67; textbooks used in, 96–108
Freeman, Sarah and Kate, 13, 75, 78, 80, 109, 113, 124
Friendly Counsels for Freedmen (Fisk), 101
Friendly Counsels for Freedmen (Waterbury), 97, 100
Friends' Freedmen's Association (FFA), 47, 87, 111
Frothingham, O. B., 30
FTP. *See* Freedmen's Teacher Project
Fugitive Slave Act of 1850, 88

Gardner, Anna, 60
Garrison, Ellen Jackson, 49
gender, education and, 145n2. *See also* teachers; women
General Assembly, North Carolina, 33, 100, 123, 125
General Order No. 8, 100
Genovese, Eugene D., 42
Georgia, scorched earth policy in, 11–12
Gill, Emily, 109
Goldhaber, Michael, 119–20
Goldsboro Messenger, 127
Gorham, Frances A., 28
Graham, John, 34
Graham, William Alexander, 55, 83
Grant, Ulysses S., 17
Graves, Frances, 77
Green, Harriet L., 48
Green, Hilary, 2, 127
Greene, George N., 54
Groner, Sophia, 92–93

Hale, Janice E., 32–33
Hall, Edward Payson, 66, 89
Hamilton, J. G. de Roulhac, 82
Hampton Institute, 128
Hancock, Noah, 93
Hanly, Joanna P. R., 74–75
Harris, Blanche Virginia, 53

INDEX

Harris, James Henry, 16, 22
Harris, Robert, 23, 39, 43, 51, 68–69, 76, 86, 111, 118
Haskell, Samuel, 30
HBCUs. *See* Historically Black Colleges and Universities
Henry J. Biddle Memorial Institute. *See* Biddle Institute
Hews, Chaney, 44
Hiatt, John C., 61
Hill, Nathan H., 65, 87
Hill, Orlando, Aaron, 65
Historically Black Colleges and Universities (HBCUs), 1, 10, 17, 20, 48, 52, 60, 66
Holden, William Woods, 16, 86, 120, 123
Hood, James Walker, 16–17, 23, 28, 30, 35, 38, 50, 53
Horton, Abby H., 60
Horton, Goerge Moses, 105
Hosmer, Susan A., 29, 54
Howard Band of Hope, 77
Howard School, 23, 143n46
Howard, Oliver O., 24, 26, 74, 77, 80
Hubbard, Luther C., 50
Hughes, Samuel, 37
Hunter, Charles N., 38, 91–92, 127

industry, lessons on, 101–2
Institute for Colored Youth, 52

Jacobs, Harriett, 105
James, Elizabeth H., 13, 73, 110, 113
James, Horace, 15, 19, 31, 41, 74, 78, 88
Jerkins, Michael P., 112
Jim Crow laws, 114, 123, 127
John Freeman and His Family (Brown), 102–3, 107
Johnson C. Smith University, 60
Johnston, Joseph E., 13
Joint Committee on Reconstruction, 80, 161n57
Jones, A. H., 63–64
Jones, Maxine, 49
Juvenile Miscellany, The, 105

Kellogg, Martha L., 78, 88
Kennedy, Crammond, 32
King, Francis, 62
Kirk-Holden war, 123
Knight, Edgar W., 2
Ku Klux Klan (KKK), 47, 86, 120–24, 126

Lane v. Stanley, 37
Lea, John G., 122
Lee, Robert E., 12
Leland, Eunice S., 84
Lincoln University, 53
literature, proliferation of, 88–89
Locker, Wallace Porter, 48
Louise, Sarah, 85

Mann, Horace, 57
Mannin, Cornelius Max, 45
Mapps, Grace A., 147n18
marriage laws, enforcement of, 99–100
Martin, Robert, 86
Mayo, A. D., 128
McDowell, Franklin, 48
McLean, Grace Ann, 47
McPherson, James, 142n33
Mendenhall, Delphina E., 64
Mendenhall, Judith Jemima, 63
Merriam, Annie P., 77
Methodist Episcopal Church, 91
Miller, Randal M., 24
Miller, Willis L., 29, 63, 66, 69, 70, 76, 117
Mitchell, Samuel, 103–4
Moore, Miranda Branson, 107
Morgan, W. W., 91
Morris, Alfred W., 19
Morrow, Robert, 41–42
motivation (of teachers), interrogating: abolitionists, 87–89; acceptance of freedpeople's education, 82–83; ameliorating degrading effects of slavery, 75–78; benefitting from postwar economic conditions, 86–87; Biddle

motivation (of teachers) (*continued*)
Institute furnish particular type
of teacher, 72–73; commitment to
free-labor ideology, 78–81; contributing
to education of Black race, 89; demand
for Black teachers, 91–92; evolution
of preconceived notions, 78; financial
necessity, 92–95; freedpeople's schools
as mechanism for social control, 81–82;
patriotism, 91; preserving antebellum
social order, 84–86; proliferation of
sentimental literature, 88–89; promise
of spiritual salvation, 73–75; racial
elevation/advancement, 86–89; racial
paternalism, 89–90; reforming style
of worship of former slaves, 69–70;
religious duty, 68–69, 74–75; sustaining
Presbyterian Church, 71; teaching as
respectable occupation, 92; working on
plantations, 83–84. *See also* teachers
Mount Holyoke Female Seminary, 58, 75
Myers, Barton A., 11

National Freedman, The, 76
National Freedman's Relief Association
(NFRA), 28, 30, 41, 48, 50–52, 54–55,
59, 75, 109
NEFAS. *See* New England Freedmen's Aid
Society
New Bern, North Carolina, 7, 11, 13, 18, 20,
25–29, 42–44, 48, 54–55, 61, 77, 80, 97,
109, 131
New England Freedmen's Aid Society
(NEFAS), 27, 47, 54–55, 60, 79, 91, 111
New York Times, The, 11, 22
Newcomb, George, 77
NFRA. *See* National Freedman's Relief
Association
Nickerson, Samuel, 59
North Carolina General Assembly, 125
North Carolina Historical Commission,
122
North Carolina Manumission Society, 63
North Carolina Presbyterian, The, 70

North Carolina Yearly Meeting of Friends,
26, 63
North Carolina, freedpeople's education
in: anti-literacy laws, 42–44; continuing struggle for educational equality,
125–30; establishing public school system, 33–38; following Civil War, 11–19;
interrogating teacher motivations,
68–95; life in Reconstruction North
Carolina, 109–24; overview, 1–10; quest
for education, 20–40; Reconstruction-
period North Carolina, 11–19; teachers,
41–67; textbooks used in schools,
96–108
North Carolinian, The, 16
Norton, Hannibal D., 62

O'Hara, James Edward, 16, 26, 54, 92, 127,
149n35
Oberlin College, 58, 85
Oberlin Preparatory School, 46
Orange County, North Carolina, 25, 37,
42, 121
organization of industry, term, 79
Outlaw, Wyatt, 123
Owen, Miranda C., 56

Parker, David, 15
Patterson, Chanie Ann, 46
Patterson, John Eaton, 46
Patterson, Mary Jane, 46
PCMF. *See* Presbyterian Committee on
Missions for Freedmen
Peabody Education Fund, 55, 125
Pearson, Sarah Elvira, 62
PEFC. *See* Protestant Episcopal Freedman's Commission
Pennock, Elizabeth, 113, 116
Pennsylvania Freedmen's Relief Association (PFRA), 52, 55
Perkins, Eliza P., 55–56
Pettigrew, James J., 42
PFRA. *See* Pennsylvania Freedmen's Relief
Association

Index

Phillips, Charles, 33, 72–73
Phillips, John T., 61
Plain Counsels for Freedmen (Fisk), 100, 101, 104–5
plantations, 14, 18, 24, 79–80, 98, 102, 108, 158n30
Plessy v. Ferguson, 33–34, 86
Plessy, Homer A., 34, 86
poverty, North Carolina and, 13–14
Prentice, Alison, 57
Preparatory High School for Colored Youth, 46
Presbyterian Committee on Missions for Freedmen (PCMF), 27–28, 48, 57, 63, 69–70, 72
Presbyterian Publication Committee, 97
Protestant Episcopal Church, 26, 31
Protestant Episcopal Freedman's Commission (PEFC), 63, 79
public schools, 1, 8, 10, 17, 20, 44, 47–48, 50, 73, 82, 85, 120, 125, 130; establishing, 33–38

Quaker Belt, 3–4. *See also* North Carolina, freedpeople's education in
Quakers, 3–4, 61, 63, 66

race, lessons on. *See* white supremacy, promoting
racial pride, attempts at fostering, 105–8. *See also* textbooks
Raleigh Sentinel, 33, 34–35
Ransome, M. C., 38
Reconstruction, 1, 7–10; Black teachers working during, 113–15; class sizes, 110–11; early days of freedom, 109–10; financial limitations, 111–13; focusing on educational matters, 110; interrogating teacher motivations in, 68–95; North Carolina during early period of, 11–19; North Carolina life in, 109–24; and quest for education during, 20–40; rise of Ku Klux Klan, 120–24; securing accommodations for teachers, 113–14;

teachers in North Carolina during, 41–67; teachers relying on each other during, 115–17; textbooks used during, 96–108; white hostility during, 117–19. *See also* freedpeople's education
Red Shirts, 120, 126
Redeemers, 10, 123, 171n1
Redemption, period, 17, 125, 149n35, 171n1
religious aid societies, 27–28. *See also* aid societies
religious organization, 27, 30, 57, 111
Republicans, 33–34, 122, 127, 130
Revels, Hiram Rhodes, 45
Rienshaw, Adora, 43
Roanoke Island, North Carolina, 11, 13, 41–42, 49–50, 76, 78, 80, 109–10, 113
Rodman, William B., 35
Roman Catholic Church, 30–32, 57
Roper, Ella, 91
Roulhac, Lewis, 44

Sanderson, George O., 15, 80
Schooling the Freed People (Butchart), 2
Scotia Seminary, 60
Second Great Awakening, 70
secular organization, 27, 30–31
sentimental literature, proliferation of, 88–89
Sewart, Sam T., 44
Seymour, Horatio, 17
Shaw University, 39, 52, 60
Sherman, William T., 11–12
Sinclair, James, 71, 90–91, 161n57
slavery. *See* anti-slavery
Smith, Margaret R., 55
Soldiers' Aid Society, 55
Soper, Sylvester, 47
South Carolina, scorched earth policy in, 11–12
Span, Christopher C., 2, 101
Special Field Order No. 120, 12
Spenser, Cornelia Phillips, 12
Stanley, Edward W., 61
Stanley, Sara G., 5

State Colored Normal School, 23, 125
State Equal Rights League, 22
Stearns, Nellie F., 115, 124
Stephens, John W., 122–23
Stoneman, George, 12
Stono Rebellion, 42, 145n4
Stowe, Harriet Beecher, 21, 88–89
summer, teaching during, 155n7. *See also* teachers
Swain, Jordan, 90
System of Modern Geography, A (Mitchell), 103–4

Talley, H. C., 94
teachers: and anti-literacy laws, 42–43; attending schools in North, 45–46; backgrounds of, 53–54, 61; barriers faced by, 47; education of, 52–54; engaging in freedpeople's education, 49–52; female teachers outnumbering male teachers, 151n42; first teachers working in North Carolina, 41–42; gender imbalance of, 48–49; gender participation, 65–67, 151n42; home states of, 48; hostility toward freedpeople's education, 62–65; and lack of educational opportunities, 44–45; male teachers, 59–60; northern teachers working in South, 55–56; overrepresentation of women, 57–59; peak year of participation by, 150n41; professionalization of, 38–40; running for public office, 54–55; secretly teaching freedpeople, 43–44; southern white teachers, 61–62, 66–67, 152–53nn57–61; sponsorships of, 47–48, 55; summer teaching, 155n7
teaching credentials, lack of, 151n45
textbooks: attempts at fostering racial pride in, 105–8; challenging naming of, 98; explicitness of, 96–97; industry lessons, 101–2; lack of critique of racial slavery in, 104–6; lessons of morality in, 98–99; and limitations on funding, 97; perception as political instruments, 96; promoting white supremacy in, 102–4; on relationship between wealth and happiness, 102; teaching about marriage using, 99–101; tone of, 97
Theobald, Marjorie R., 57
Thorpe, Margaret Newbold, 113, 116
Thurston, A., 83–84
Ticknor and Fields (publisher), 105
Tomlinson, doctor, 26, 63
Tourgée, Albion W., 16, 34, 60, 86–87
Tupper, Henry Martin, 60
Tuskegee Institute, 128

Uncle Tom's Cabin (Stowe), 21, 88–89
United States Congress, 1
University of North Carolina, 129

Vance, Zebulon B., 125
Vaughn, William P., 65
violence, localization of, 117–20
Vogell, H. C., 93–94, 97, 119
Vogelsang, Peter, 50
voting, right, 17–18

Wake County, North Carolina, 44, 118
Walker, David, 42
Warner, Yardley, 87
Warrick, Charles, 52
Warrick, Louisa, 52
Warrick, Lydia, 52
Warrick, William, 52
Washburn Seminary, 112
Washington, Booker T., 128
Waterbury, J. B., 100
Waterbury, Jared Bell, 97
Waugh, Caroline, 28
wealth and happiness, alternate messages on relationship between, 102
Webster, Noah, 96
Welborn, William C., 63
Western Freedmen's Aid Commission (WFAC), 64
WFAC. *See* Western Freedmen's Aid Commission

Wharton, Francis, 79
Whipple, George, 31, 82
white people, 35, 70, 82, 84, 90, 103, 117; hostile whites, 117; navigating advances of white men, 100–101; northern whites, 18, 62, 128; northern white teachers, 7, 55–56, 59, 61–62, 69, 73, 87–89, 113, 116, 145n2, 150n41; poor whites, 20, 29, 92, 128; southern whites, 24, 33, 79, 90, 114, 119–20, 128; southern white teachers, 61–62, 66–67, 152–53nn57–61; white flight, 129; white hostility, 117–20
white supremacy, promoting, 102–4. *See also* textbooks
Whiton, Samuel J., 22, 69
Whittemore, James O., 74–75

Whittlesey, E., 14, 113, 117, 119
Wild, Edward A., 11
Williams, Esther A., 48
Williams, Heather A., 2, 96
Williams, Lucelia Electa, 55
Willson's Third Reader, 97
Wilson, Henry, 105
women: gender imbalance of, 48–49; joining paid workforce, 65–67
Woodward, C. Vann, 116–17
Worden, W. H., 83

Yankee schoolmarm. *See* freedpeople

Zion Wesley Institute, 17

AnneMarie Brosnan is Associate Professor in the History of Education at Mary Immaculate College, University of Limerick, Ireland. Her research interests include African American history in the US South, the Civil War and Reconstruction period, and race and ethnicity in the nineteenth century.

RECONSTRUCTING AMERICA
Andrew L. Slap, series editor

Hans L. Trefousse, *Impeachment of a President: Andrew Johnson, the Blacks, and Reconstruction.*

Richard Paul Fuke, *Imperfect Equality: African Americans and the Confines of White Ideology in Post-Emancipation Maryland.*

Ruth Currie-McDaniel, *Carpetbagger of Conscience: A Biography of John Emory Bryant.*

Paul A. Cimbala and Randall M. Miller, eds., *The Freedmen's Bureau and Reconstruction: Reconsiderations.*

Herman Belz, *A New Birth of Freedom: The Republican Party and Freedmen's Rights, 1861 to 1866.*

Robert Michael Goldman, *"A Free Ballot and a Fair Count": The Department of Justice and the Enforcement of Voting Rights in the South, 1877–1893.*

Ruth Douglas Currie, ed., *Emma Spaulding Bryant: Civil War Bride, Carpetbagger's Wife, Ardent Feminist—Letters, 1860–1900.*

Robert Francis Engs, *Freedom's First Generation: Black Hampton, Virginia, 1861–1890.*

Robert F. Kaczorowski, *The Politics of Judicial Interpretation: The Federal Courts, Department of Justice, and Civil Rights, 1866–1876.*

John Syrett, *The Civil War Confiscation Acts: Failing to Reconstruct the South.*

Michael Les Benedict, *Preserving the Constitution: Essays on Politics and the Constitution in the Reconstruction Era.*

Andrew L. Slap, *The Doom of Reconstruction: The Liberal Republicans in the Civil War Era.*

Edmund L. Drago, *Confederate Phoenix: Rebel Children and Their Families in South Carolina.*

Mary Farmer-Kaiser, *Freedwomen and the Freedmen's Bureau: Race, Gender, and Public Policy in the Age of Emancipation.*

Paul A. Cimbala and Randall Miller, eds., *The Great Task Remaining Before Us: Reconstruction as America's Continuing Civil War.*

John A. Casey Jr., *New Men: Reconstructing the Image of the Veteran in Late-Nineteenth-Century American Literature and Culture.*

Hilary Green, *Educational Reconstruction: African American Schools in the Urban South, 1865–1890.*

Christopher B. Bean, *Too Great a Burden to Bear: The Struggle and Failure of the Freedmen's Bureau in Texas.*

David E. Goldberg, *The Retreats of Reconstruction: Race, Leisure, and the Politics of Segregation at the New Jersey Shore, 1865–1920.*

David Prior, ed., *Reconstruction in a Globalizing World.*

Jewel L. Spangler and Frank Towers, eds., *Remaking North American Sovereignty: State Transformation in the 1860s.*

Adam H. Domby and Simon Lewis, eds., *Freedoms Gained and Lost: Reconstruction and Its Meanings 150 Years Later.*

David Prior, ed., *Reconstruction and Empire: The Legacies of Abolition and Union Victory for an Imperial Age.*

Sandra M. Gustafson and Robert S. Levine, eds., *Reimagining the Republic: Race, Citizenship, and Nation in the Literary Work of Albion W. Tourgée.* Foreword by Carolyn L. Karcher.

Brian Schoen, Jewel L. Spangler, and Frank Towers, eds., *Continent in Crisis: The U.S. Civil War in North America.*

Raymond James Krohn, *Abolitionist Twilights: History, Meaning, and the Fate of Racial Egalitarianism, 1865–1909.*

Hilary N. Green and Andrew L. Slap, eds., *The Civil War and the Summer of 2020*.

Ian Delahanty, *Embracing Emancipation: A Transatlantic History of Irish Americans, Slavery, and the American Union, 1840–1865*.

AnneMarie Brosnan, *A Contested Terrain: Freedpeople's Education in North Carolina During the Civil War and Reconstruction*.

www.ingramcontent.com/pod-product-compliance
Lightning Source LLC
Chambersburg PA
CBHW020407080526
44584CB00014B/1219